Blessed Anastácia

Blessed Anastácia

Women, Race,
and Popular Christianity in Brazil

JOHN BURDICK

ROUTLEDGE
New York and London

Published in 1998 by
Routledge
29 West 35th Street
New York, NY 10001

Published in Great Britain in 1998 by
Routledge
11 New Fetter Lane
London EC4P 4EE

Printed in the United States of America on acid-free paper
Design: Jack Donner

Library of Congress Cataloging-in-Publication Data

Burdick, John, 1959–
    Blessed Anastácia : women, race and Christianity in Brazil /
by John Burdick.
        p.   cm.
    Includes bibliographical references and index.
    ISBN 0–415–91259–8 (hc.). — ISBN 0–415–91260–1 (pbk.)
    1. Women, Black—Brazil—Religious life.   2. Brazil—Religious life and
customs.   3. Race—Religious aspects—Christianity.   4. Brazil—Race relations.   5. Brazil—Politics and government—1985–   6. Brazil—Social
conditions—1985–   I. Title
BR675. B87   1998
306.6'7810829'08996—dc21   98–16293
                                                            CIP rev.

Contents

Preface and Acknowledgments

In the early 1980s I was active in the solidarity movement with Latin American revolutions. It was an exciting period. Fighting against tremendous odds, the social revolutions of the region embodied, for me and many of my generation, the best and brightest hope for freedom and democracy in the Southern Hemisphere. The role of the Catholic Church in this process seemed fundamental. When it came time for me to define a doctoral project, it felt inevitable that I should witness firsthand the revolution in consciousness that, under the auspices of Catholic liberation theology, was supposed to be sweeping Latin America. I went to Brazil.

My encounter with the Brazilian grass roots between 1984 and 1988 was a sobering experience. What had started as a study of radical consciousness turned into an effort to explain why so few people were interested in liberation theology, while so many were passionate about evangelical Christianity. Many of the latter, I began to understand, found liberation theology too abstract to heal the wounds of their everyday lives. What I found most remarkable was the gulf between Catholic theologians' claims that the evangelicals were mindless dupes, and my experience of them as no more duped than anyone else. Indeed, I met evangelicals deeply involved in progressive social movements, who explained their involvement as due to divine inspiration. Some of the most successful local neighborhood associations, it seemed to me, were precisely the ones in which Protestants and Catholics struggled side by side.

Three lessons from this experience have shaped my perspective, and inform every aspect of this study. First, I learned that political activists may not always be the best-informed informants about the nature and range of popular political consciousness; second, that a movement's ideology should be understood not only for its power to resonate and mobilize, but also for its tendency to marginalize and alienate; and finally, that textured local knowledge about political consciousness should be useful to people who desired to build bridges across the religious divide.

I did not go to Brazil intending to study the question of race. I had, in fact, largely accepted the image of Brazil as a society where race was unproblematic. It did not take long for me to be set right. The issue of color was, I saw, a constant presence in how men and women looked at each other, chose their lovers and spouses, modeled their bodies. It was there in the daily round of jokes, banter, insults, and accusations. It was there in how people talked to and about each other, in how they touched or did not touch each other. And it was present in the stories men and women, especially women, told me, of hurt, anger, and healing.

Yet it was also a constantly elusive presence, which slipped out of my fingers whenever I thought I had finally grasped it. For every person who recounted stories of pain and suffering in connection with her color, another would declare that despite her color she had never suffered a moment's discrimination in her life. For every person I considered "black" who spoke of her slave ancestry, another would matter-of-factly deny being the descendant of slaves. The world of race and color in Brazil was rather different from the one I was familiar with.

1988 was the centennial year of Brazil's abolition of slavery. The issue of racism was all over the media, and the *pastoral negro* (black pastoral) of the Catholic Church was a growing force in Rio de Janeiro. As I accompanied the young black clergy struggling to bring the issue of racism into the everyday life of Catholic Bible groups, I felt I was engaging in some of the deepest problems about politics, religion, and the legacy of slavery in the hemisphere. Between 1993 and 1996, I was lucky enough to carry out sixteen months of research on these problems.

Through this research, I came to feel that I needed to listen carefully to the experiences of *negros* who said they had never suffered from color prejudice as well as to those who said they had. The important thing was to respect the reality of both experiences and to try to understand what made both socially possible. In the United States, I had grown up surrounded by strong evidence that being non-white inevitably included the experience of racism. As a white Jew from a liberal family deeply involved in the civil rights movement, I had learned that racism was the single most important issue in U.S. society. But why should I expect Brazilian nonwhites to have a North American-style experience? Why not instead accept the possibility that they were accurately describing their experience?

Accepting this in no way diminished for me what I was hearing of the deep wounds of those *negros* who had suffered from color prejudice, nor rendered less disturbing what I was learning about the systematic marginalization of nonwhites. Whenever I heard that social prejudice in Brazil was based on class, not color, all I had to do was think of the poor Afro-Brazilian women I had met who could barely choke back tears as they recalled from their childhoods the preferential treatment their lighter-skinned sisters had received, or their feelings of ugliness during adolescence, or of being ignored by a godchild in the company of white people. Of one thing I was increasingly sure: for many Brazilians, the color of their skin and the texture of their hair were cruelly oppressive. Yet in the midst of this oppressiveness, glimmers of light always seemed to shine through. This book is a record of both the oppressiveness and the glimmers of light.

My debts in writing this book are many and deep. The book could not have been realized without the painstaking work of my two research assistants, Marcia Pinheiro and Ruth da Silva. Nor could it have been written without a leave of absence from Syracuse University. My thanks to Douglas Armstrong for that.

For the warm welcome I received at the Program on Race and Ethnicity at the Federal University in Rio de Janeiro in 1996, and for creating a wonderfully stimulating atmosphere there, I am grateful to Peter Fry and Yvonne Maggie. Also at the Program I thank Olivia Cunha, Flavio Cunha, and Laura Moutinho. I benefited in Rio from talks with Patricia Birman, Marcia Contins, Caetana Damaceno, Maria das Dores, Rubem Cesar Fernandes, Clara Mafra, Cecilia Mariz, Regina Novaes, Pierre Sanchis, Livio Sansone, and Gilberto Velho. Among the non-Brazilian scholars who passed through Rio while I was there, I appreciated the chance to talk through ideas with David Lehmann and Kenneth Serbin.

A number of people aided me in invaluable ways unrelated to providing personal interviews. In connection to the devotion to Anastácia, I want to thank Milton Gonçalves, Isabel Fillardis, Ubiraja da Silva,

Luzia Salles, Lady Francisco, Luiz Duarte, Marcos, Marinete, Lurdes Singelo, Zé-Limar, Victoria de Rosário, Rivanilda Santos Gomes, Adão Tiago dos Santos, and the late Nilton da Silva. In the arena of pentecostal churches, I am thankful for the help I received from Pastor Aristom, Irmã Celia, Irmã Maria, Pastor Sergio, Hernani Francisco da Silva, Ariovaldo Ramos, Pastor Ezekiel Teixeira, Pastor Edson Menezes, Gerson Martins, Antônio Olimpio e Sant'Anna, André Mello, Sergio Gonçalves Pereira, Carlos Roberto da Silva, Pastor Selmo, Paulo Cesar Reynaldo, Pastora Rute, Ruth de Almeida, Marcos, and Alexandre. In the area of the *pastoral negro*, I am grateful to Frei David Raimundo dos Santos, Padre Pepe, Dona Aurelina, Dona Ana, Dona Elza, Gegê, Dona Donata, Jeany and Inoque, Sr. Paiva, Luana, Catia, Fernanda, Cosme, and Baiano. Among Rio de Janeiro's black movement organizations, I am indebted to Julio César, Ana Bia de Andrade, José Junior, Josina, Helena Theodoro, Sandra Almada, Ivanir dos Santos, Rosa, Jurema Batista, Benedita da Silva, and Amaury de Souza. Also thanks to Sean Bishop. And a very special thanks to Daniela.

In the United States, the ideas developed in this book have benefited from the criticisms of George Reid Andrews, Diana Brown, Madeleine Cousineau, Anani Dzidzienyo, Marc Edelman, Arturo Escobar, Carmen Ferradas, David Hess, Ted Hewitt, Aisha Khan, Sierra Khan, James Lorand Matory, Robin Sheriff, Amy Simpson, Orin Starn, and Caroline Tauxe. I am especially indebted to my colleague Pramod Parajuli, who for years has helped me to challenge my own thinking about social movements in tough and helpful ways. I am deeply grateful to all these people for allowing me to sharpen my wits in their presence. They will all be relieved to know that for anything I have written that is blameworthy I hold them blameless.

This research was supported in 1993 by the Maxwell School of Citizenship and Public Affairs of Syracuse University. In 1994 it was supported by a summer grant from the National Endowment for the Humanities. And in 1996 it was supported by grants from the Rockefeller Foundation, the Department of Education (Fulbright-Hayes), and the Social Science Research Council. I am very grateful to all these institutions.

Above all, I want to thank my wife Judy, our son Ben, and our daughter Molly, for doing such a crazy—but I hope memorable—thing.

Introduction

Brazil's *Movimento Negro* and the Search for Resonance

THE PROBLEM

Devastating and quotidian, malignant and normal, attitudes of prejudice and acts of discrimination against nonwhites in contemporary Brazil infiltrate city halls and executive suites, corner bars and beauty salons, kitchens and bedrooms, hospital waiting rooms and public school classrooms. Long swept under the ideological carpet, the fact of Brazilian color prejudice and its consequences for the everyday lives of millions of men and women can no longer be denied. Since World War II, three generations of scholars have produced a shelf of studies that reveal the reality of Brazilian discrimination on the basis of color. Starting with the UNESCO studies of the 1950s,[1] continuing through the São Paulo studies of the 1950s and 1960s,[2] efflorescing once again in the census studies of the 1970s,[3] and culminating in the statistical and attitudinal studies of the 1980s and 1990s,[4] the question is no longer *whether* a Brazilian's color influences her life chances, but *how.*

We now know, for example, that nonwhites are three times more likely than whites to be illiterate,[5] and that whites are five times more likely than *pardos* (people of visibly mixed ancestry) and nine times more likely than *pretos* (people who identify themselves to census-takers as "black") to obtain university degrees.[6] We know that the darker the child, the more often he is allowed to drop out of school by the fourth grade,[7] and that whites have access to the highest-paying jobs, earning up to 75 percent more than *pretos,* and 50 percent more than *pardos.*[8]

We know that police brutality and prison sentences continue to be applied disproportionately to nonwhites[9] and that state governments continue to budget almost nothing to offices treating judicial cases of racism.[10] And we know that nonwhites, who are the majority of Brazilians, are virtually absent in the halls of political power.[11]

Not surprisingly, women are the most disadvantaged segment of the nonwhite population. We know that nonwhite women, and especially *pretas*, continue to be sterilized, and their children continue to die from disease and violence at rates far exceeding those for analogous groups of whites; that nonwhite women, and especially *pretas*, continue to be paid less, occupy lower-status jobs, and receive less education than do white women;[12] and that nonwhite women, especially *pretas*, die from debilitating diseases far more often than their white counterparts.[13] The more we know, the worse the picture gets.

Such are the injustices that Brazil's black movement is committed to fighting. The movement, which first appeared in the 1930s, had new life breathed into it in the early 1970s,[14] when a whole generation of nonwhite students found themselves caught in the contradiction between the promise of upward mobility and the reality of continuing to be treated in the job market as second-class citizens.[15] It was a period that saw the explosion of the "Black Soul" dance craze[16] that popularized the physical carriage of self-confident, militant black North America.[17] It was also a time when the struggles to decolonize the Portuguese possessions of Angola, Guinea-Bissau, and Mozambique sent a symbolic message: Portuguese-speaking blacks were courageously shaking off the yoke of white domination.[18] In this context, Rio de Janeiro saw the founding of a number of black cultural groups, some of which, initially to avoid repression by the military, styled themselves "research centers" such as the Instituto de Pesquisas de Culturas Negras (IPCN) and, later, the Centro de Estudos Afro-Asiáticos (CEAA).[19]

By the end of the decade, the military had begun the process of "opening" political space, which social movement groups began to occupy.[20] Among black activists this new self-confidence showed itself when in 1978, in protest against the murder by police of Robson Luiz, a black taxi driver, activists in São Paulo called a major demonstration. This became the founding event for the *Movimento Negro Unificado* (MNU, the United Black Movement), which would serve as the center of black movement organizations in Brazil for the next decade.

No one can doubt that the black movement has had a tangible effect on Brazilian society. The past twenty years have witnessed changes in Brazil's landscape of attitudes about color/race identity and relations, many of which can be attributed to the movement. Institutions throughout Brazilian society have, for example, increasingly questioned the notion that Brazil is a racial paradise.[21] The 1988 Constitution makes racism unconstitutional, and the 1989 Caó Law makes it a crime.[22] President Fernando Henrique Cardoso has stated that Brazil is a racist country and asked Congress to implement some version of affirmative action.[23] TV Globo recently aired the first Brazilian soap opera about a middle-class black family, and *Fantástico*, the most-watched television show in Brazil, now periodically features dark-skinned hosts. Beauty salons specializing in *cabelo crespo* (nappy hair) are proliferating in urban areas, and on city streets one can see women sporting an impressive variety of nontraditional hairstyles, including rasta dreads, braids, and Afro permanents.[24] And on newsstands in major cities one now finds glossy magazines targeting a self-identified *negro* audience.[25]

While such trends are promising, many activists regard their promise as far from fulfilled. They see recent changes as fragile and contingent, as more an expression of fashion than a real turnabout in attitudes, behavior, and institutional power. They point out that all too often the people who spout the appropriate line about Brazil's being a racist country have difficulty identifying racism in their own experiences, speak mainly of individual rather than institutional racism, and do nothing to stop either.[26] They point out, too, that all these changes have not yet affected the socioeconomic indicators that continue to find people with the darkest skins at the bottom of the social pyramid.

Activists in the *movimento negro* thus believe that their work, far from over, has really only just begun. To achieve lasting changes in the status of Afro-Brazilians, they say, will require changes in, among other things, Brazil's legal system, access to education and health care, and police behavior. Bringing about such changes, they say, will require a strong black movement. As the National Congress of Black Organizations recently stated, "the black movement in Brazil . . . is one of the most crucial elements in the process of democratization of society."[27]

By *movimento negro* I mean groups that place an explicit emphasis on struggling against racism and building a positive black identity.[28] These groups do not speak with one voice. One may, to begin with, distinguish between groups that focus on the judicial and legislative arenas, such as União de Negros pela Igualdade (UNEGRO) or Movimento Negro Unificado (MNU), and groups that focus on cultural work, such as musical *blocos afros* like Olodum or Agbara Dudu. Groups that emphasize an essential black identity rooted in an African cultural/racial lineage, such as Instituto de Pesquisas Afro-Brasileiras (IPEAFRO) or

Centro Nacional de Africanidade e Resistência Afro-brasileira (CENAREB), need to be distinguished from those that emphasize a black identity rooted in the New World experience, such as Rio de Janeiro's Grupo Cultural Afro-Reggae. It is also useful to differentiate between those groups whose audience tends to be middle-class professionals and intellectuals, such as the Instituto de Pesquisa da Cultura Negra (IPCN), the Centro de Estudos Afro-Asiáticos (CEAA), and those which pride themselves in having "gone to the bases," such as the Centro de Articulação de Populações Marginalizadas (CEAP), Agentes de Pastoral Negro, and the Catholic Church's pre-vestibular courses for black and poor communities. Finally, since the late 1980s the growing number of organizations focused on the concerns of women, such as Criola in Rio and Geledes in São Paulo, may be distinguished from traditionally male-dominated *movimento negro* organizations.

Yet an ideological core to the black movement does in fact exist. All activists believe that the North American model of hypodescent—the one-drop rule of black identity—should be adopted in Brazil. Furthermore, they invariably claim that the image of Brazil as a society with easygoing race relations was concocted by the white ruling class to keep the black masses ignorant and docile. They all agree that a key struggle is to convince black men and women that they are beautiful. And with only a few exceptions, activists believe that in order for the Brazilian black to shake off centuries of internalized inferiority and self-hate, he must come to value his African heritage.

While groups espousing these views have proliferated, the actual number of participants in them is not very large. It is in fact a matter of concern to black activists that their organizations remain fragmented and small.[29] To the extent that the leadership and social base of the movement are mainly limited to urban, middle-class, and professional *negros*,[30] a common refrain of movement activists is that they want to mobilize the mass of Afro-Brazilians, but that these resist mobilization.[31] "[T]he near absence, or let us say the relative weakness, of a *movimento negro*," writes Howard Winant, "is rather striking. . . . The Afro-Brazilian movement's failure to present itself has thus come to constitute a rather glaring challenge to those of us who have so eagerly awaited it."[32] Given the extent of racial injustice in Brazil, this "failure" is a matter calling for careful assessment. If color prejudice and discrimination are so pervasive and severe in Brazil, why is it that, as Carlos Hasenbalg has said, "the great masses of the black population . . . are not very receptive to the *movimento negro*'s message"?[33]

Efforts to answer this question have tended to cluster around one or more of the following explanations. First, in contrast to the dichotomous racial classification system of the United States, in Brazil the social perception of race exists along a continuum that encourages passing toward whiteness, making it difficult to forge a unified non-white identity.[34] Further, the myth of "racial democracy," which teaches Brazilians to interpet inequality mainly in class, not color, terms, remains powerful.[35] Twine, among others, has argued that Afro-Brazilians do "not possess a conceptual scheme to interpret and analyze their experience [of color prejudice]."[36] In addition, the relative lack in Brazil of clear geographical segregation by color makes it difficult, as Hasenbalg has put it, "to establish the connections between racial discrimination and social position. The poor black does not necessarily perceive the connection between his racial condition and his poverty."[37] Finally, in a society in which misery is an overwhelming social reality, blacks tend to be less concerned about color prejudice than they are about basic economic issues.[38] As Hasenbalg contends, "[t]he themes that appear in the *movimento negro*—denunciation of racism, retrieving a black identity through culture—are things that seem very abstract and distant for that great mass of the black population that confronts very elementary problems of survival."[39]

Together, these explanations go some way in helping us understand the limited force of Brazil's black movements. But are they exhaustive? I do not think so. To these explanations, I believe, should be added one more: namely, that *movimento negro* activists adopt stances that marginalize and alienate many people in their targeted constituency who otherwise are sympathetic to their goals. The previously cited explanations focus on only one kind of demobilizing force, namely the lack of consciousness of blacks in Brazilian society. These explanations' common underlying claim is that lack of popular black participation in the *movimento negro* can be best understood as expressing Brazilian blacks' ambiguous or vague awareness of color identity and color prejudice. This view presumes that there are no sizeable potential constituencies of blacks that might be tapped if only the *movimento negro* were to refine its own consciousness and tactics. In short, this view fails to ask: Are there men and women in Brazilian society who identify themselves as *negro*, perceive color discrimination in their everyday life, yet steer clear of black movements? If such men and women exist, what is it about the *movimento negro* that fails to resonate for them?

THE FIELD OF POPULAR CHRISTIANITY

In any study of how political movements relate to popular culture, it is advisable to pay attention to religiosity. Religion often fills the days, evenings, and weekends of people, affecting their private thoughts and their public behavior. This is especially true in Brazil, where religiosity is a pervasive presence.[40] Furthermore, any study of popular Brazilian religious culture must examine Christianity. Eighty percent of Brazilians identify themselves as Catholic, and the country has seen a rapidly growing presence of Protestants, especially pentecostals (15 percent). In seeking to depict the religious experience of Brazil's blacks, most anthropological work has focused on the "Afro" religions.[41] If the figures published by Datafolha for 1994 and by the Instituto de Estudos de Religião for 1995 are considered, however, it becomes clear that the majority of people who identify themselves as *negro* or *preto* are practitioners of some form of Christianity. The national survey of 1994 found that 71 percent of the six hundred respondents who identified themselves as *preto* (out of a total of five thousand respondents) identified themselves as Catholic, and 10 percent identified themselves as pentecostal.[42]

This is the context in which I learned, in 1988, that Benedita Da Silva, the rising star of the *movimento negro*, was a member of the pentecostal Assembly of God church. I was becoming aware of the depth of the Brazilian black activists' antipathy toward the Protestants, whom they excoriated as hostile to black pride. Blacks who became evangelicals, they said, were trying to become white. What then, I wondered, did they make of Benedita's religious identity? "Benedita is an idiosyncrasy," an activist told me. "She is exceptional. Her black identity has really nothing at all to do with her being a *crente.* . . . We think she must have gone through some kind of crisis, and that was how she went in. But to tell you the truth, most of us wish she would leave that religion." Such remarks left me feeling skeptical. Having grown up in the United States, it was difficult for me to accept the claim that black pride and evangelical belief were inevitably at odds with each other. What complex connections might in fact exist in Brazil between evangelical and black identities?

As I began to formulate this question in 1988, I attended a rally organized by the *movimento negro*, where I saw a large canvas painting of a black woman with blue eyes, her mouth muzzled by a facemask. It did not take long to learn that the image of this woman was the object of a huge Catholic devotion. She was known as Escrava Anastácia, and she commanded a massive following not only in Rio, but throughout Brazil. Her face provoked in me a myriad of questions. Who was she? What was her story? What did she mean to her devotees? Did devotion to her influence the devotee's ideas and sentiments about color and race? How could this Catholic icon, the image of a tortured, silenced woman, be used as a symbol by the *movimento negro*? How successful was this attempt on the part of the movement to link to a phenomenon of popular Christian culture? Was the movement able through this devotion to gain adherents, making up for its losses to pentecostalism?

Then, in that same year, I witnessed the Catholic black pastoral's effort to create a celebration of the Eucharist that incorporated elements of African culture. Black Catholic leaders, who enjoyed sympathy from the secular *movimento negro*, were insisting, I heard, that this inculturated Mass would become the cornerstone of their struggle to raise popular consciousness about the value of Afro-Brazilian culture. Yet I was also hearing grumbling about the inculturated Mass from practicing Catholics. Why were these people grumbling? Who was being drawn to this form of the Mass, and who was being alienated by it? What was the impact of this innovation on the attitudes about color and race of the people exposed to it?

What first arrested my attention about each of these three domains was the particular stance adopted toward them by the black movement. Activists had strong opinions about the political meanings of each, opinions that led them to specific postures of hostility, ambivalence, or support. How fair were these opinions? What were they getting right, and what were they getting wrong? In what ways were they successfully identifying connections between popular Christian belief and black identity, and in what other ways were they missing them? In remaining hostile or ambivalent toward some forms of popular Christianity, while emphasizing others, to what extent might the *movimento negro* be contributing to the marginalization of pools of potential sympathizers?

Such questions derive from, and are enriched by, more general views about social movements as simultaneously articulatory and marginalizing practices, and about their situatedness as one set of practices among several in a field of cultural alternatives. It is to the task of explicating these views that I now turn.

THEORIZING SOCIAL MOVEMENTS' RELATIONSHIP TO POPULAR CULTURE

Social movements are clusters of ideas and practices that build upon the ideas and practices already present in the world they inherit, in order to move toward ideas and practices of a world they seek to create.[43] Thus, for instance, in order to move toward the idea and practice of racial equality and integration, the civil rights movement in the United States built from the idea of equality expressed in the Declaration of Independence and Gandhi's idea of civil disobedience.[44] As a movement struggles to move from that which it inherits to that which it creates, its activists strive to deepen and expand their support among those people whom the movement seeks to serve. All social movements work at the cusp of representing and constructing social groups, of moving from groups "in themselves" to groups "for themselves." Activists are simultaneously engaged in acts of expression—of articulating what they take to be the group's felt needs and grievances, and in acts of persuasion—getting people to think of themselves as belonging to a group, or to think in a new way about their everyday experiences.

Activists present to prospective constituents what sociologists call, following Goffman,[45] a "collective action frame," a series of claims about which experiences are important, how they should be interpreted, and what should be done about them.[46] A social movement's collective action frame may be as modest as a union organizer's framing of the shortness of a lunch break as an attack upon workers' rights, or as sweeping as "master frames"[47] about colonial oppression or capitalism. Whatever their breadth, such frames are always calls to a targeted constituency to articulate certain of their experiences and ideas, and to marginalize others. Such moving between articulation and marginalization is particularly clear in the frames deployed by identity movements.[48] These frames commonly call upon members of a constituency to highlight one aspect of their lives while setting aside and "forgetting" others. Alberto Melucci has called this the tendency to ask people to "turn their backs on complexity."[49] Thus, for example, the Kayapo indigenous movement seeks to teach young Kayapo men to set aside tribal loyalty and emphasize pan-Indianness;[50] the British Carnival Development Committee (a black cultural affirmation movement) sought in the 1970s to teach inner-city black youth to set aside gang loyalties and to think instead of a pan-African identity;[51] the Citizen Action for Health, a New England movement to reopen prenatal clinics, sought to teach women of various races and ages and education levels to set these aspects of their lives aside and to transform themselves into "community" and "low-income" women.[52] The Brazilian black consciousness movement, meanwhile, expects nonwhites to pay special attention to their descent from slave and African forebears, and to set aside their other ancestries; it calls upon them to reinterpret experiences once understood as having been shaped by personal idiosyncracy or class prejudice as having been shaped by racism; it asks them to place a special value on their bodily response to drumming, while marginalizing their bodily response to, say, violins; it urges them to be especially appeciative of Afro-religious practices such as the worship of the *orixá*s (Afro-Brazilian spirits), while distancing themselves from the practice, say, of wearing the suit acquired in a Baptist church.

Emphasizing some ideas and experiences and marginalizing others can, of course, evoke a positive response. Some people responded favorably to the claim, made by certain sectors of the nuclear disarmament movement, that the elimination of nuclear arms was so important that it required activists to suspend struggle on other fronts until all nuclear arms were destroyed.[53] When a collective action frame is able to line up like this with the existing ideas, beliefs, and concerns, sociologists speak of "frame resonance."[54]

A frame can, however, fail to resonate. There were people who found the claims of the nuclear disarmament movement alarmist and insensitive to the need to work on other issues as well.[55] As Snow and his colleagues remind us, "[p]otential constituents are sometimes galvanized and mobilized; on other occasions framing efforts fall on deaf ears and may even be counter-productive."[56] Activists sometimes fail to grasp important meanings in their audience's myths and cultural practices; or the framings they choose may carry unintended messages or be heavy-handed, rigid, and emotionally problematic for some in their audience.[57] As Tarrow has noted, the process of frame resonance "is not always easy, clear, or uncontested," partly because "movement participants often have their own 'reading' of events that differ from those of their leaders."[58] Rhetorics of ethnic identity are notorious for failing to resonate evenly among those at whom they are directed; indeed they often are experienced as quite "dissonant."[59] Audré Lorde has pointed to this dynamic: "As a Black lesbian feminist comfortable with the many different ingredients of my identity . . . I find I am constantly being encouraged to pluck out some one aspect of myself and present this as the meaningful whole, eclipsing or denying the other parts of self."[60]

The perspective of frame resonance is useful for analyzing the work of Brazil's black movements because it allows us to move beyond the view that the movements fail to persuade segments of their constituency primarily because people in these segments are confused, hegemonized, or alienated. Our question should be not just "Why don't they respond?" but also "What is it about the movement's framing of issues that fails to resonate for them?"

Reframing the question this way opens a new perspective on the logic of activism. It reminds us that activists need to get to know their constituencies well. Many activists know little about their targeted audience except that they belong to the category of people their movement is supposed to benefit. Sometimes their knowledge is made up primarily of stereotypes and bits and pieces culled from hearsay. As they strive to resonate, they choose items of popular culture that seem relevant to their own collective action frames. Their effort to resonate is rarely a clear, unambiguous process; it is, rather, thick with presupposition, bias, and shooting in the dark. It is highly interpretive.

Interpretation has consequences for where activists choose to concentrate their energies. As Klandermans has pointed out, given the limited resources of many social movement organizations, activists tend to prefer tactics in which

> no time and effort is wasted on people who do not sympathize with the movement to begin with. Therefore, like advertisers, movement organizers apply their knowledge and engage in target group segmentation: they canvass in neighborhoods where they know many sympathizers live, they advertise in newspapers and magazines they know sympathizers read, they go to events sympathizers attend and they use mailing lists of organizations that sympathize with the cause.[61]

In trying carefully to husband their resources, activists are not averse to dismissing as lost causes entire groups of people.[62] Sometimes such dismissals are prudent and well advised. Yet because activists' knowledge of their constituencies can sometimes be spotty, dismissing whole groups of people may be a mistake. This is one of the problems of social activism: the tendency to preach to the converted, become sectarian, and fail to devote time and energy to tough outreach efforts that cross taken-for-granted divides and barriers.[63]

A shift in perspective can be helpful here. Activists sometimes fail to appreciate that sympathizers with their cause often exist in unexpected places, not only as individuals, but also in informal networks. Some activists are sensitive to the role of culture and the networks and collectivities it generates as forming oppositional consciousness and pools of potential sympathizers.[64] Thus, for example, black political groups in Britain were keen in the 1970s to develop linkages to Trinidadian steel bands, because they recognized that "the steel band transforms the people who play in it and dance to it, and fosters links between them."[65] Similarly, black consciousness groups in Brazil have developed complex linkages to reggae-samba, hip-hop, and Afro-music bands, as well as to *candomblé* houses.[66] Yet such linkages are typically narrow, and frequently crowd out alternative and potentially rich sites of resonance. The choice of which groups, cultural practices, and networks to seek out and align with is often determined less by textured knowledge of where the most sympathizers are than by the presuppositions of movement ideology.

When we examine a social movement organization's cultural politics and its choice of appropriate sites for linkage, we need always to keep in mind three questions: How correct are the activists that this cultural site is indeed hostile to the development of sympathy with the movement? To what extent might activists find that people at the site, while unsympathetic with some parts of the ideology, are sympathetic to others? And how might activists' own views evolve, deepen, and expand by entering into a direct encounter with people who are not the usual suspects?

To address these questions, it is helpful to reimagine social movements as belonging to a field of popular social thought and action, in which they are not privileged carriers of oppositional consciousness. Once we think in terms of a field,[67] we can shift our focus away from the social movement organization itself, to the constituency it is striving to serve. In this way, our perspective becomes more panoramic, expanding to consider a social movement group *alongside* other social practices in the field. This encourages us to examine the social movement in the same way we examine other practices, as perpetuating old ideas and experimenting with new ones.

This raises the question of how to read the political meanings of popular culture. Although James Scott is certainly right to insist that the socially weak often believe and do things that resist domination,[68] subalterns can and often do think and act in other ways as well. Not all beliefs and practices have to do with domination and resistance. Like the complex sets of beliefs about plant magic documented among the Aguaruna, some beliefs have more to do with the intricate relationships between people and their natural environments. These may, quite obviously, sometimes find themselves caught willy-nilly in larger political struggles, but they may also be examined and understood in their own terms, as cosmovisions that enjoy their own specificity.[69]

Even for beliefs and practices directly implicated in the social relations of inequality, there is much that is left out of the view that all is resistance. The poor and oppressed sometimes say things that are splendidly quotable as examples of resistant and oppositional views; but they also sometimes say things that are embarrassing to an ideology that prizes agency and collective action. The socially weak sometimes resist and sometimes do not; sometimes embrace with great passion norms they have learned from the socially powerful and sometimes do not; sometimes do both simultaneously; and sometimes feel unsure, like anyone else, what in the world to do. The reader may, with justice, supply Gramsci's point that the consciousness of the socially disempowered is frequently contradictory, a site of the coexistence of, and struggle between, hegemonic and counterhegemonic views. The task of the analyst here is not to claim that the socially weak do mainly one thing or the other, but to document the range of, and to trace the lines of social influence upon, what they in fact do.[70]

Fair enough. A thoroughgoing Gramscian will find the unappealing, hegemonic stuff to originate mainly from above in powerful institutions, and the appealing, counterhegemonic stuff to originate mainly from below, in popular horizontal practices.[71] It might be desirable if the local social relations of neighborhood fostered only egalitarianism and moral economies,[72] but we also know that they can foster hierarchy and patriarchy.[73] It might be comforting if the power of the state, whether colonial or national, only fostered attitudes of deference, dependency, and patron-clientelism,[74] but we also know that the state can foster, through political parties, education, and land policy, combative attitudes of citizenship and agency.[75]

More problematically, the Gramscian view does not help us to understand why dominant points of view develop such persuasive power among subordinated classes. Certainly there is no denying the influence of powerful institutions like schools and churches to teach people to accept illusions and lies. But there is something peculiarly unsatisfying about such an account. Not only does it deny subordinate classes the ability to exercise a critical faculty, but it dichotomizes the world into the collision of true and false ideologies. A more respectful view, in my opinion, recognizes that powerful ideologies—such as the claim that Brazil is a racial democracy—derive some of their power from being partly true. That is, for people to continue to believe a myth, it must fairly describe some important part of their everyday lives. It is precisely an ideology's partial rootedness in accurate descriptions of everyday life that makes it possible for those who embrace it also to accept those parts of it that have no such accuracy.

In even the most sensitive treatments, popular consciousness is frequently read off of practices and myths, without paying due respect to the fact that practices and myths are often understood in significantly different ways by different subgroups within the population that deploys them. Bourdieu has sensitized us to the power of *habitus*; let us hope he has not desensitized us to our informants' powers of reflection, critique, interpretation, consciousness, and even indifference. In recent analyses of religion, for example, it has become common to invoke a certain romance of memory, in which the researcher's task is to discover the core of religious belief in dramatic reenactments of colonial histories.[76] While such discoveries are important, it is crucial to remember that our informants' interpretations of these ritual scenes and myths run the gamut from indifference to passion, and that their understandings include, but are not limited or reducible to the splendid accounts of colonialism the anthropologist may have discovered. The claim by some informants that their religion allows them to transcend history altogether must also be respected as a genuine expression of religious experience.[77]

HOW WE CARRIED OUT THE STUDY

From its inception, I knew a project of this scope should be undertaken by a team of researchers, and that it would be important for the perspectives of black Brazilian researchers to have an impact on the formulation of questions and the completion of the interviews. As a white male middle-class North American Jew about to embark on a project in which most of my informants were to be poor black Brazilian Christian women, I needed all the perspective I could get.

Through Patricia Birman, an anthropologist at the Universidade Estadual de Rio de Janeiro (UERJ), I was able to recruit two research assistants, one a master's student in anthropology, the other the holder of a recently completed bachelor's degree in anthropology. Since I already had some sense that the difference between being white, *morena*, and *negra* was bound to be significant to the project, I was grateful that one assistant had grown up identifying herself as *morena* while the other assistant had always identified herself as a *negra*. I assumed that such differences would eventually come to play some role in our definition of research strategies and in the data we would collect. (The term "*morena*" will be discussed in Chapter 1.)

Marcia, Ruth, and I began planning the project in June 1993. We devoted six weeks to interviewing and participant observation in May and June 1994; between 1994 and 1995, they carried out occasional interviews while I was in the United States. Then, from January to December 1996 we worked jointly on all phases of the research, with them devoting ten hours per week each to the project. I paid them at a rate comparable to what they would have received from a Brazilian university fellowship.

Working in a team was an extraordinary experience. I was exhilarated by sharing the minute details of sampling, interviewing, observation, question formulation, and preliminary analysis. The fact that they were Brazilians with extensive knowledge of the *movimento negro* and deep personal experience with issues surrounding race and color made working with them irreplaceable and unforgettable. During the early phase of the project we met daily to discuss issues, questions, and strategy. Later we kept our meetings to monthly day-long events. At every phase, they challenged my assumptions, subjected my interpretations to criticism, and were a great fount of ideas and suggestions. If this book has any merit, it is due to my having had the good fortune of working with Marcia and Ruth.

Between mid-1993 and the end of 1996, we interviewed men and women in the metropolitan area of Rio de Janeiro, in the Zona Sul, Zona Norte, and Baixada Fluminense. Rio de Janeiro, with a population of nearly six million, is the second largest city in Brazil, after São Paulo. It is a place of breathtaking, seething contrasts. The city is a dramatic embodiment of Brazil, a country with the dubious distinction of having one of the most unequal distributions of wealth in the world. Excruciatingly beautiful black crags of granite rise in impossibly sheer cliffs from the ocean. From Ipanema beach, with its shady palms, picturesque bistros, and shining white hotels, it is a ten-minute walk to the winding narrow corridors of the bare brick shantytown of Cantagalo. On a Sunday afternoon, well-heeled patrons of the movie theaters in Copacabana walk past large groups of barefoot street children begging from blankets set out on the sidewalk.

The city is divided into two main zones. There is the southern zone (Zona Sul), which includes the great upper-class neighborhoods of Leblon and Ipanema, and the middle-class neighborhoods of Copacabana and Botafogo. The Zona Sul is the site of most of the city's cinemas, luxury hotels, stores, restaurants, beach culture, and nightlife. Tourists rarely venture beyond the Zona Sul. The zone is ringed on the mountainsides by huge *favelas*, the largest of which (Rocinha) is home to a half million inhabitants. The *favelas* are armed camps, controlled by drug gangs, in a state of tense truce or open battle with the municipal police. Warfare between gangs or between gangs and the police periodically explode into exchanges of machine-gun fire inside and between *favelas*, and stray bullets sometimes end up on the floors of nearby penthouse apartments.

To the north of downtown Rio lies the sprawling northern zone (Zona Norte), which until two decades ago was almost entirely poor and working class. Since the rise in Zona Sul's rents, the middle class has begun to migrate to the northern zone. The Zona Norte is now a mix of working- and middle-class homes and apartment buildings. In contrast to the Zona Sul, the Zona Norte has few parks or trees.

Beyond the Zona Norte lies the Baixada Fluminense, the great expanse of Rio de Janeiro's poor suburbs, including the major cities of Duque de Caxias, Nova Iguaçu, and São João de Meriti. Residents of the Zona Sul shudder when the name of the Baixada is mentioned, for it is associated with horizontal *favelas,* drugs, crime, and misery. While these blights do exist, the reality of the Baixada is better understood as a stretch of major urban centers separated by expanses of deserted land, and interspersed with hundreds of small working-class towns. Each town or *bairro* includes hundreds of brick and plaster houses, built by their owners. While most people in the Baixada have running water and plumbing, electric power outages are frequent and garbage disposal and bus service are spotty. Women who are not at home or working as maids toil in the numerous metallurgical, petrochemical, and pharmaceutical plants that make the Baixada the most industrialized region of Brazil outside of São Paulo.

Over the course of three years, we conducted one- to three-hour-long interviews with one hundred sixty-six people. One hundred thirty of these interviews were with women, and thirty-six were with men. We did our best to speak with people throughout the range of age: about 45 percent of our informants were between the ages of fifteen and forty, 30 percent were between forty and sixty, and 25 percent were over sixty. Given our focus on the poor and working class, most of the people we spoke with lived in the districts of the Zona Norte and the Baixada Fluminense, rather than in the Zona Sul. Indeed, about four-fifths of our sample lived in these areas, and identified themselves as *pobre* (poor), or, at best, *razoável* (reasonable).[78] Our female informants worked as domestic servants, housewives, nurse's aides, retail clerks, elementary schoolteachers, factory workers, and in the informal sector as putting-out workers. The men were construction workers, factory workers, drivers, retail clerks, teachers, informal-sector workers, and unemployed.

As our research proceeded, it became clear that most of our informants would be women. In part this was due to the usual force at work in ethnographic research of this type: it was simply easier to locate and talk with women in their homes. But the pattern was also due to the objective demographic makeup of the religous groups we were studying. As a recent survey has concluded, seven of ten evangelicals in the greater Rio de Janeiro area are women.[79] Among devotees to Anastácia, the proportions we saw at temples were about ten women to every man. The predominance of women among participants in the inculturated Mass was also clear: at four different Masses, we counted a preponderance of women over men at a rate of about four to one.

Naturally we were not constrained by these proportions, and could have sought more aggressively to expand our sample of men. I decided not to. As the depth and richness of women's accounts began to emerge, and the patterns of difference in experience between white, *morena*, and *negra* women began to surface, I began to feel that our effort would be better rewarded by deepening our knowledge of these contrasts, rather than making efforts to expand the male sample, when the payoffs for such efforts were unclear.

Later I began to turn methodological necessity into theoretical virtue. As I became more immersed in the literature on race produced by Brazilian scholars, the lack of a textured, ethnographic analysis of women's experience became quite glaring. The use of the term "black" in that literature glossed over the specificities of gender-bound experience. The works that did treat of black women specifically were mainly statistical studies.[80] And despite the depth and importance of beauty, dating, and marriage in the construction of Brazil's gender/race system, not only were these topics absent from analytic view, but empirical research on their specific emotional impact on women was virtually nonexistent.[81] I began to feel that a deeper engagement with women's experiences might hold an important key to Brazil's enigmatic world of race and color.

This work does not purport to be comprehensive in its coverage of the experience of color in Brazil. It focuses on the lives, travails, triumphs, and ambivalences of women. The speech and experiences of men have been included mainly where these help situate and shed light on the lives of women. I do not doubt that a fuller ethnographic treatment of white, mulatto, and black men's lives and attitudes is urgently needed, and that a fuller, more nuanced portrait of race in Brazil will only emerge when the accounts of men and women are represented simultaneously.[82] If the present work does nothing more than persuade the reader of the desirability of such fuller treatments, it will have performed a useful service.

The Color Terms of the Interviewees
The image of Brazilian color terminology that has dominated the academic literature until recently is that it is enormously variable and con-

textually fluid.[83] This literature relies heavily on the lists of color terms published by the UNESCO studies of the 1950s and by the census of 1976, to show that, in contrast to the United States, Brazilian racial classification is very subjective and changeable.[84] Recent research suggests, however, that the contextual quality of Brazilian color terminology may have been overstated. Nelson Silva's work has made it clear that the majority of the terms in those long lists are rarely used in primary self-identification. Most Brazilians, he shows, identify themselves either as *branco, preto, moreno,* or *mulato,*[85] while the other terms are used only secondarily to qualify, intensify, or "soften" one of the primary terms. Other research suggests that Brazilians in fact distinguish between the terms they most consistently apply to themselves and the more fluctuating set of terms that may be applied to them by others. In a careful pragmatic study of color terms in a Rio de Janeiro shantytown, Robin Sheriff found among inhabitants "a distinction between what they seemed to perceive as one's 'real color' and the words people conventionally used when talking about a specific person's color."[86] It was common, for example, to hear informants say things like "I am *preta*. People call me *morena* but I think I am really *preta*."[87]

A variable rarely taken into account in earlier studies is how a person's term of self-reference has, or has not, changed over time.[88] One might assume that this variable is important in any discussion of "identity," for only by getting a sense of how durable the usage of a primary term is in a person's life can we gauge its relationship to identity. Many people, for example, who call themselves *preta* have gone through long periods of their lives vacillating between this term and saying they are "*morena*," while others have used the term "*preta*" unflinchingly their whole lives. To get at such patterns, there is no substitute for life-historical interviews.[89]

The Terms our Informants Used

With regard to color, we asked each informant, "What is your color?" and how long ago she had begun using this term. We were not satisifed here with short answers, but insisted on probing memories and details. In addition, we sought to understand the various terms other people used to refer to the informant. We found that in most cases, informants drew a clear distinction between the terms with which they most closely identified and the terms used in daily conversation, whether in the contexts of humor, euphemism, or insult.

Twenty-six of our female informants identified themselves as *brancas* (whites). The actual range of terms they used in self-reference included *clara, branquela, branquinha,* as well as *branca.* All these women claimed to have used one or another of these terms their entire lives.

Thirty-two of our female informants referred to themselves by using one of the terms that clustered around *morena,* including *morena clara, marrom bom-bom, morena escura,* and *mestiça.* Five said they regarded themselves as *mulatas.* It is important to distinguish in this group between those who used such middle-range terms with self-confidence and certainty, and those for whom the term involved anxiety and uncertainty. The self-confident *morena* does not need to engage in the process of hair straightening (at least, that is what she says). Other women, meanwhile, self-identify as *morenas,* and engage in hair-straightening as a way to confirm this identity. It is an anxious, uncertain identity, not a self-confident one, because the woman knows the truth about her hair, and is engaged in an elaborate process to alter it.

The remaining seventy-two female informants referred to themselves by one of the terms associated with the darkest-skinned, kinkiest-haired, most "African"-featured end of the somatic continuum: *preta, retinta, escura,* or *negra.* Of these, fifteen said that they had once called themselves by a middle-continuum term such as *morena* or *mulata,* or had vacillated for years between this and a darker-continuum term, but had finally opted definitively to call themselves *negra* in the recent past, during the last decade, due to the influence of the media, the *movimento negro,* friends and family, or religion. I will refer to such people, as they refer to themselves, as *negras assumidas* (assumed *negras*). The remaining fifty-seven female informants claimed to have used one of the darker color terms without vacillation, though not necessarily proudly, all their lives. I will call these women *pretas, escuras,* or *negras,* depending on what they called themselves. These women's appearance placed objective limits on their ability to claim for themselves any durable identity other than that of *preta* or *negra.* They tended to occupy that part of the phenotypical continuum that Clovis Moura calls "indisputably . . . black":[90] very dark skin and visibly kinky hair. Several blacks told us that they could never have entertained the idea of trying to pass into lighter color categories, even if they had wanted to. "I am *preta,*" went a typical comment. "I have always been *preta.* Nothing can change that. Look at my skin: I am dark, and my hair is *seco* [dry]. So I am *preta.* That is all."

A key source of subjectively felt color identity is what one knows to be the truth about the natural state of one's hair. Many who self-identify as *preta* engage in hair straightening as a way simply to be more acceptable aesthetically and to compete more effectively with *morenas.* Straightening for this group does *not* entail coming to think of or identifying oneself as *"morena,"* precisely because they are aware, as they devote considerable time and money to the process, that they do not possess naturally soft hair.

Some of the *negras* said that they had always felt at home in their *negra* identities, that being *negra* had never been a source of shame for them. Others acknowledged either having endured a long period in their lives when being *negra* had been a heavy emotional burden for them, when they had felt the desire to hide themselves away. A few even admitted to still having such feelings now. But none of these women had undertaken a sustained effort to identify themselves as anything other than "what I am": *negra.*

Some of these women used the term *preta* or *escura*; others used the term *negra*. The word *negra* refers directly to the inner, unchangeable essence of a person, her "blood." *Preta* or *escura,* in contrast, refers to that superficial quality, the color of skin. Until the 1980s, *negro* was generally avoided as a self-referential term. The 1980s saw a change in the connotative penumbra of the word *negra*. Due to the influence of the *movimento negro,* but also to the growing presence in Brazilian markets of U.S. black popular culture, especially hip-hop, *"negro"* increasingly became a term of self-affirmation and pride.[91] By the 1990s, the term had entered into common public discourse. It should thus not surprise us that the younger black women, especially those under thirty, who came of age in the 1980s, use the term *"negra"* to refer to themselves. Women over thirty either use the term *"preta"* or else say that they used to say *"preta"* but now say *"negra."*

The Religious Sites

We conducted interviews with forty-three women who belonged to four pentecostal churches. In the working-class neighborhood of Bairro Cera-mica where Ruth grew up, we focused on the Renovated Baptist Church, a congregation of two hundred people, including a sizeable contingent of visibly dark *negros*. The church became Ruth's primary responsibility as researcher. She had known many of the members from childhood. Her prior acquaintance with many of the dark-black women of the congregation, in addition to her own obvious identity as a dark-black woman, gave her special access to the experience of dark-black women.

Marcia assumed the task of carrying out interviews and developing an ethnographic relationship with the Jesus is the Truth church, a congregation of about seventy members on Governor's Island, a neighborhood in the Zona Norte near the international airport. Marcia had gained entry to the church through a friend, and quickly came to be accepted as a researcher carrying out a project on a variety of issues among evangelicals, including youth, women, and color. This church was poor and working class as well, mainly female, and also had a sizeable black contingent.

Aside from these congregations, I got to know two others. I periodically visited a small Assembly of God church in Abolição, a lower-middle- and working-class neighborhood in the Zona Norte. The church had sixty mainly working-class members, a large black contingent, and was pastored by a dark-black man. I also got to know a smaller congregation of the Assembly of God located in the Zona Sul *favela* of Cantagalo. Here, the leaders were mainly black women, aside from the dark-black male pastor, and almost all the members were dark-black or *mulato*. Everyone was poor and working class.

We conducted interviews with thirty-two women who had strong personal relationships with Escrava Anastácia. Initially, our plan was to conduct interviews at the Escrava's shrines, but we quickly realized that those settings were not conducive to high quality interviews. We turned to the less hurried at-home interviews with key informants, who in turn introduced us to other devotees.

There were three principal Anastácia shrines, two in the Zona Norte, the other downtown. In the middle- and working-class neighborhood of Vaz Lobo, a renovated garage has been turned into a pilgrimage site of the slave saint. A life-sized statue of Anastácia stands inside a glass case, receiving the visits each day of hundreds of devotees seeking blessings and giving thanks. We started visiting this locale in 1993, but were obliged to reduce our involvement in 1995 when a split took place and a new temple was established in Olaria, a middle- and working-class neighborhood in the Zona Norte. The temple in Olaria, an impressive structure built by a priest of the Eastern Orthodox church, became popular very quickly, and by mid-1996 was drawing hundreds of devotees each day. We also frequently visited Anastácia's original shrine, the Museum of the Negro, in the annex of the Church of Rosário in downtown Rio de Janeiro.

We interviewed thirty women with some direct experience of the Catholic inculturated Mass. The first women we spoke with we contacted through the black pastoral leader Frei David. Through these women we came to interview family members, friends, and neighbors with a less intense relationship to the inculturated Mass. This allowed us to sample the views of women both central and peripheral to the Mass. We also spoke to women who were quite opposed to the Mass.

THE ARGUMENT OF THE BOOK

This work explores how women's experience of color in Brazil is articulated in three different contexts within the Christian religious arena. The argument is that, contrary to the views of major segments of the *movimento negro*, Christianity is an important and viable idiom for imagining and articulating black ethnic identity and antiracism. We found that both pentecostalism and the devotion to Anastácia have generated complex ways of understanding and coping with the experience of blackness in Brazil and that the inculturated Mass, while expressive of black identity, is problematic in its relation to black women.

After describing each of the three religious contexts, I examine how black Brazilian women encounter the social arenas of beauty, love, marriage, family, and work. I contend that these arenas create deeply troubling experiences for them, qualified in some ways by relations of intimacy and affection. I then turn to an in-depth analysis of the ways the Catholic inculturated Mass has created a space both for the articulation of some black women's deepest longings and desires for memory and wholeness, and the marginalization of others who have fears of Afro-religion, mistrust the Mass's spectacularization of the woman's body, and resent the requirement that they focus exclusively on their African ancestry.

I develop the view that the inculturated Mass, despite its opposition to certain dominant cultural codes, in fact extends and deepens the definition of woman's body as site of pleasure, above all as the pleasure of spectacle and object of male desire. The logic of ethnic politics is the logic of women's bodies serving as vehicles for drawing black men back from white women, and for reproducing and strengthening the black "race," through fertility and the family. Thus, although the standards of female beauty promulgated by the inculturated Mass are alternative to the codes of whiteness, they are not alternative to a conception of female that discovers her value in her body as source of pleasure for men. While the inculturated Mass provides black women a way to liberate themselves from the white aesthetic, it seeks neither to assist women in transcending the need/desire for bodywork, nor for coping with the social consequences—in continued male objectification of them—of such bodywork.

I go on to focus on the *movimento negro*'s great enemy, pentecostalism. Here I find a complex, contradictory field of meaning in relation to blackness. On the one hand, this form of spirituality does indeed appear to dilute black identity and a concern with this-wordly injustice, for some. Yet I document another strong tendency in pentecostalism, which places considerable value on black identity—the valuing of black women, the creation of a courtship arena in which black women can compete on a more even playing field than outside the church, and a language through which the struggle against racism can be imagined as divinely inspired. I document a number of recent collective initiatives to join pentecostal and black identities together.

At a more general level, and in contrast to the inculturated Mass's spectacularization of the female body, pentecostalism proposes the idea of the woman's body as container, as shell, as vessel for what really matters: the sacredness of the soul, and, above all, of the Holy Spirit. By conceiving of women's bodies as vessels into which the Holy Spirit can be poured, pentecostalism effectively shifts the gaze from without to within. Pentecostalism has its own female aesthetic, but it is an aesthetic designed to draw attention to the space within, to the part unseen, manifested through the body as kinetic vehicle. This is a body that is released from the male gaze, from its status as a satisfier of male desire. Although in practice pentecostal women continue to think of their bodies in ways that perpetuate the dominant logic of Brazilian society—that is, themselves as objects of the male gaze—this thought must in pentecostalism confront the logic of sacred containerhood.

As for the devotion to Anastácia, I find there ideological and spiritual forces that push the devotee away from focusing on her blackness and the antiracist struggle. But I also find compelling symbolic resources through which black women can build self-respect for their natural black beauty, cope with the problems of domestic violence, and recreate imaginatively a story of Brazil through which they emerge in triumph. In particular, by conceiving of the woman's body as subject to pain, the devotion to Anastácia dares to tread where the inculturated Mass dares not.

The devotion to Anastácia draws attention to the female body as the site of physical affliction and suffering. Her body suffers violence, torture, rape, disease, dissoluton, and death. But the devotion does not imagine the female body as pure pain: it is a body that endures, that is tough, dense, and resilient. While the inculturated Mass has little space to articulate a rejection of male rights to women's bodies, and little space to appreciate the black woman's power to endure and overcome pain, these themes are central to the devotion of Anastácia. Her body's meaning, its experience in the world, cannot be reduced to that of conventional motherhood. In this devotion the female body's subjection to and transcendance of pain and physicality are not limited by the notion of childbirth: Anastácia never has children. Her body too, like that of the pentecostal, becomes a site of and vehicle for, ultimately, absolute freedom.

I end the book by describing my attempt to make known my findings in different contexts of discussion and debate with black movement activists, in the hope that they might in some way contribute to the ongoing evolution of movement identity, tactics, outreach, and goals. I discuss these efforts in detail, in the expectation that I will be criticized for my naiveté and audacity. If my discussion of these issues does nothing more than to stimulate the reader to reflect further on the dilemmas of translating knowledge claims into practice, it will have been worth the effort.

ONE

The Everyday Wounds of Color

Negras in Love, Family, and Work

MAPPING THE EVERYDAY WOUNDS OF COLOR

Many years ago I was sitting in the kitchen of a poor working-class home on the outskirts of Rio de Janeiro, talking to Dona Maria, a woman who called herself *preta*. I had known Dona Maria for just over six months, during which time we had spoken of religion and politics and death and the best way to prepare rice and beans. The one subject we had not broached was color. I was unsure how to introduce the subject, or whether it was a subject to be introduced at all.

At the table that hot morning, I had just finished off a glass of water. I was still thirsty, but there was no more cool water to be had. Except for Dona Maria's own glassful.

"I'm so thirsty, Dona Maria, would you mind if I had some of yours?"

She made as if to pour some from her glass into mine, but it was too late: I had already seized her glass and was quickly draining it. When I looked up, I could see her eyes were moist.

"What's wrong, Dona Maria?"

A few seconds passed before she regained her composure.

"No one has done that before."

"Done what, Dona Maria?"

"No one who is white—to put their lips there, where mine have . . . been."

After that, as the day drew on, and the week, and the year, Dona Maria drew me into spaces of pain and longing and silent earthquakes. These are the small everyday spaces where the pain of color prejudice occur in Brazil. She told me of the moment when her goddaughter refused to say in public that she was her godmother; of the time in her twenties when the boy she loved left her for a girl with softer hair than hers; of the supercilous looks she used to get from her cousins, who were from a lighter-skinned family; of having to take her meals apart from the family in the house where she worked as a maid for ten years. These things were not supposed to bother her: she was a magnificently faithful Catholic, and all adversity was supposed to rest lightly upon her shoulders. But bother her they did, and mightily. Her tears testified to that.

No one from the black consciousness movement needed to explain to Dona Maria that these things were the work of color prejudice.

It is to a few of these spaces that I turn in this chapter, to shine a small lantern into them. I have chosen to focus here on three arenas of social life where the experience of color for self-identified black women (*negras* or *pretas*) is particularly pronounced and consequential: the world of love, dating, and marriage; the world of sibling relationships; and the world of work. These spaces are not, of course, loci of pure experience. I endeavor to represent them as complex fields of image, sign, and fantasy, in which what is at stake are not just black women's direct experiences, but how those experiences are framed by powerful ideas, norms, and stereotypes about themselves, which they always partly believe and partly disbelieve.

It is not my intent to represent black women in isolation, nor as encountering a world of unremitting adversity. Neither representation would be a fair one. The experiences of black women in these three social arenas emerge in sometimes tense, sometimes warm, but always intimate relation to white women, *morena* and *mulata* women, and men of all colors. These experiences are "softened" and qualified in various ways by these other people's empathy, solidarity, communication, and love. It is precisely because such moments of communion are possible that the wounds their absence inflicts are all the deeper.

WHAT IS THE COLOR OF LOVE?

It is frequently claimed that in Brazil "love knows no color." A young dark-skinned man told me, as if it were the most self-evident thing in the world, that at young people's dances, especially the *funk* and *charme* dances that have been all the rage in Rio de Janeiro since the early 1980s, "there is no discrimination at all. Go there and you will see: the thing you see most often are interracial couples."[1] The idea that youthful urges transcend color prejudice is, in fact, common in Brazilian popular media. A recent spread of glossy photos in the national magazine *Manchete* displays couples at a *charme* dance, accompanied by the caption "in these dances, prejudice ends and interracial couples find their natural habitat."[2] In the magazine *Raça Brasil*, a feature article about "interracial relationships" declared cheerfully that "here, where love reigns, prejudice and racism ends."[3]

There is, however, room for doubt. A second glance at the photographs in *Manchete* and *Raça Brasil* brings home the point: they all are shots of pearl-white women with dark men. When I asked the young man who sang the praises of *funk* dances' color-blindness to describe the interracial couples he was thinking of, it turned out he was referring exclusively to black men with white women. Black women, in these cases, remain invisible.

Just beneath the surface of the arenas of flirtation, dating, courtship, and marriage lies a deep well of color discrimination. In general, the dark hue of *pretas'* skin and the nappiness of their hair destine them, in the awful calculus of the heterosexual romantic economy, to be the ones last chosen and the ones first abandoned. *Negros* and *pretos* with any claim to special status—the fine dancer, the snappy dresser, the one with the car—will do what any self-respecting young Brazilian man will do: he will find himself a *morena*, or, better still, a *branca* with long, flippable hair. Any young black man who frequents the *funk* dances around the city could echo the comment of Rodrigo, a *negro* who on Saturday nights heats up the dance floor in the Zona Norte: "If you're successful, you want to stand out," he says, "there is no other way about it: you have to have a *branca* on your arm. Preference: blonde."

The Beauty of Whiteness

To be a moderately attractive white woman in the working-class courtship arena of Rio de Janeiro means falling heir to a potent array of images that construct her as a token of social honor and power. Walk down any main street in the city, and you are bombarded by images of attractive white women: at every intersection, hundreds of them look at you from newspaper stands, emblazoned on the covers of glossy magazines. Their very ubiquity proclaims their power to occupy— unchallenged—public space. There they are, proclaiming right of eminent domain, looking all passersby straight in the eye, presenting their skin and hair as the self-evident standard by which all female beauty must be measured.

The connection between white women and social power is reinforced in the media through the use of white women's images in association with material wealth. The most socially prestigious products, advertised in magazines and on television, require models who are not only white, but blonde. The wealthiest male icons (such as Romário the soccer player, Ayrton Senna the race-car driver, and Pelé the legendary soccer king) set themselves apart by choosing women with blonde hair. So do successful drug traffickers. The notorious case of Marcia Vieira, a middle-class golden-haired model who ended up dead because she knew too much as the favored wife of a drug kingpin, was a highly publicized example of a common pattern.[4]

The white woman is made by the media to evoke class power through her symbolic connection with physical health. Hers is a body associated with the good nutrition, hygiene, and medical care available only to the middle and upper classes. White women, primarily blondes, are the models of choice for advertising hygiene products and "natural" and "nutritional" foods. This pattern prevails even when the advertiser recognizes that a large part of their market is nonwhite. Early in 1996, for example, O Globo, the most widely distributed newspaper in Brazil, published a supplement that offered readers "complete orientation to improve nutrition, stay in shape, reduce stress and prevent health problems." In this ten-page guide, every model was white. Or consider Astro-Cream's selection of whom to approach to model their body-toning lotion on national television. Although demographic research reveals a large market for such creams among nonwhite women, Astro-Cream recruited not Isabel Fillardis (currently Brazil's most famous mulata model) but the blindingly blonde Xuxa.[5] It is undoubtedly blonde women's association with hygiene and health that has led three out of the four top Brazilian children's show hostesses to be the bearers of golden tresses.

If the motives of the black men who seek out white women are fairly clear (social honor and power are strong inducements, after all), what do white women expect in return? The matter is complex, and I do not presume to have plumbed its depths here. I spoke at some length to three young white women about the question. All agreed with Marta, a wiry youngster with long brown hair who wore the regulation funk uniform of halter and super-shorts: "What can you say? Those negões [large black men], dressed so well, they're irresistible. Their bodies, the way they move. They are hot. Hot." Her girlfriends made the "mm-mmm" sound. Marta added: "And they know how to treat a woman." The others nodded, sucking a little air through their lips.

"What do you mean, 'know how to treat a woman?'" I asked.

Laughter all around.

Marta again: "They are happy to have you with them, they show you much *carinho* [tenderness].Very sweet. A white man [*o branco*] takes you for granted."

I heard this opinion quite often. It was a widespread perception that black men treated their lighter-skinned girlfriends and wives with a solicitude they rarely showed to dark women. I was at a barbeque once when a black man married to a white woman excused himself to return home. His drinking buddies started to harass him. "Ah, man, you should have married a black woman!" "Then you wouldn't have to go running off, like a slave!" The man bristled. "Go fuck yourself!" he said. "It doesn't have anything to do with it." This comment was met with general hilarity. I had witnessed the whole exchange at the side of a dark black female friend. "Put that in your notes," she said, "that is the truth. They treat their lighter wives with so much *carinho*, and us they treat like dirt."

The *Mulata* and *Morena* in the Courtship Arena

If the blackest men are on the lookout for the fairest-skinned and softest-haired women, the lightest men have their pick of darker women, but avoid the darkest. For them, the ideal is the *morena* or the *mulata*. "I like *morenas*," said Duglass, a well-dressed young white man. "They are really beautiful. We Brazilians love a woman who looks like that, you know, the *mulata de exportação* [export-quality *mulata*]." The young men he was with laughed. "Good in bed," they said smirking.

How to identify a *mulata* and distinguish her from a *morena*? The answer is fairly complex. For starters, *morenas* and *mulatas* have two physical features in common, defined in contrast to the *preta*. Although the color of their skin can vary, it cannot be *retinta*, that is, very deep brown or black. Their color has in fact been endowed in Brazilian culture with certain mystique. The ideal images of the *mulata* and the *morena* are rooted in nineteenth-century romantic novels, and were codified in Brazilian popular culture in the twentieth century through the lyrics of the sambas sung at the annual festivities of Carnaval. These odes to sensual beauty portray the *mulata* as the woman who attracts the male gaze effortlessly, without lifting a finger. Royalty, divinity, and magic are routinely invoked in reference to her. The first recorded samba lyric dedicated to her rhapsodizes, "If the *mulata* did not exist / We would have to create her / Whoever invented her deserves / A throne, a scepter, an altar."[6] The same mystical language was applied to the *morena* starting in the 1940s. The contemporary hit song "Marrom bom-bom" ("very beautiful brown"), sung by the Morenos, proclaims "there is magic in your color."

Morenas and *mulatas* also share the feature of hair. Their hair cannot be *"crespo"* (nappy), but must be long, or soft, or gently undulating. Ideally, the hair of a *mulata* or a *morena* behaves this way naturally. The centrality of hair in the image of the *mulata* has been present since the nineteenth century. It was, for example, present in Bernardo Guimarães's novel *Escrava Isaura*, first published in 1875. This is the story of Isaura, a very light octoroon slave, whose "flowing, undulating hair fell gently upon her shoulders in thick and shining curls, and as if a black frieze entirely hid the back of the chair in which she sat"[7] in contrast to her arch rival, a slave named Rosa, who had "black and tightly curled hair . . . worn short and frizzy like a man."[8] Today, to become a professional *mulata*, one of the women who dance the samba in Rio de Janeiro's famous "shows de *mulata*," a woman must be the bearer of long, glorious locks.[9] Every weekend, millions of households tune their televisions to variety shows set to backgrounds of dozens of gyrating young women, all with straight or shoulder-length tresses.

This much the *mulata* and *morena* have in common. What distinguishes them is that the *mulata* cannot deny her *"sangue negro"* (black blood), which supposedly expresses itself through her body's sensuality and natural *"swingue"* (rhythm). The term *"mulata"* itself draws attention to descent, originating during the slave period in the comparison of the offspring of a white-black union to the mule, the issue of a horse and a donkey.[10] Though shorn today of this bestial connotation, the association with hybridity remains. This association, in effect, embodies the male sexual fantasy of uniting the white woman's respectability with the black woman's stereotyped lubricity and powerlessness.[11]

It is the *mulata*'s ability to fulfill the male sexual fantasy of hybridity that endows her with her symbolic power, a power expressed, in part, through her control of the sexual encounter. The *mulata*s in Jorge Amado's novels control the timing, pace, and possibility of sexual pleasure. In the famous television version of Guimarães's novel, Isaura refuses her master's advances, and he cannot bring himself to force himself upon her, as he would were she a *preta*. Similarly, the *mulata*s who dance at Carnaval stand on platforms, to be gazed at rather than possessed—at least not initially. And when Vicente Paiva's samba pleads "Come here, *mulata*," her reply is "No, I'm not going."[12]

This subtle synthesis of white unattainability with the availability of the black woman is at the heart of the *mulata*'s sexual appeal. It should thus not surprise us that although the term *morena* is fast becoming the single most common term of self-reference in Brazil, the prostitutes interviewed by Aparecida Moraes do not use it; instead, they use *mulata* in reference to themselves.[13] It should also not surprise us that in a national survey conducted in 1995, white men declared, by an order of three to one, that *mulata*s were "better in bed" than *pretas;* for young white men the order was closer to five to one, and two out of three young *negros* were also of this opinion.[14]

The importance of race-power fantasy in the construction of *mulata* identity is well illustrated in the careers of *mulata* models and actresses. Few if any are hired to market health or hygiene items; instead their images are used to sell lingerie, beer, or musical events. Isabel Fillardis, for example, is an actress with classically *mulata* features and long hair she claims not to straighten. She began her career at sixteen as a model in lingerie commercials, and her subsequent roles on television were defined by her sexual appeal. In February 1996 she became known as the *mulata* queen who danced Carnaval on national television. In April of that year, in a widely watched television soap opera, Fillardis played the most desirable of the three wives of a magus. By the end of the year, she was the cover girl of the Brazilian edition of *Playboy* magazine.[15]

What distinguishes the image of the *morena* from that of the *mulata*? It is not that the former is about color and the latter about ancestry; for at bottom, they are both about degrees of descent from *negros*. The *mulata* without *sangue negro* would cease to be a *mulata*. "The difference is that *mulata*s have more black blood," said a young *morena*. "The *morena* may have some, but not nearly as much." *Morenas* sometimes deny or "forget" having African or slave ancestors at all, and emphasize rather their descent from European stock, or from the heroic Indians who ran away or died rather than be enslaved. The *morena*'s ability to distance herself from Africa allows her to be socially construed as a respectable girl, whose physical appeal derives not from her body, but from her face and hair.[16] She may have to work harder to stir up the few drops of *swingue* in her body, she may need to be taught how to dance the samba, she may need even more persuading than the *mulata* to give in to the pleasures of the flesh. At the same time, precisely because the degree of black blood in her veins is uncertain, a *morena* may at any time discover that she is a bit more *mulata* than she thought. Thus Maria, a young *morena* told me: "I am *morena*. But sometimes, let me tell you, I really feel like a *mulatinha*!" How could this be, I asked? She smiled. "It's in the blood. You may not know. But you find out." Could it be that she was "really" a *mulata*? "No," she replied. "I am *morena*. I would have to have a lot more black blood to be a *mulata*." The term *"morena"* thus has a broad range as a signifier, accommodating, depending on the woman herself, psychosocial dips into mulatismo without making it a way of life.

Pretas: Beauty, Love, and Marriage

I asked several young men at a dance what they thought of *pretas* as prospective love partners and mates. One made a face; the others were pensive. "Depends on how she looks," said one of them. "If she has a knockout body, fine. But the brillo hair has to go." The young man who made the face commented: "I can't go for one. I don't like *pretas*. When there are so much better-looking women?"

Twenty years of cultural struggle on the part of the black movement have not succeeded at shaking the deeply set Brazilian stigmatization of the looks of the dark-black, nappy-haired woman. In July 1996, a small-time circus performer, a man named Tiririca, released an album on the Sony record label that included the song "Veja os cabelos dela" ("Look at her hair"). Here are some of that song's immortal lyrics:

> Look, look, look at her hair
> It looks like steel wool
> When she walks by, I give a look
> But her hair just won't do.
> Look, look, look at her hair
> She stinks to high heaven
> Like a zoo animal

Despite black movement leaders' success in getting a judge to rule this song a violation of the Constitution, and to order it off store shelves, the effect of the publicity was to make sales of the record skyrocket nationwide, and to lead Sony to scoff at the Constitution by keeping the record on sale in Rio. The chorus in the media was that the case was much ado about nothing instigated by humorless politicians and self-righteous judges.[17]

The song, and the widespread view that it was not worth taking seriously (no newspaper, for example, saw fit to seek the views of a *preta* on the subject), point to the influence in *carioca* (Rio) culture of at least two ideas about the young *preta*. First, what most sets her apart, making her subject to the taunts of others, is her hair, which is "like steel wool." And second, despite her hair's socially defined ugliness, her body remains an object of desire.

Twenty years ago, a national magazine characterized Zezé Motta, the famous dark black actress, as "ugly" because she refused to straighten her hair.[18] In the 1990s the message is much the same. Untreated frizzy hair remains known in everyday speech as *cabelo ruim* (bad hair) or *cabelo feio* (ugly hair). The growing importation from the United States of black hair-care products has only reinforced the high value placed on chemically treated hair.[19] In a 1995 survey of 283 *pretas*, more than a fourth said they would alter their hair if they could.[20] "The modern *negra*," declared a national hair magazine in 1996, "and any woman with *cabelo crespo*, suffers in her skin, or rather, at her roots." Up to 95 percent of all the advertisements in magazines devoted to black pride are for hair relaxers, straighteners, and other chemical means of treating "hard hair."[21] "*Cabelo crespo* is no shame," insists an advertisement for a relaxer, "the shame is not to treat it!"

Ten years ago, black movement militants were vocal about the need to abandon all chemical hair treatments and instead to wear hairstyles that required no invasive chemical alteration, such as the "Angela Davis" natural, dreadlocks, or braids. In the last decade, however, partly because they met resistance from women who felt their hair was no one's business but their own, some activists (both male and female) have adopted the stance of looking the other way. Some have decided to stretch what they mean by "going natural" by accepting the (expensive) practice of implanting and weaving in long, soft "natural" hair imported from China and Indonesia. Others, impressed by the ability of women in the United States to combine a strong black identity with elaborate permanents, have grown more sympathetic to these, too. They personally prefer dreads or braids. (To have braids done well can be quite expensive, too, and there are only a handful of salons in Rio that specialize in them.) Those who become public figures, like Benedita Da Silva or Jurema Batista of the Workers' Party, prefer slightly more conservative, close-cropped naturals or fewer, thick, large braids, known as the "Afro braid." In general, black movement activists no longer place much value on the larger, puffed-out versions of the Afro, because, they say, it is too difficult and time-consuming to manage.

In any case, in Brazil, as in the United States, sporting locks or braids is no longer a guarantee of the radical consciousness of the wearer. For many women these hairstyles have become simply one more fashion statement, a way to imitate Isabel Fillardis's long braided tresses, or to be able to achieve flippable hair without chemical alteration.[22] I met women with braids who were firm believers that racism did not exist in Brazil; and I met at least one woman who wore locks because she was pregnant, and so had been obliged to stop applying harsh chemicals to her hair. She said, however, that for her the locks were the next best thing to straightening. "This way I can get some length," she said.

Activists still reserve tough criticism for chemical straighteners, which they regard as a capitulation to the values of whitening. "These products," an activist told me, "tell a *negra* that the only way she can be acceptable to society is if she damages, burns, and destroys her hair." "The point of all this chemical alteration," said another, "is to make the hair look like the white woman's. So it is another way *negras* have learned to deny their true selves." Yet another complained: "If an attractive man comes into the room, watch what happens: all the black women will start trying to flip their hair, even if they don't have hair to flip! They learn that from white women."

Hair straightening in Brazil thus has a different set of political meanings than in the United States, where black women cannot use straightened hair as a means of passing into a nonblack category. As a North American black woman told me: "When I straighten my hair, I am not trying to be white. I am trying to be a black woman with straight hair. That's all." While such statements may in fact occur in Brazil more commonly than activists realize, as I will indicate shortly, it is nevertheless true that they occur within a larger social context where passage out of blackness into the category "*morena*" remains a possibility.[23]

From the point of view of activists, hairdressers who specialize in black hair are unreliable allies in the struggle against whitening. Four of the black beauty salon owners we spoke with had no qualms about reinforcing, through word and deed, the idea that nappy hair was intrinsically inferior. They all said that women who wished to be beautiful should overcome their nappiness; the photographs they used to illustrate the hairstyles they offered were all of white women. Many black beauticians have, it is true, increasingly called for greater technical respect for natural hair. They now discourage invasive chemical straightening, advising instead that their customers try out the gentler techniques of "relaxing" and wearing the North American "Afro" permanent. Yet they are, in the end, subject to how waves of fashion shape the market, and in Brazil, the biggest player in fashion is neither the hairdresser nor the activist: it is the soap opera. "We are run by television," said Janir, a black hairdresser in the Zona Norte. "If tomorrow all blacks on TV had permanents, that's all I'd be doing. But now straightening is all the rage, because women will come in wanting a cut from the eight o'clock soap opera, even if it doesn't suit her. So what do you do? You give them what they want."

Activists who say black women who straighten are subjecting themselves to discomfort and even danger make a fair point. Chemical hair treatment can inflict direct harm and pain. From older women, who remember the *chapa bahiana*—the traditional scissors-like hot iron used to straighten nappy hair—we heard more than one story of fingers burnt and hair singed. Stories circulate, too, about women who suffer negative reactions to caustic straightening gels, and who have lost hair, gone bald, had their scalps burned, and, in one case, lost vision as a result of the chemical dribbling into her eyes.[24] Use of chemical straightening products, even of Henné (a gentler, herb-based paste), can be the cause of embarrassment, because such products tend to run when the woman sweats. I spoke to one woman who referred to the stress of being forever on guard against little brown rivulets. "It's a pain," she said. "I have to be careful not to walk in the rain, or run too fast."

Furthermore, keeping nappy hair manageable and in style means an investment of time and energy above and beyond what is required of non-nappy-haired women. A person who wishes to straighten using Henné will have to apply it for a full year—twice a week, in half-hour sessions of applying, rolling, and massaging—before the desired effect is achieved; and then she will have to sustain the twice-weekly sessions indefinitely. A woman who wishes to switch from Henné to another straightener has to wait two years while the Henné grows out of her hair. Stronger agents work more quickly, but have to be reapplied every three months, and require constant maintenance. If her hair is damaged to begin with, she will first have to undergo four weekly sessions of three to four hours each, of hair rehabilitation and massage, plus periodic treatments thereafter. One woman spoke of feeling irked by how much she had to visit the beauty salon. "It is suffering: to spend a whole day at the hairdresser's. Sometimes I look at a woman with straight hair and I say, what have they done to deserve that?"

All of this, of course, costs money. Although there are no statistics on the subject, it is probable that a woman with nappy hair who wishes to be in style must spend more money than does a non-nappy-haired woman with the same desire. While a woman who uses Henné will generally spend fifteen dollars per month on the product (by working-class standards no small sum), hair care is more costly for women who use straighteners, activators, protective gels, oil sheens, relaxers, and special shampoos, most of which require a visit to the beauty salon. A basic straightening treatment will cost a woman twenty *reais* (about $20) once every three months. A permanent that uses a high-quality product, imported from the United States, will cost one hundred fifty *reais* ($150) over the course of four months. "I have clients," explained the manager of a major black beauty salon in the Zona Norte, "who earn seventy *reais* in two weeks, and spend it all here. And she will come back in four months." In one salon that targets a working-class clientele, about half the customers earned under one hundred fifty *reais* per month, and up to half of that salary went once every three months to hair care. "When they are going to do their hair," explained one beauty salon owner, "that month they do not buy shoes for the kids, they will give up paying some bills." A mother with several daughters will stagger hair care to follow cash flow: she will bring in one daughter per month. Christmas season is especially busy in hair salons, as working women are flush with holiday bonuses. "Then," said a black hairdresser, "the salon fills up, because mothers are bringing all their daughters at the same time!"

For all these reasons, chemical treatment of black women's hair may with some justice be regarded as oppressive, time-consuming, expensive, and even dangerous to black women. Yet this view does not express the range of how *negras* and *pretas* feel about chemical alteration. While I certainly met women who spoke negatively about straightening, most of the black women I knew did not consider altering their hair a purely negative experience.

To begin with, most of the black women we interviewed do not straighten in order to pass into a new color category—from *preta* to *morena*. Rather, they said, they want the freedom straight-haired women have to do whatever they wish with their hair. Many of the women we spoke with have clear notions of themselves as *negras* or *pretas*, and say they have personally felt discriminated against because of their color. "Look at the woman with straight hair," said one black woman. "She has all the choices. She can curl her hair, or let it go long and soft. So why can't I do what I want?" From this point of view, saying that a black woman should be content with nappy hair feels to these women to be tantamount to declaring that they should have less freedom than straight-haired women.[25] One woman who applies a bleaching agent to the hair on her legs laughed when her aunt accused her of wanting leg hair like white women's. "Does blonde hair on a black leg look like a white woman's leg? No! That's not the point." Another black woman who straightens said: "The black woman who wears a permanent wants to show that she too can wear her hair like any woman. But with the permanent, you are not abandoning your race. It's just that your hair has the same ability as any white woman's for you to do anything with it you like. Why should the black woman be restricted in her choices, if the white woman is not?"

Furthermore, in many women's accounts, the rationale for doing their hair is not primarily to please men (although they usually want to do that, too), but to please themselves. "I am doing this for *me*" is a common refrain. "Most of the women who come here," said Janir, "earn their own money, and they feel that their hair is none of their husband's business." Husbands know this, and resent it. One woman's husband actually followed her to the beauty salon to make sure she was not really with a lover.

While this pattern could be interpreted as a sign of the completeness of the dominant ideology's interpellation of black women, it may also be read as a site of double consciousness, in which women are simultaneously enacting a practice imposed upon them by men, while also destabilizing it by changing its rules: the woman engages in an act of self-beautification to satisfy herself, not the other.[26] It is thus worth noting that many informants were able to move from this destabilizing space of consciousness to an explicit critique of what they took to be the black movement's authoritarian discourse about hair. Their feelings went beyond the notion that everyone should have a right to do their own thing,[27] although they thought that too. One woman put her view clearly: "If someone says that I need to value myself, that I need to have self-esteem, I say: I am doing that! I am taking care of myself, I am not letting myself go. I want to be beautiful. It is only the woman who doesn't care about her looks at all, who feels hopeless, who refuses to go to the beauty parlor."

Hair straightening is not however just a matter of self-esteem, freedom, and equality. It is also a social activity. Many of the black women spoke fondly of the experience of hair straightening at home or in the beauty parlor, as a site of sensual pleasure, of tactile interaction with other women, as a place of bonding, intimacy, information exchange, and affection.[28] "When I apply Henné, I always ask my sister to do it with me," said Angela. "We make something to drink, and we do this, and talk." In the beauty salon, the long hours spent with other women is often experienced as some of the most enjoyable time of the week, spent away from the stress and obligations of the household. "Some women," said Janir, "think of it as an outing, of taking the day off." "I look forward to my visit to Janir's," said Camila. "because here we chat, we have *cafezinho* [coffee], someone always brings cookies or a snack. During the day at home there is no one to talk to, I am very distant from my neighbors. Here we talk about everything."

My own visits to Janir's confirmed this. The place was constantly humming with conversation and laughter. Here women spoke to each other about health, about diet, about family problems, about men. On one occasion, a woman passed around the card of a cosmetic surgeon, provoking a long and often heated free-for-all on the benefits and dangers of such surgery. I tried to think, but could not, of other sites in Brazilian society where such an easygoing, informative, and multiple-voiced conversation among female nonkin might have taken place.

We must therefore be careful to avoid the conclusion that the treatment of hair is an arena in which black women experience nothing but oppression. They do experience oppression there, but that is not all they experience. It would also be too simple to conclude that whatever these women experience that is positive in hair treatment is nothing but a crumb, plot, or strategem to draw them into a regime of power over which they have no control. Again, it does do that, but not only that. What we are witnessing in the arena of haircare is the deep tension between structure and agency that continues to inform most social arenas in which black Brazilian women move.

In Brazilian culture, the bodies of *negras* and *pretas* are regarded as the seat of primitive, uncontrollable sexuality. "The *preta*," goes a gibe common today, "has fire under her dress."[29] I have seen young men lean out of bus windows and make obscene remarks to dark-skinned, nappy-haired black women, while saying nothing to lighter-skinned ones. One *preta* told me, "I can't walk down the street without hearing what they are going to do to me. They don't respect the *criolla* [black woman]. They won't say these things to someone who is lighter-skinned than me, with good hair. They think they need to respect them more. But the *criolla,* who cares? They think we'll spread our legs for anyone."

The image of the *preta* who spreads her legs has long been projected onto the screens, large and small, of Brazilian popular culture. In 1959, in her most famous movie role, Léa Garcia played in *Black Orpheus* the part of a voluptuous *preta* who, in a memorable scene, hurls herself wantonly at her lover.[30] In 1975, Zezé Motta, then as now one of Brazil's few nappy-haired stars, played the title role in Cacá Diegues's film *Xica da Silva*. Xica, an eighteenth-century slave, not a striking beauty, is unable at first to make her charms felt by the master. Only when she literally throws her raw sexual power at him is she finally able to win him over.[31]

From their perspective, *pretas* do not experience themselves in the courtship arena merely as passive objects of the male alternation between lust and avoidance; they engage in active avoidance themselves. In particular, they endeavor to minimize situations in which they will be subjected to humiliating comparative gazes. At dances, *pretas* tend to cluster away from *morenas, mulatas,* and *brancas.* "The black *funkeiras* are always by themselves," said Carlinha, a teenage *preta,* "dancing alone and with each other." The pattern is visible not just at dances. In any social situation where flirtation is in the air, such as at house or block parties, girls tend to gravitate into darker and lighter groups, while groups of boys tend to remain mixed in color. I asked several young people about this. "Yes," said a *preta.* "It is hard to stand next to *uma menina mais clara* [a lighter girl] at a party. A guy passes by, he looks not at you, he looks at her, he says something to her. I like to stand with my friends who are my color."

Avoiding humiliation is also why *pretas* often actively reject the advances of lighter boys. Elinete, a *preta* in her twenties, said: "I never went out with a white boy." "Why not?" "There was actually a boy next door, who was lighter than me, who was interested in me; but I was afraid, I didn't want to get involved. I thought like this: that boy, so light and good-looking, he can't really be serious about me. He certainly wants something else." Another *menina escura* was more explicit. "I won't go out with a white boy because all he wants is sex. And if he gets angry, he'll throw your color right at you, calling you *nega* [pejorative term for *negra*], insulting you."[32]

Despite such anxieties, young *pretas* and *escuras* also have fantasies about being accepted by handsome light-skinned men. "I thought that if I could find my white Prince Charming," said Madalena, a young *escurinha,* "I would never feel ugly again." For young *pretas* came the elation of being found attractive by someone who, they think, could have had someone else. "This made me feel beautiful, that someone wanted me, me," said Ruth, a *preta* in her twenties. "Ulysses could have had any other girl, lighter, prettier than me, with long beautiful hair. I would look in the mirror and say: 'You better count your lucky stars.'"

Some dark-skinned girls entertain the fantasy of "lightening the line" or "cleansing [or purifying] the womb."[33] While this fantasy originated in the fact that the offspring of master-slave miscegenation often obtained privileges, today it has to do with the recognition that lightness means social power.[34] "I have always preferred white boys to black," explained Elielma, a young *preta.* "My cousin said I wanted to lighten my children. Well, that's true. Why not? Why not want a better future for them?" A similar sentiment was voiced by Adriana, a *negra* who was dating a white boy: "I want to have children who are lighter than me, whose hair is better. I think that will be good for them, that they will be happier that way. I was called '*neguinha horrorosa.*' I have wanted to lighten my children, so they won't have to live with that."

Such hopes are not, however, necessary in order for a *preta* to pursue a relationship with a lighter boy. Perhaps the most compelling reason offered in conversation is the simple desire for the same freedom experienced by other girls to pursue love. "Why," asked Sandra, an eighteen-year-old *preta*, "should I have less choice than other girls?" Said Caetana, a twenty-year-old *preta*: "I have never thought about having lighter kids or anything like that. I just love him."

Such love can of course be rewarded. I spoke to several young white men who were dating *pretas*, and asked them what, if any, relevance color had for them. "None at all," said Ulysses. "I do not see her color." Said Rodrigo: "What I value is her as a person." Yet, sadly, more common were stories of stress, betrayal, and failure. Sometimes the relationship was fraught with tension, as the girl worried that the boy was dissatisfied, and was waiting for something better. As Alessandra explained, "I went with a white boy who was very handsome. And every day I thought: 'Why is he with me, an ugly black girl? How can he want to be seen with me?" Indeed, he apparently wanted to be seen with her only when they were safely tucked inside a dance hall. "He accepted me, I think, but I always felt shame when I was with him, because I felt I was ugly and he was beautiful."

The boy may not really be serious after all. He may have heard that *pretas* have fire under their dresses, and wanted to try one out; or he may simply have been playing the scene. In the context of dances, a *preta* often only gains access to one of the high-status men by having to share him with other women. In the case of Alessandra, "he dumped me for a prettier, lighter girl. He was only using me for a time." This kind of boy confirms *pretas*'worst fears. "After that," she said, "I decided never to be with another *clarinho* [light-skinned boy]."

Yet even when the relationship is a strong one, the young *pretas* we spoke with never felt out of the woods, for they had always to contend with forces outside the relationship itself, with the piercing gaze from lighter-skinned girls, or the disapproval from their own or the boy's family. "When I was twenty years old," recounted Tania, "I started liking a boy who was *moreno*. Now, a white woman stood in my way saying that he was too good for me, a *preta*. She did everything to prevent our relationship and set him up with a girl who was much lighter, with long brown hair. She saw him every day and worked on his emotions, drawing him away from me."

Pretas in relationships with lighter men thus often feel surrounded by jealousy and surveillance. "If you are *preta*," said Tania, "and you are in the street with a white man, everyone will be looking at you. Lighter girls will think: there is any easy mark. I'm going to steal that guy away from that girl. So a black woman going into the street with a white man will feel that white girls are flirting with him." Irane, a *pretinha* in her teens, told Marcia that "I myself have gone through this here, in the neighborhood, with my boyfriend. Women look a lot at him. Black women are jealous. Because getting a white boy is a scarce thing, they are jealous. And the lighter girls gossip and say "Why is he with that *neguinha*?""

A *preta* is sometimes received coolly or not at all by the boyfriend's family. "I know girls," said Alessandra, "who were with white boyfriends, and were rejected by their families. Because whites will say they are not racist, and they aren't—until the day their son brings a *nega* home." Such parents are afraid of various things. Some say they do not want grandchildren with nappy hair. Others say that black women tend to be harder for men to control, hard to trust, promiscuous, and insubordinate. Some parents stand directly in the way of light-skinned sons' becoming involved with *pretas*. One *moreno* who was dating a black girl was so sure his parents would disapprove that he kept the relationship a secret. Unable to hide it, he brought her to meet his family. "They treated her well while she was in the house," he reported. Once she had left the premises, however, they laid down the law. "They said to me, 'Don't ever bring that *criolla* into our house again.'"

For the *preta* the question is always: Will the boy succumb or will he come through for her? In the case just mentioned, the young man buckled under. Another case was recounted by Alessandra. "I knew a boy who was *claro*. But his family said I was a cocky *preta*—just because I wanted to date their son. And he didn't want to go against the wishes of his mother. So always there is that uncertainty: Would he or wouldn't he listen to her? The neighbor told me that his mother was saying this and that against me, because of my color. So in the end he left me, because he couldn't say no to his mother."

She fell silent. Her voice broke. "Look at how hurt I still feel!"

Once married, a common anxiety among *pretas* is that their husbands, whether light- or dark-skinned, have more of a roving eye than most. For these women, the danger of being replaced by a "more attractive" woman keeps them on edge. I met black women who spoke of the need to keep her hair chemically treated precisely to reduce the competition presented by *morenas*. Marlene expained why she spent extra time fussing with her hair: "My hair is naturally very bad. I don't want Carlos to run his hand over that brillo pad, and say 'What's this? What did I marry?' [laughter] Because there are many *morenas* with beautiful hair out there waiting if I don't."

The other side of this sentiment is the suspicion among black women that somehow their husbands, and especially their lighter-skinned husbands, were obliged to settle for them, that they had tried their luck with more beautiful women and had failed. Denise, now raising two children on her own, spoke bitterly of her ex-husband, a white man. "He was a drunk, he wasn't worth very much," she said. "Especially when there was a fight. And he would say the worst things, really cruel. Then I was a damned *neguinha, criolla danada*. He would take my color and hurl it at me. 'God-forsaken, ugly creature!' he would say." Tanya was married for several years to a dark-skinned black man who never let her forget her color. "It was always a joke, an insult, always on his lips. 'Ah, with all the blondes in the world, why did I end up with you?' So I would say to him: 'Good for nothing, then why don't you go out and find one?' And we would go around like that. Finally he left and found himself one."

While these tensions are all quite real, it would be a mistake to characterize *pretas*' experience of marriage as always anxiety-ridden. Not only are there "good men," but the relationship of marriage itself can create opportunities for bonding, intimacy, growth, and a mutual respect that black women can find affirming, even liberating. Older women whose children were grown could still feel grateful to their husbands "for having chosen them," but it was a gratitude now enriched with years of common experience, exchange, and trust. Dona Edith, a *preta* in her sixties, spoke tenderly of her white husband's willingness to be with her: "There, a man with his looks, so handsome, pretty hair, he could have gone with any woman he wanted, but he chose me. And our love over the years bloomed." I asked: "Did he ever treat you in way differently because of your color?" "Never!" she replied. "That is what I love about him. For him, black or white, there is no difference."

The experience of *pretas* in love and marriage is thus fraught with contradictory forces. On the one hand, color prejudice and the aesthetic ideal of light-skinned and straight-haired women place special emotional stress on marital relationships. On the other hand, there can be no doubt that marriage can sometimes bring people together in humanizing and equalizing ways. Women who do not experience these more positive forces in their own marriages often have friends or relatives who do. Black women who have seen lighter husbands stand down the racism of their own families, have seen them grow in respect and love, or have experienced their families come around, will have a hard time simply dismissing the claims of racial democracy out of hand.

THE FAMILY: SECRET OF BRAZIL'S RACIAL DEMOCRACY?

The great secret of Brazil's race relations, Carl Degler argued a quarter century ago, lay in the presence within families of people of all colors.[35] This judgment has remained central to both popular and academic understandings of color relations in Brazil. In the final analysis, because of her presence in the family alongside her lighter-skinned siblings, the Brazilian *negra* "cannot be totally excluded."[36] This, it is argued, is especially true of working-class families, which are more chromatically mixed.[37]

It would be strange indeed if the experience of family life had no effect whatsoever on attitudes about color.[38] It is probably difficult to accept dehumanizing images of a group of people when you have spent years under the same roof with them, shared meals day in and out, shared cooking utensils, beds, and bathrooms. With time, bonds forged by facing common crises, as well as sharing moments of joy and accomplishment, inevitably touch the lineaments of relationships and reshape prejudices, stereotypes, and images. I well remember Neide, a *branca* in her fifties, interacting lovingly with her teen-aged dark-skinned daughter. Neide had supported her daughter's desire to pursue her schooling seriously, and was trying to get her to study English or French. I also recall Sandra, a white mother who took every opportunity to tell her nappy-haired daughter how beautiful she was. Other examples also come to mind. On the other hand, it is precisely because of the strength of emotion present in families, of the high expectations within them for love, unconditional acceptance, and affection, and the fact that one is, as it were, stuck in them, that experiences of differential treatment within them create deep psychic wounds.

Stories about parents giving preferential treatment to lighter-skinned children are not hard to find. Take, for instance, the story of a working-class woman in the Baixada who gave birth to twin girls, one of whom was much darker and nappier-haired than the other. When the daughters were older, according to a neighbor, the mother assigned household chores to the darker-skinned one, while making sure the lighter one had ample time for schoolwork. "Only the *pretinha* is like a servant in the house," a neighbor explained. "She's the one who does everything: she cleans the house, washes the clothes, and makes the food; while the *branquinha* gets to study, read the newspaper, magazines."

Another family's story was more dramatic. A mother of two daughters, one with nappier hair than the other, constantly fussed over the beauty of the softer-haired one. "You should see what she does," reported a neighbor, "the one with nice hair is always nicely dressed, her clothes are always clean and ironed, and she always gets her way. The older one—ha!—she would go about with her hair uncombed, because her mother would not comb it. She said: 'To hell with that hair, there's nothing to be done for it.' And that older girl was never dressed as well, or in clean clothes, or ironed."

Then came the incident. "One day, that woman took an electric razor and shaved off every hair on the nappy-haired girl's head," recounted the neighbor, sighing deeply. "When we objected, she just said: 'That hair was wrong, it had to go.' Just one day, the girl comes home, and unsuspecting, gets her hair shaven: she was bald!" The woman telling me the story looked at me sadly. "So this girl comes next door, crying, crying, crying until all she could do was sob. She refused to go back to the house. She couldn't show her face at school for a week."

Although I could not speak to this girl, I got a vivid sense of some of the pain she may have felt from a long conversation I had with Marilene, a *negra* in her late twenties, a woman of working-class origin who struggled to make it to university, and is now an elementary school teacher. Marilene had very nappy hair and the features of a *preta retinta*. She referred to herself as *negra,* and said she was proud of her color. When she told me her story, she made sure to take me to an outdoor table in the family home's backyard, out of her mother's earshot.

"My sister Daniela was always called 'pretty,'" she told me, "she was always praised by everyone. And not me: I was the ugly duckling. The relatives all were invited to praise Daniela, how she walked so well in the street, Daniela was lighter, and prettier, I don't know what else. I always went about with a small mirror in my pocket. I wondered why no one found me pretty. They all thought Daniela was pretty, but not me. They would say that!"

Marilene stopped speaking. When I asked if she wanted to continue, she said, "No, please. I can't talk about it any more. That's enough."

THE EXPERIENCE OF *PRETAS* IN THE LABOR MARKET

Observers of the labor market in Brazil have avoided analyzing the contrast between dark and light nonwhite women, tending to submerge the difference between them into the larger category of *negra* or "*não-branca*," which they contrast with data on white women. For example, although the tables Marcia Lima published attest to the contrast between *pretas* and *pardas* (the census category for nonwhite women who do not identify themselves as *preta*), her text elides it. While her tables show a significant difference in access to skilled professions between educated *pretas* and *pardas,* Lima's text reports only that "black women [*as mulheres pretas*] are unable to reach the level of social mobility normally due to investment in education."[39] With this small eliding stroke—declaring educated *pretas* and *pardas* to belong to the same category—Lima effectively diverts attention from the largest contrast here, which is not between white and nonwhite women, but between *pardas* and *pretas*.

The most recent national statistics on women's participation in the labor market quite clearly reveal that *pretas* are at a disadvantage in relation to *pardas*. Census data from 1990 show that *pardas* are about twice as likely as *pretas* to work as skilled professionals. *Pardas* are almost 30 percent more likely than *pretas* to be in a semiskilled profession, while *pretas* are about 16 percent more likely than *pardas* to be working in a manual occupation.[40] The contrast is even more striking among women who have completed high school. While education is usually touted as the ticket to occupational mobility, the ticket is awarded more often to lighter than to darker women. The 1990 census data reveal that if you were a *parda* with a high school education, you would be about twice as likely to become a skilled professional than if you were a *preta* with the same education. If you were a *preta* with a high school education, you would be about 70 percent more likely to end up in a manual job than if you were a *parda*. Educated *pardas* are actually closer sociologically to white women than to *pretas*: white women with high school educations were only about 10 percent more likely than were their *parda* counterparts to become skilled professionals, while they were 210 percent more likely to do so than their educated *preta* counterparts.

Appearance in Retail Clerking

Pretas are less represented in the occupation of retail clerking and cashiering than are *morena* and white women. This pattern is evident to anyone who visits the nonfood stores of Zona Sul, Zona Norte, suburbs, and periphery. As Maria Bento has noted, clerking requires extensive contact with customers, visibility, involvement with money, and the use of computerized machines. These aspects remove retail clerking from the domain of pure manual labor or the caretaking of lighter-skinned bodies. These factors, combined with the general supposition that clerks are the first representatives of an enterprise to outsiders, conspire to make "good appearance" a prime requisite for the job.[41] Consequently, the majority of cashiers in nonfood stores are *morenas* and *brancas*. In stores that sell items directly involved with the creation of image, beauty, and status, the lightest-skinned clerks predominate. Stores that seek to project an image of seriousness, prestige, and intellectualism, such as bookstores, paper goods stores, and large department stores, also prefer to hire lighter-skinned women. Some stores have the unstated policy of hiring only white girls or *morenas* as cashiers.

A seventeen-year-old white girl, with long wavy golden-brown hair, explained the importance of color among the cashiers at a downtown paper goods store where she worked. "For me," she insisted, "there is no difference. But we all know that the managers want the prettiest girls, blonde and blue-eyed, up front." How did she feel to be regarded as one of the pretty girls who could be up front? "I don't think about it," she replied. "I just do my job." She paused and smiled. "Who doesn't like being pretty?"

Pretas who have bucked the odds and ended up as clerks and cashiers in such stores sometimes face antagonism, not so much from *brancas* as from the *morenas* who do not want to be associated with them. One *preta* told Ruth how after she became a clerk at a major dry-goods store, she faced various awkward situations. "The manager told me that if I wanted a drink, to go to the refrigerator and get a soda. And there they had cups that everyone used. Only I saw how the other girls felt uncomfortable with me using the same cup as they did. They wanted me to set my cup to one side. I couldn't stay in a place like that." Another young *preta* who tended the cash register at a department store recalled somberly her run-in with a *morena* coworker. She remembered:

> The girls were always primping themselves. And they would give me looks, but I didn't pay attention to that, I just minded my business. Then one day a woman left her pocketbook. I took it to the manager, who looked inside it, and we contacted the woman: and she saw I hadn't taken a single penny. Well, the next thing I knew, the manager wanted to make me chief cashier. One of the lighter girls, she said: "What? A *neguinha* as head cashier? You should go back to being a maid. What are you doing here?" And stuff like that. The manager said I should do the job. But I couldn't take all the gossip. So I left.

The attitude toward *pretas* as cashiers is rather different in large food stores, where it is common to hire them. Grocery stores are not usually purveyors of status. Doing the marketing for food preparation, cooking, and feeding the bodies of whites are all still acceptable activities for *pretas*. In addition, since maids do most of the food shopping, having more *pretas* as cashiers in food stores avoids the socially awkward situation that would be created were light women systematically to wait on *pretas*. A *preta* cashier at a food store gave this account: "I guess there are more *pretas* coming into the food store than into Lojas Americanas [a department store], and they want them to feel at home."

The Domestic Servant

Domestic service is the backdrop to virtually any other job held by *pretas*. Nationally, nearly half of all *pretas* who work in manual jobs work as domestic servants, while only one-third of *pardas* in manual jobs are in this occupation.[42] A *preta* in a manual job is about one and a half times more likely to be a domestic servant than is her *parda* counterpart. In Salvador, the one city for which we have statistical data, 7 percent of domestic servants are white; 37.6 percent are *pardas*, and 55.3 percent are *pretas*.[43] Although domestic servants can now earn more than they did a few years ago due to the emergence of the day-labor market for cleaning women, as well as the improved enforcement of laws governing payment of social security taxes to domestic servants, the job still remains at the bottom of the status hierarchy of the Brazilian labor market.

Pretas' presence in this occupation both reinforces and is reinforced by the image of the simple, robust, noble, loving *preta* maid, which originated under slavery. This is an image that appeared in Jose de Alencar's mid-nineteenth-century play *Mãe* (Mother) and soon became a stock character in Brazilian folklore.[44] Today the image of *preta* as maid continues to be one of the most durable in Brazilian popular culture, reinforced through everyday practice, as well as by storytelling, media, schoolbooks—and even by the figure of the *preta velha* (old black woman) in the religion of *umbanda*. In elementary school textbooks, black women are frequently presented as wearing headkerchiefs, the unmistakable symbol of domestic service, or engaged in ironing or washing, while white women wear recreational clothing.[45] In clothing store windows, the mannequins are all white, with the notable exception of black mannequins used to display maids' uniforms. In *umbanda* and *candomblé* centers, black mediums often do most of the cooking.[46] And Brazilian television continues to offer to *preta* actresses almost exclusively the roles of maid, nursemaid, and babysitter.[47] When Zezé Motta began her TV career, all she could find were maids' roles. After attaining international stardom, she refused to play any more maids, but was told by a producer: "My dear, I understand your feelings, but get real. If you insist on this posture, you will no longer do any television."[48] He was right: she never did.

Nursemaid, Healer, and Nurse

The job of nurse's aide has in recent years turned into one of the fastest-growing labor markets for *pretas* in the greater Rio area. Although the central nursing union does not keep records on the color composition of the job category, conversations with leaders of the union, as well as with a dozen nurse's aides, paint a picture of an occupation in which *pretas* are overrepresented. A white nurse who had worked in various hospitals throughout the region observed the same patterns as did my other informants: "I can tell you that it is true," she said. "Most nurse's aides are *pretas*. Just go into any hospital and you can see that." She clarified what she meant by *pretas*: "I mean really dark, you know, with hard hair, the ones who are indisputably black. Not *morenas*, not *mulatas*."

To the extent that this is true, it is useful to grasp both why Brazilian society makes this role so readily available to *pretas*, and why so many *pretas* are eager to enter the role. Ruth, a *preta* in her thirties who has worked as a nurses' aide for five years, began: "Most of the nurses at the hospital are *preta*: society accepts us in this role. As the healers of suffering, caretakers. That thing about helping. We are accepted as helpers. To nurse others. To really give of ourselves. We have nursed children who are not our own. So obviously, we are a people ready to sacrifice for others."

This image can be traced to that most contradictory of roles, the slave wet-nurse. This role figured prominently in *The Masters and the Slaves*.[49] Freyre devotes page after page to a loving description of the black nursemaid in her daily round, telling stories to the master's children, coddling them, feeding them, bandaging their scrapes and cuts. His image of her takes shape around a series of gifts of personal substance, of affection, music, language, food, the sweat of palms. His is

> [t]he pleasing figure of the Negro nurse who, in patriarchal times, brought the child up, who suckled him, rocked his hammock or cradle, taught him his first words of broken Portuguese, his first "Our Father" and "Hail Mary," along with his first mistakes in pronunciation and grammar, and who gave him his first taste of pirão com carne . . . as she mashed his food for him with her own hands.[50]

The black nursemaid's transfer of her "strong blood" through her breastmilk to the children of the white ruling class is part of a larger set of images and practices through which blacks symbolically contribute, through donating their blood, to the health of the nation. This symbolism could be seen, for example, when the Oswaldo Cruz Foundation, in collaboration with the black consciousness movement, organized in May 1988 the "Pyramid of Black Blood," a motorized blood bank that took donations from marchers in a major political demonstration.[51] In the absence of a nationalist war in which the act of shedding blood can symbolize fealty, donating blood to the national supply seems to take on added symbolic meaning.[52] It could also be seen in the outpouring of popular response to the last episode of the telenovela *Corpo a Corpo*, which aired in the early 1980s.[53] In that soap opera, the white patriarch tries to disown a son who seeks the hand of Sonia, a black woman. The tension builds to breaking point. Then, when the patriarch survives a near-fatal car crash, the only person with the correct blood type to save him is Sonia. She rallies and offers the salvific blood. Upon recovery, he repents, opens his arms, and welcomes her into the family.[54]

Pretas have, however, motivations for entering the occupation of nurse's aide other than the symbolism of the role. It is one of the few respectable occupations available to poor and working-class black women: training takes only two years and does not require absenting oneself from income-generating activity. Most of the nurse's aides I spoke with had worked as domestic servants and regarded the move to nursing as a major step up. This was clear in the testimony of Irane, a *preta* in her thirties. "I started working as a domestic at ten years of age," she said. "Now, as a nurse's aide, I work for a company, not an individual. I am treated with greater respect. If you say to someone 'I am a maid,' you are treated with that, you know, without respect. But now, when I say 'I am a technical assistant to a nurse,' I am treated differently. Sometimes I make less than a maid, even, but the job is much more valued, more status. The treatment is much better."

The very *habitus* of the nurse's gait—head held high, available to people only on her own terms—stands in powerful contrast to the subservient, self-effacing persona of the *preta* so often cultivated in the public spaces of lobbies, elevators, the street, grocery stores, and the employer's apartment. The hospital corridor belongs to the nurse's aide. "Patients respect the profession," said Irane, "they have to cooperate. Now I can say to the patient—whoever she is, whether she is a queen or a poor person—'Hey, she just washed you, now try to cooperate with her.' Never are such things possible for a maid to say. When you are maid, you don't say 'no'; but as a nurse's aide, you can say 'no' to a lot of things. When I was a maid, I wanted so many times just to walk away. But I couldn't. Now, if a patient is driving me crazy, I walk out, and assign someone else."

At perhaps an even deeper level, the occupation has a less direct appeal: its trappings, including the clean, pressed white uniform, stand as public negations of the image of the slovenly *preta*. "To be a nurse was for me a dream of my childhood," Irane said. "To be dressed all in white, I thought it was so beautiful. To be all pretty. I saw this on TV: all white, all pretty. I love white, because it symbolizes peace. I love peace."

But the job also exposes black women to racial tension. None of the nurse's aides I spoke with referred to tension with doctors, who were just too distant and powerful. The relations that tended to be more stressful were with the nurses for whom they worked as aides. Full nurses tend on average to be lighter-skinned and white. While the general ideological context of the hospital, of curing, caring, survival, and health, tends to overrule various everyday tensions, the relations between aide and nurse could at time become burdened with resentment tinged with color prejudice. Recounted Ruth: "Just the other day, one of these nurses who is so proud of her looks, long brown hair, that she is always combing, snapped at that [aide]. . . . And she said, 'Go upstairs right now and get a scissors.' Like she was a slave. Like she was some mistress on the plantation, and telling her to get a scissors like that. I tell you, it made me sick."

Yet in the end, if the *preta* sometimes feels she is encountering color prejudice from nurses, what she mainly experiences are mobility, status, mastery, pride, and the reliance upon her of her social "superiors." The experience of being a nurse's aide thus reduces the emotional plausibility of blanket claims about the oppression of blacks in general, and black women in particular. If racial democracy is for such women not quite a description of their everyday lives, neither is in blatant contradiction to it.

I have attempted in this chapter to introduce a few of the everyday fields of meaning and experience encountered by black women in Rio de Janeiro. But while I have tried to give the reader a sense of some of the pain and longing that these fields generate for black women, I have tried to avoid painting a portrait of monolithic suffering. For although these social fields do too often bring white and *morena* racism as explosions upon black women's senses, these social fields also make possible moments of joy, intimacy, and triumph. Being fields populated by real human beings, they could do little else.

TWO
Spirited Languages

The Field of Popular Christianity in Rio de Janeiro

THE FIELD OF POPULAR CHRISTIANITY

The variants of Christianity in Rio de Janeiro extend far beyond the three groups I shall focus on here. In the Protestant field alone, the city is host not only to traditional pentecostal churches like the Assembly of God, but to a whole generation of newer super-churches like *Renascer em Cristo* ("Be Reborn in Christ") and the Universal Church of the Kingdom of God, which have their own distinctive reading of the Bible, and have been referred to as "neo-pentecostal."[1] The Protestants also include various historical denominations, such as the Baptists, Lutherans, and Methodists. In the Catholic Church, the movements of the *pastoral negro* and inculturated Mass are but two of that institution's numerous current trends, which include not only the Charismatic Catholic movement, but also liberationist, reformist, and conservative tendencies as well.[2] Innumerable popular saintly devotions also occupy the religious landscape.[3]

My focus on the inculturated Mass, the devotion to Anastácia, and the traditional pentecostal churches is thus in no way exhaustive of the range of possibility and meaning in Rio's Christian sphere. It is, rather, an effort to engage interpretatively with three religious traditions that have a tangible effect on the assumption and articulation of *negra* identities and antiracism. It is also an attempt to engage critically with religious traditions that have evoked specific ideological concerns and hopes on the part of black movement activists.

I have sought in this chapter to accomplish two tasks: first, to convey something of the process of each religious tradition's historical emergence; and second, to capture some of the feel of each tradition's ritual and spiritual relations. My hope is that by coming to appreciate, even if only partially, the subjective symbolic world of participants in these traditions, the reader will better understand the particular race and color meanings that have emerged in each tradition, which are the subject of chapters to come.

THE PASTORAL NEGRO AND THE INCULTURATED MASS
The Emergence of a Black Pastoral[4]

The story of how, in the late 1960s, Brazil's Catholic hierarchy began to offer political shelter to progressive theologians and priests, has often been told. [5] Less familiar is the connection between the progressive Catholic movement and the emergence of the Catholic black consciousness movement. Once exposed to the theology of liberation, it would not be long before young nonwhite seminarians began to sense inconsistency between clerics' claim to be liberated, and their failure to appreciate the cries for racial justice coming from the black movement. Many of these young seminarians were, like David Raimundo dos Santos, light-skinned blacks, who had taken advantage of their social privilege by entering seminary, but who lacked at the time a well-developed consciousness of their *negritude*. Once inside, the color dynamics of clerical advancement had a radicalizing effect on many of them. For while white students were preparing to enter the ranks of the clergy, nonwhites found themselves on the receiving end of advice to enter the regular orders instead. It was understood, implicitly, that as members of orders they would not compete directly with white priests for ecclesiastical preferment.

A decade earlier, such advice might have been received without comment. In the context of the mid- to late 1970s, however, the contradiction between this advice and the Church's own liberationist pretensions was simply too much for many nonwhite seminarians to bear. A current leader of the *pastoral negro* remembers:

I hadn't really thought of myself as *negro* before entering the seminary. But there, I felt all of a sudden treated as a *negro*: because we knew we would never have the same opportunities as our white colleagues. So we began to meet and talk about these things amongst ourselves. Pretty soon we had a few black priests, and laypeople, and religious, and seminarians, all talking together. We were very inspired by what was happening all around us, by the IPCN and the MNU. . . . And we thought: this Church which says that it wants liberation, let it assume this responsibility fully, let there be no hypocrisy. And hypocrisy there was, and plenty.

Already in these groups a distinction could be drawn between those who saw themselves as headed for clerical careers, and laypeople whose primary commitment was to the secular black movement. While the former saw their role as influencing racial attitudes within the Church, the latter saw themselves as working through the Church to change Brazilian society. Another current leader remembers:

> At that time the difference had not really emerged yet. We were all equally concerned about ending racism in Brazil, about building black self-confidence and identity. But some of us felt that what we needed to do was work on the part of Brazilian society that was closest to us, where we lived, where we had the most at stake. That is, the Church. And there were others who saw it mainly as a instrument of change. But they didn't really trust it even as that.

The event that stimulated these groups to become formally organized came in late 1978, during preparations for the major Latin American bishops' conference in Puebla, Mexico. The document the Brazilian bishops planned to present at the meeting fell into the hands of the black seminarians, who found it wanting. A current leader of the black pastoral recalls:

> At no point did the document state that the physical face of the "poor" it championed just happened to be mainly black and indigenous. So we entered into contact with the bishops, especially Dom Paulo Evaristo Arns, and we challenged him. We said: "Look, you have not had the courage to say openly that the people you are defending have this physical face."

Dom Paulo responded by announcing that the National Brazilian Bishops' Conference (CNBB) would append an additional document, which recognized the ethnic composition of the Brazilian people. This appendix would be the first time in its history that the Brazilian Catholic Church had publicly recognized the issue of race.

The appendix set off a rapidly unfolding political process. The group of black clerics found they had affected the content of a document representing the Brazilian Church as a whole. One of the early leaders recalls:

> We suddenly felt that we could make a difference. We felt that it was our responsibility, as black men and women, to pursue a whole new path in the Church. That we should not simply wait for things to happen. So this was how it started. Priests in other cities knew what was happening with us, we were in touch with lots of people; and so these meetings took place all over.

The chief proposals to the Bishops' Conference that emerged from these meetings were: that the Church should recognize the specificity of black experience and suffering; include a call for racial justice in its social agenda; work to educate at the grass roots about racism and racial inequality; and encourage blacks to take pride in their culture and history. And there was something else, an idea that, in the late 1970s, was still embryonic, but that would eventually mature into a fully-fledged project: that the Church should work to integrate black culture into the Catholic liturgy.

Despite misgivings, the progressive members of the CNBB were not unreceptive to these ideas, which coincided with their own goal of giving voice to the voiceless. Yet the very willingness of some bishops to cede legitimacy to the fledgling black movement in their ranks led many black laypeople to be on their guard against co-optation. The tensions between these laypeople and a clergy grateful for the opportunity offered by the Church came into the open in 1981, on the occasion of the first national assembly of black priests, religious, and laypeople in Brasilia. "People came from throughout Brazil to this meeting," recalled a priest, "and it was here that a group said: "We do not believe that the Church, which oppressed blacks for so many hundreds of years, all of a sudden is going to become a trustworthy partner now.'"

The laypeople who articulated the anti-Church position dominated the assembly. They ensured that the principal objective of black Catholics would be the creation of projects outside of the Church, in alliance with other secular groups in the movement. The outcome of the assembly was the formation of the Grupo de União e Consciência Negra (Group of Black Unity and Consciousness, GRUCON) and the marginalization of the effort to create a black pastoral internal to the Church.

The fight, however, had just begun. Those priests and religious who still believed in the possibility of working toward a black pastoral called a meeting in 1983 in São Paulo. "There," recalled Frei David, "we united everyone with a commitment to the pastoral, and to black identity. And so we formed a new phenomenon: *agentes de pastoral negros*, or APNs (black pastoral agents)." The term was felicitous, for it allowed for a clear identity, while holding out the promise that some-day there might be an official Black Pastoral sanctioned by the Church, to which one could become attached as an "agent."

By the mid-1980s, the groups belonging to GRUCON had grown weak through infighting over finances and the question of how closely to work with the infrastructure of the Church. The initiative of the movement was quietly passing toward the APNs, who steadily thrummed away at the need to make the Church internally more responsive to the needs of its black members.

In 1986, the APNs captured the imagination of a large segment of the clergy and laity when they sought to convince the CNBB to adopt the issue of racism and black identity as the theme of the 1988 "Brother-hood Campaign."[6] The APNs argued that because 1988 was the cen-tennial year of abolition,[7] the media would be focused on the issue, and the Church should not be left behind. The bishops agreed, by a vote of forty-three to two.

The APNs put an enormous amount of energy into the campaign, which some invested with near-millennial overtones. Many APNs believed they were standing at a watershed in history, at which the Catholic Church was becoming a major force for change in Brazilian race relations. But when it became clear that at the grass roots parish-ioners were less than swept away by the politicized tone of the cam-paign, the APNs entered into crisis. Some left the Church; others threw up their hands at the depth of the "alienation" of the masses; others turned to tilling other political vineyards, such as the pastoral of youth.

The end of the 1980s was a period of crisis for the political left in general, and many APNs became disillusioned with ideological projects of any kind. Only a core of true believers remained. What they had learned from the campaign was the necessity for long, slow education at the grass roots, and the need to focus not on political rhetoric but on what they believed really mattered to people: the symbolic, the ritual, the liturgical aspects of the Church. Starting in 1990, a small group of APNs in Rio de Janeiro began serious work on a project first outlined a decade earlier: the creation of an institutionalized Black Pastoral, that would have as its centerpiece a thorough reconstruction along Afro-Brazilian lines of the high Mass: the "inculturated " or "Afro Mass."

With the naysayers gone, and with the resistance of GRUCON

reduced to grumbling on the sidelines, those APNs who stuck through the crisis began energetically to pursue their liturgical project. They could count on passive acceptance from the ecclesiastical hierarchy, both conservative and progressive. Conservatives knew that for the better part of a decade Pope John Paul II had insisted that the Church must be more embracing of cultural difference.[8] And progressives knew that in the supposedly post-Marxist world, bases of identity other than class were increasing in political legitimacy. The APNs were at long last rewarded with an institutionalized national Black Pastoral in March of 1996.

It is in this context that the work of the inculturated Mass has proceeded at the parish, diocesan, and national levels. As one of its major theoreticians, Frei David, explained:

> One thing has become clear over these long eighteen years of struggle: the ritual of the inculturated Mass is indisputably the best instrument, the greatest of instruments, to stimulate the sprouting of a consciousness of blackness among the blacks who participate in the Church. Making this Mass a common occurrence throughout Brazil, to make the masses aware of it, through their neighborhoods, communities, the media—this is one of the black pastoral's top priorities, if not the top priority.

The Ritual Structure of the Inculturated Mass

Over four months, from September to December 1996, Marcia, Ruth, and I accompanied the preparation and performance of four inculturated Masses in the parish of São João de Meriti, the epicenter of Rio de Janeiro's black pastoral movement. In 1996, there were about twenty such Masses held throughout the archdiocese in which São João is located. This particular parish is the most frequent host to the Masses, because Frei David has worked assiduously there for the past six years, training a cadre of pastoral agents who are knowledgeable and skilled coordinators of the Mass. They in turn guide and orient lay liturgy teams at the level of base communities whose members desire to carry out the ritual. The communities where the Mass is performed are home to lay leaders who have already begun to think politically about black identity. While each community-level liturgy team has some latitude for deleting or rearranging particular elements of the inculturated Mass, overall the parish-level pastoral team keeps fairly close reins on the process. People of all color identities are involved. The preparation and performance of the inculturated Mass is not exclusively an activity of people who identify themselves as *negros*. Later I will discuss in some detail the motives and understandings of nonblack participants in the Mass.

At the most general level, the inculturated Mass is, its theoreticians claim, an attempt to salvage the history and culture of Afro-Brazilians from the oblivion to which racist society seeks to consign them, by imparting knowledge about African culture, especially its dances, rhythms, instruments, dress, and food; its relations to nature and the earth; and about the history of slavery, especially the names and stories of the great martyrs. "The inculturated Mass is about salvaging a people's culture, its race, its origin," explained a lay leader. "To teach blacks about themselves, about their own history, about their own values and the value they have for themselves."

The first thing one notices about the inculturated Mass is that the whole two- to three-hour ritual (twice the length of the traditional Mass) is accompanied, from beginning to end, by the loud rhythmic drums called *atabaques*. These tall cylinders are widely associated with the music of samba, as well as with the irredeemably un-Christian religions of *umbanda* and *candomblé*. It is therefore not surprising that most witnesses, when asked to comment on the inculturated Mass, think first of the drums. They remark on how unusual it is to see such drums— whose very mention provokes a shiver in some—inside the sacred precinct of the church. They also comment on the drums' constant din, the fact that they are played far more during the inculturated Mass than any musical instrument is played during the traditional Mass.

When asked to explain the presence of the drums, theologians of the *pastoral negro* point to the Psalm of David that incites the believer to praise the Lord "with timbrel" (Psalms 150:4). They also insist that bringing the *atabaque* into the church is an act of cultural revolution, in which the demonized instrument is finally winning the respect it deserves. "For too long," said Frei David, "the *atabaque* has been seen in Brazil as the tool of the devil. So by bringing it into the Mass, we are declaring its value, saying 'No! It is a valuable part of African and Afro-Brazilian culture. It is nothing to be ashamed of. It too must take its place in the sun.'"

The constancy of the drumming derives from the black pastoral's interpretations of popular culture. "Our understanding," said one black priest, "of sacred rituals in Africa is this: in contrast to European rituals, which value silence at the most sacred moments, there they value the most intense music, noise, and drumming. So in order to show that the whole ritual is sacred, that there are no profane moments, it is appropriate to keep the drum going throughout." Further, it is assumed that *negros* instinctively like drums that are "lively" and "festive." "We are making a Mass," explained a lay leader, "that captures the festiveness of our people. This is a people that hears music every day, hears the samba drum in the street every day. So this is corresponding to their culture. There is no reason to silence these drums, for they are the voice of the People."

If the drums are the source of the inculturated Mass's energy, the dance is the Mass's body. Everyone in the church is encouraged to follow the lead of the celebrants, who sway their torsos and swing their arms in tight semicircles. This is the distinctive motion of *ginga*, the semi-mystical, deeply felt internal rhythm supposedly inherited from Africa.[9] Novices to the Mass are easy to spot by their reluctance to attempt the motion, or their awkward, self-conscious attempts to imitate it. Participants who have attended inculturated Masses before may have mastered the motion but rarely perform it without self-awareness. I could always catch performers of *ginga* looking down at their own arms or feet, or shooting glances around to see who was watching them.

The *ginga*, so simple to an outside observer, carries heavy connotations. The motion is associated in urban Brazil with the movements performed by spirit mediums in *candomblé* as they promenade in a circle prior to becoming possessed by spirits. It is awareness of this association that leads many celebrants to introduce idiosyncratic variations to the motion, such as sweeping arms above the head, or snapping fingers, or clapping, so as gesturally to distance themselves from the *ginga* of a religion they have learned to think of as the work of the devil. To no avail. The association is so strong that many witnesses to the inculturated Mass continue to denounce its introduction of "*macumba*" into the Church.

If small movements are viewed as shocking by some, larger ones can be even more scandalous. Many variants of the inculturated Mass celebrate the "Afro-dance" with troupes of up to a dozen young female dancers, dressed to evoke "Africa," in brightly colored fabrics wrapped so as to display arms, thighs, and midriffs. The dancers wear jewelry, makeup, and headbands; their hair is usually unstraightened; and they include a high proportion of dark-skinned women. The idea is to convey an image of "African female beauty," different from that of the European aesthetic standard.

The women perform "African" dances at various points throughout the Mass, often in opposing lines, mirroring each other's large and expansive movements, deploying their hips, legs, and necks. While the young women dance, Mass-goers are transfixed by the spectacle of any kind of dance, let alone one with such sensual overtones, inside the church. This is precisely the effect the orchestrators of the Mass are seeking to achieve. Although they point to various passages in the Bible as providing a charter for the dance (including Exodus 15:20–21), their main goal is to capture attention and to teach respect for this African cultural inheritance.

The inculturated Mass calls upon celebrants, especially the presiding priest, to wear "African" colors and garments. The priest wears a long, brightly colored shawl, and a "kepi"—a round, flat, multicolored head-dress strongly associated in Brazil with the black movement and some-times with *pais-de-santo* (ritual leaders) in *candomblé*. His assistants, other celebrants, and the dancers all wear clothing supposed to evoke "Africa" by virtue of their vibrant colors and loose, flowing fabrics.

The notion that bright colors are somehow peculiarly "African" is paramount. One priest went so far as to claim that "in Europe, white symbolizes peace. Of course, it is the Pax Britannica! But we feel this is a continuation of the idea that only white can be good and peaceful. So we were very pleased to learn that in Africa, quite to the contrary, it is not white, but the combination, in harmony, of many different bright colors that represents peace. In Africa the idea is not a single, overpowering white color, but the coexistence of many colors." Often, too, the clergy and laity say that Brazilian blacks naturally prefer vibrant colors.

The use of colorful garments in the inculturated Mass is among the least controversial of its ritual innovations. In part, this has to do with the lack of strong religious associations with multicoloredness. But what is more important, the leaders' desire to *avoid* white clothing sits well with many participants. For white—as all Brazilians know but as the framers of this Mass seem to have temporarily forgotten—happens to be the most sacred color of *candomblé*; too much white would, once again, raise the spectre of introducing the religion of the devil into the Mass.

One of the most distinctive moments of the inculturated Mass is the invocation of the martyrs and ancestors. This segment substitutes for the section in the traditional Mass during which the priest prays for the deceased. It is the most explicitly political moment of the Mass. The celebrant begins by asking the congregation to remember those of their ancestors who have died struggling for the freedom of their people. Most of the congregation remains silent, while those who know the list of "martyrs" recite it. The list includes, first and foremost, Zumbi; but also Luiza Mahin, the rebel leader of the Islamic slave uprising in Salvador in 1835; Martin Luther King Jr.; and Padre Genuino, who was murdered several years ago in the Northeast.

The importance of Zumbi, the leader of a seventeenth-century runaway slave community, is hard to overstate. His image, which is also the most important icon of the secular black movement, can be seen everywhere in association with the inculturated Mass: on the T-shirts of celebrants; on the buttons worn by congregation members; on posters; on the covers of songbooks; in songs. The most popular of all inculturated Mass songs declares: "Hey, Zumbi, Zumbi Ganga my king; you are still in me; you have not died."[10]

The image and name of Zumbi come close to being sacralized by the inculturated Mass. In some celebrations, larger-than-life depictions of Zumbi's (imagined) face are brought to the altar. In others, dirt shipped from Alagoas near where Zumbi's *quilombo* (slave community) of Palmares was located is distributed and made into the sign of the cross on participants' foreheads. Several lay leaders explicitly said that they regarded Zumbi almost with the same emotion they did Jesus. "As Jesus was our savior," said one woman, "so too was Zumbi." In many celebrations of the Mass, Zumbi's name is repeated more often than Jesus'.

While I heard much grumbling about the presence of drums and *ginga* in the Mass, I never heard a complaint about the invocation of

"Zumbi and the Inculturated Mass."

the martyrs. I was surprised to hear people who otherwise were critical of the Mass singing the praises of this ritual moment. It was, in their eyes, a statement of the importance of steadfastness and courage, and was a lesson to all Christians to fight for what they believed in. "This is a value that is very important to the Christian," said Geraldo, an elderly white man who otherwise had little use for the inculturated Mass. "I like when they talk about the martyrs. That is something that the black can bring to the Mass that is very positive."

Directly following the distribution of the host, or as a substitute for it, bowls and trays of food are carried into church, to much dancing and singing, and arranged upon the floor in front of the altar; these are offerings to the spirit of love, brotherhood, and community. Frei David says that the ritual division of this food not only announces the Christian Kingdom of God on earth, when everything shall be shared equally among all people; it also is designed to continue the African custom of reconstituting the community's relation to divinity through commensality. The foods are supposed to be "popular," and must be consumable with the fingers. Items such as cornbread, cake, and fruit are favorites. What is regarded as most "African" is the placement of the offerings on the ground. This, according to the Mass's planners, "recuperates the Afro cosmovision, that sees the earth as the origin of all life." It also echoes the nativity of Jesus, in its association with the receipt of gifts on the floor of the manger.

A last ritual practice that distinguishes the inculturated from the traditional Mass is the use of African language. Nagô, the language of *candomblé*, is incorporated in homily, song, and imagery. Most dramatically, the Yoruba names of some of the *orixás* of *candomblé* are invoked at various moments, including Oxalá, Oxumaré, and Olorum, with the accompanying claim that these names are the equivalents of Jesus and God.

The inculturated Mass, as it is performed in the Rio area, cannot be understood without appreciating its spectacular quality. It has, for instance, been a priority of its coordinators to maximize the size of its audience. They actively court television and media coverage, and advertise and schedule the Masses to draw the largest possible crowds. In fact, many of those who attend are not regular Mass-goers. It is exciting for many lay leaders to command large crowds, read press reports and reviews, and be on television. And certainly in preparatory meetings, coordinators assume that the objective is to create a memorable experience that the public will enjoy.

The result is the ambience of the "show." In contrast to other events in the church, video and flash photography is encouraged: during one such Mass with about six hundred people present, I counted almost a hundred flashes over the course of three hours. During rehearsals, participants are reminded to bring cameras and to urge their friends and family to do the same. During the actual performance, participants look for friends and family in the audience, and wave coyly to them. In some of the larger performances, semiprofessional music troupes contribute their time to play background music for the dancers. After the Mass is over, there is a period of open dancing, as members of the audience come forward to congratulate participants, to dance, and to share a celebratory post-performance meal.

This atmosphere of spectacle has led to some negative backlash within the ranks of the black pastoral itself. I met several young lay leaders who were critical of the effort to make the inculturated Mass into a media event, and were upset that the ritual seemed to be coming unhinged from its primary function, of raising consciousness. "The inculturated Mass is not a very effective instrument for raising consciousness," complained one lay leader. "Because most of the people who go in there now, they are there for the show, and you never see them again. The inculturated Mass should be the end result of a long process of consciousness-raising; as it is, it doesn't express anything, and it is slipping into folklorization." By this, she meant that the political content of the inculturated Mass—its valorization of black identity and African roots—was being crowded out by its appeal to simple curiosity.

But Frei David had little patience with such criticism. He declared:

> Those who say such things tend to be elitist. They think that the inculturated Mass should be for card-carrying members of the black pastoral, like them. But we must know how to work with the masses. I prefer to think optimistically about this. We are reaching more people this way. If out of a crowd of six hundred only a dozen people feel the desire to pursue in greater depth the issues of black identity and racism, I say this is a victory, these are twelve people we would not have reached any other way.

In a later chapter I shall treat in detail how the inculturated Mass is understood by local nonwhite women, as well as its impact on them. Here I wish to make a few comments on how whites feel about the ritual.

Frei David and the leaders of the black pastoral are emphatic in their insistence that the inculturated Mass is not only for blacks. As

Catholics, after all, they believe fervently in a single Church that unites people across all social cleavages. They are therefore fond of pointing out that in any given inculturated Mass one can see a large proportion of whites not only in the audience, but among the celebrants. Indeed, I also found that some of the inculturated Mass's strongest supporters were long-standing local church leaders, who were white.

Christian universalism provides the ground upon which whites stand in support for the inculturated Mass. Yet white acceptance of the Mass remains largely contingent upon two things: that its various non-European practices be readily translatable into more familiar terms; and that the valorization of black identity not be emphasized as an end in itself, but as a means to the formation of a more all-embracing Christian community based on racial unity and harmony.

The whites we spoke with were mainly concerned with translating black culture into recognizable European and Christian terms. In effect they sought to minimize or even deny that *negro* values were substantially different from those of white European culture. Elza was explicit on this point:

> When you think of it there really is no important difference between the inculturated Mass and the traditional Mass, in terms of values, the things that are symbolized. These are all universals. Zumbi struggled for a cause. There is no difference between Zumbi and Saint Francis! Saint Francis also struggled for a cause. Maybe his struggle looked different from Zumbi's but it is the same thing! Francis gave up riches, he struggled against the wealthy of his day. And he defended the weak of his day. And Zumbi, too, he struggled defending the weak of his day. So it was the same thing.

The black pastoral's effort to legitimize Afro-religiosity involves selecting out and focusing on those elements of Afro-Brazilian religion that may be interpreted as rooted in "African values," the "*negro* way of being," or resistance to the social and cultural conditions of slavery, but above all that express values convergent with a Christian worldview.[11] For example, in the months leading to the acceptance by the CNBB of the Black Pastoral, a document was circulated, authored by Cardinal Bernardin Gantin, the head of the Sacred Congregation of Bishops in Rome, discussing "Universal Values in the Traditional African Religions."[12] Gantin highlights such theological convergences as antimaterialism; immersion in the spiritual dimension of life; belief in a supreme creator god; the attitude of gratitude, dependence, and submission to the supreme God; the view of all human relations as deriving their meaning from their relation to the supreme God; and the belief in spiritual equality before God, and hence of universal human dignity.

Much of the nervousness among practicing Catholics about the inculturated Mass derives precisely from such thinking, and its manifestation in the Mass's apparent similarities with many of the rituals of *umbanda* and *candomblé*. This nervousness has led numerous laypeople to look upon the inculturated Mass with hostility and to give it a wide berth. "Nowadays," observed one layman, "with the Protestants criticizing us on all fronts, I am totally amazed that some priests want to give them even more artillery by doing something like this." In some communities, these views have effectively kept the inculturated Mass entirely out of the question. In others, they have led to rifts, as congregations become divided between pro- and anti-inculturated Mass factions. In the seat of São João de Meriti, the respectable old guard will have nothing to do with the young practitioners of the black pastoral who support the introduction of the devil's ways into the Mass. In a few places, where emotions have risen to boiling point, outsiders have been asked to come in to ease tensions. Frei David himself, though associated with the inculturated Mass, is considerate and respectful of opposing views and has often come to communities to smooth ruffled feathers back into place after an inculturated Mass has been performed.

On such occasions, David's approach is familiar. He reminds everyone that, despite superficial appearances, the inculturated Mass does *not* import the practices of *candomblé* or *umbanda* into the Church. He insists that those features of the inculturated Mass that resemble aspects of these religions, such as the use of the *atabaques*, the swaying of the body, "Afro" dancing, the placing of the altar upon the ground, the offering of bowls of food, even the invocation of the names of Olorum and Oxalá, are not inherently religious, but are rather drawn from a larger common fund of "African culture."

"The cultural values of the African and Afro-Brazilian peoples," Frei David has written, "form a universal patrimony, just as, too, the cultural values of Japanese, Americans, Chinese, and so on are universal patrimonies. These values are there to enrich the lives of anyone who wishes to listen to them." "Culture" here becomes a kit bag filled with all the practices and values not beholden to any particular religious group. David continues: "Which came first, culture or religion? I think no one can doubt that it was culture. In order for religion to gain form, it had to turn to elements of culture that already existed."[13] In an interview, Frei David was more metaphorical. "As a theological and liturgical body, *candomblé* sought to drink at the primary well, which is African culture. We too today wish to bring into the Catholic Church that which springs from our ethnic reality: we are not drinking at the well of *candomblé*, but rather, we are drinking at the same well where *candomblé* drank: culture."

This view, of course, avoids addressing the extent to which various parts of African "culture" are in fact associated with specific religious traditions; the extent to which one is entitled to separate "religion" from "culture" at all; the extent to which the various translations from African "culture" into meanings and values palatable to a Christian audience are themselves accurate; and the extent to which one is entitled to separate out and valorize only some items of "culture" while downplaying others. Yet whatever its defensibility, the "culture prior to religion" view has successfully defused, for many participants in the inculturated Mass, the "macumba question."

If this view seems a delicate one, Afro-Catholic theologians have another, even more delicate, item on their agenda. While insisting that *candomblé* is not a source of elements for the inculturated Mass, they wish still to valorize the religion as an expression of the values, identity, and historical struggle of the Afro-Brazilian people. They thus have sought, with some trepidation, to encourage a de-demonizing attitude toward Afro-Brazilian religion. In practice, this has meant leading reflection groups in discussions about *candomblé* and inviting *pais-de-santo* to lead workshops with the Catholic laity. In the earlier phase of the movement, in the 1980s, this effort included leading field trips to Afro-religious temples and inviting *pais-de-santo* and *candomblé* priests to participate in ecumenical services in the Catholic Church. Not surprisingly, these practices have been discontinued because of the uproar they caused.

THE DEVOTION TO ESCRAVA ANASTÁCIA
A Brief Eventful History of the Devotion to Anastácia[14]

The twentieth-century devotion to Slave Anastácia arose within a religious tradition that began at least two hundred years earlier. Relations with dead slaves originated in Brazil's black brotherhoods, in connection with their practice of seeing to the burial of members, both free and enslaved.[15] As is still true today, a person who died with bitterness in her heart was believed to wander and to require purification, while whoever had faced worldly suffering with resignation was thought to become an *alma bendita*, a blessed soul, whose proximity to the saints would allow her to intercede on behalf of the living.[16]

Religious representations of the suffering of virtuous slaves emerged among the black confraternities in the nineteenth century, influenced by the tradition in Catholic culture of portraying in graphic detail the bloody suffering of martyrs. An iconography of torture began to appear in the brotherhoods' processionals, with images copied from book illuminations, which may have included abolitionist literature. In a procession of the church of Nossa Senhora das Dores in Porto Alegre, for example, a chromolithograph of a male slave bearing the marks

"Anastácia Bust at Her Shrine in Olaria."

of torture was borne aloft for all to see.[17] On the eve of abolition, a religious procession of the black brotherhood of Our Lady of Remedies in São Paulo prominently featured a painting of a tortured slave.[18]

After abolition, the knowledge of torture under slavery remained widespread among the first and second generation of slaves' descendants through storytelling, as well as through family visits to abandoned plantations. Old men and women recounted to us how an uncle or grandparent would take them on outings when they were children to see the decrepit ruins of slave quarters, where they gazed in horror at the rusty remains of chains and neck braces.

Four elderly women and one man indicated to us, entirely independently of each other, that they remembered in the late 1940s and early 1950s having seen in the homes of relatives the image of a female slave with a neck-iron, perhaps even a face-iron—an image that was the object of religious devotion. In addition, a woman in her sixties had clear and distinct memories of hearing the name "Anastácia" in connection with such an image when she was a teenager in Minas Gerais. "When they were dancing in the streets celebrating the end of World War II," she said. "I had already seen the image and heard the name of Anastácia."

It is likely that the name "Anastácia" was common enough among Brazilian female slaves. The name of a well-known European saint, it was probably deemed especially appropriate for newly baptized slaves, coming as it does from the Greek meaning "one who is reborn through baptism." By the 1940s the name was widely associated with black women, after the popular writer Montero Lobato began publishing his *Tales of Auntie Nastacia* in the 1930s. So close was this association that some older Brazilians continue to refer to the slave Anastácia as "Auntie Nastacia."

Until the late 1960s, the devotion to Anastácia was known only among a small group of devotees. Then, in 1968, the Museum of the Negro, an annex of the Church of the Rosary of the Brotherhood of St. Benedict in downtown Rio, mounted an exhibition on the occasion of the eightieth anniversary of abolition. To prepare the exhibit, the museum's director, Yolando Guerra, an amateur historian of slavery, turned to Brazil's National Archive and discovered there a collection of clippings belonging to the Pires de Almeida family. Among these, he found a page that had been removed from the nineteenth-century memoir *Souvenirs d'un aveugle: Voyage autour du monde* (1856) by Jacques Arago, a French traveler. On the page there was a single engraved image: a person wearing a "Flanders mask," with the caption "*Châtiment des esclaves*" (slave punishment). Guerra chose the image as a good illustration of torture, and included it in the exhibition.

The museum was not yet a major point of attraction in the city, and so the engraving remained relatively unnoticed. Then in 1971 the remains of the Great Liberator of the slaves, Princess Isabel, were transported from Portugal to Brazil, to be interred at the Cathedral of Petrópolis (about an hour to the north of Rio de Janeiro). Before arriving in Petrópolis, Isabel's sarcophagus was placed for a two-week vigil in the Museum of the Negro.[19] The vigil attracted many thousands of visitors, of all social classes, most of whom had never before set foot in the museum. That is when a huge public saw Arago's drawing for the first time.

An informant named Maria, a black woman in her seventies, told me what happened next. "While Isabel was there, you could hear the humm-humm. Some were saying: This is her! This is the picture of Anastácia! They had known about her, but there she was." Apparently the "humm-humm" persuaded at least a few people to petition Arago's image for spiritual or material blessings. "Pretty soon the word got out that Anastácia was at the museum," said Maria, "and people would go there to ask for things. She is a very miraculous saint. So when one would receive a blessing, she would tell it, and then another, and another. So it passed by word of mouth."

When Guerra got wind of what was happening, he spoke to an old ex-slave who told him that the image was indeed that of a slave who had been known for a long time: she was called Anastácia. Guerra wrote several articles for spiritist magazines about what he had learned, and this drew a new group of interested people to the museum. A member of the Brotherhood of the Rosary, a white woman with spiritist leanings named Maria Salomé, was moved by Guerra's writings and instructed by the spirit of Anastácia herself to compose a history of the slave, which was published by a vanity press and sold for a nominal price. This was the first published version of Anastácia's story, which would later be altered in various and profound ways in oral, graphic, radio, textual, musical, television, and theatrical productions. Salomé's version begins:

> The slaves brought from Africa to Brazil, came from Guinea, Angola, and the Congo, bringing rosary beads with them around their necks. Only the strongest and those with the best teeth were chosen. Many died on the trip to the north of Brazil. Yellow fever and nostalgia for their distant homeland took many lives. Among the slaves were chosen the healthiest female slaves to take on heavy tasks in the plantations and sugar-mills.

Among them stood out because of her stature and the perfection of her facial traits, a young woman of Angola. She was beautiful, with white teeth and sensual lips, upon which could be noted a sad smile. In her large eyes, there was always a shining star. Because of her physical gifts, it may be presumed that she was the property of a noble family, which, upon returning to Portugal, sold her to a rich Brazilian planter. Taken to the plantation, her life underwent an abrupt change. Lusted after by men, envied by women, she was loved and respected by her brothers in suffering: old and young slaves alike found in her a sage friend.

Stoic, serene, obedient to her torturers until she died. They called her Anastácia, for she had no birth record. She said that she left in her distant homeland father, mother, and a brother. She was cruelly raped to augment the workforce, and to satisfy the instincts of monsters in the clothing of men. She was harassed constantly by the slavedriver, in whom she inspired a morbid passion, and who raped her cruelly, turning her life into a martyrdom, as if the torture of slavery was not already sufficient. Pursued by the men in the surroundings, her nights were filled with anguish, fear, and shame. Her honor, body, and dignity were sacrificed by the violence of men brutalized by instinct. Like beasts, they fought over who would possess her, like an object.

As a inevitable consequence, she had many children. Beautiful children with blue eyes, like the blue of the sky, that seemed so far away from her. In order to nurse the children of the master, she had to deny her healthful milk to her own children who, while still young, were already hard at work in the Big House.

During the day Anastácia worked in the sugar-mill. The cane-juice was denied her, as it was to the other slaves. One day she felt the desire to taste a piece of sugar. She was seen by the evil slavedriver, who, calling her a thief, placed the face-iron upon her. It was vengeance. Anastácia had never allowed him to kiss her. She was pure, innocent, and chaste. This punishment was dreadful and drew the notice of the Mistress of the house who, vain and jealous, upon seeing the strange beauty of the slave, feared that her husband might fall in love with her. Perfidious, without consulting her husband, she ordered a neck-iron to be placed upon her. She could not withstand this torture for very long. The iron, digging into her flesh, caused tetanus, which poisoned her blood and perfected her soul, elect by God who called her to the kingdom of heaven where the angels live. Anastácia died after a prolonged agony, on a pale and sad morning.

There was general grief on the plantation, reducing the productivity of the slaves, who attended her body in tears. When the fact of this sadness became known to the owner, remorse awoke too late his pity for this slave, sacrificed in the full bloom of youth.

The slavedriver and the Mistress felt pierced by a feeling of guilt that was so great that they permitted the vigil for Anastácia to be held in the chapel, while the master, filled with remorse and compassion, provided a burial worthy of a freedperson. And so the beautiful slave, covered with flowers, was buried in the Church, built by slaves, their sweat mixed with the mortar.

And today her devotees can testify that the tortured slave is a saint. I have already received many blessings and miracles from her, in the certainty that she died in saintliness, and must be in Heaven, surrounded by the angels, interceding for men. Go there, to the Museum of the Negro, and verify for yourself what I have reported here. Go and meet Anastácia. Contemplate the softness of her gaze. Ask from her a blessing and return later to thank her for the miracle.

The various themes touched upon in this early account, of Africanity, beauty, suffering, rape, and death, and how devotees conceive and feel about these themes, will all be treated in detail in a later chapter. For now I simply want to draw attention to several key points about this version. First, Anastácia is here portrayed as a "pure" black African woman. She is born in Africa, not Brazil. Second, the account makes clear that Anastácia's physical appearance—her beauty—is central to the myth. The long, loving gaze upon her face is fundamental to her meaning. Third, she is violently raped: she does not succeed in fending off her attackers. But her rapists do not include the master himself, a point that will, later, be of the utmost importance. Fourth, the face-iron is placed upon her as punishment for pilfering sugar, and as vengeance for refusing to kiss the slavedriver; the neck-iron is part of a plan by the master's wife to keep her husband from falling in love with her. Neither of these tortures are punishments for rebellion or for speaking out against slavery. Indeed, what makes Anastácia saintly is that she maintains, in the midst of the worst torture and suffering, her serenity, stoicism, and calm obedience. Finally, after Anastácia dies from infection, her torturers are overcome with remorse, and provide her with a burial worthy of a freedperson, despite her slave status. It will be helpful to keep these points in mind as we encounter more recent versions.

Throughout the 1970s, the number of Anastacia's followers remained modest, and the devotion received little coverage in the media. A current director of the Brotherhood of the Rosary who has watched the cult for nearly thirty years stated that in the 1970s "people came to the museum, but not in great crowds." One of Anastácia's elderly devotees remembered that "in the 1970s, you could still speak of Anastácia and there were people who would not know whom you were talking about."

The change came in the early 1980s. After that, as another devotee recalls, "everyone knew Anastácia." The population that led the way was the middle class. "In the 1970s," explained a white middle-class devotee, "to be a devotee of Anastácia meant being poor and black. I was exceptional as a devotee in those days." Then came a veritable deluge of white middle-class devotees in the early 1980s. "It became a rage, a real fashion, to carry her medallion."

Why the shift? For starters, Rio's black movement was having an impact on the consciousness of many white progressives. On the one hand, the movement was making blackness part of any self-respecting progressive's listing of politically important oppressions; on the other, the black movement's mobilization around the racially confrontational figure of Zumbi was met with coolly by many white progressives, who preferred symbols of racial harmony. The figure of Anastácia thus became doubly appealing, both for its rootedness in blackness and slavery, and for its not being Zumbi. "I felt more in tune with Anastácia than with Zumbi," explained one white woman. "Zumbi, I felt, was just for blacks; Anastácia was for everyone."

It was then that a series of specific events brought Anastácia to the attention not only of the middle class but of all Brazilian society. Early in 1984 a well-funded movement for the canonization of Anastácia emerged, led by two black men—Nilton da Silva and Ubirajá Silva—who believed that as an official saint she would strengthen black self-esteem, promote racial harmony, and help instill national pride in Brazil. In their effort to canonize Anastácia, the two men received support from Petrobrás, the national oil company, which subsidized the publication of the movement's booklet and the production of its T-shirts. The company had been approached for support of the Zumbi monument, and had declined. The image of Anastácia, with its appeal to harmony, may have appeared to the nationalist elite at Petrobrás to be a useful alternative to the separatist radicalism of the black move-

ment. "Petrobrás liked the univeral message of Anastácianism," Ubirajá told me, "that it didn't intend to hurt or offend anyone. It was a
'softer' kind of black identity than Zumbi."

In May 1984 the two Silvas sent their petition for canonization to
the pope. In it they retold the story of Anastácia. This retelling became
the version printed on the hundreds of thousands of small prayer sheets
distributed by Nilton's shrine to Anastácia over the course of the last
decade. Here is his version, which Nilton claims was transmitted to him
directly by the slave saint:

> She was born more or less in the period between 1770 and 1813,
> in the state of Bahia. A beautiful *negra* with blue eyes, daughter of
> adultery, of a plantation owner with a slave. Anastácia, for having
> always insisted on preserving her body—in full puberty—from the
> defiling desires of her owner, was cruelly subjected to a martyrdom
> that lasted years. In hateful spite, the master ordered her placed in
> a neck-iron and face-mask of leather. She was then abandoned in
> a dark cell. Some time later, dying, devastated by hunger and sick-
> ness, she was found. Her saviors took her to Rio de Janeiro, where
> she was given medical attention and made a member of the
> Brotherhood. Here she died and was buried. Now in this church
> there is constant celebration of masses for the souls of the slaves, of
> whom Anastácia is the only one represented in effigy in the church.
> And in compensation for the tortures of the slaves, God has given
> to the generous gaze of the portrait of Anastácia, the true power to
> ease the suffering of all those who come close to God with sincere
> goodness in their hearts, faith, charity, and love.[20]

In this version, Anastácia is no longer a pure daughter of Africa; she
has become a child of Bahia, daughter of slave and slaveowner, to
which her blue eyes attest (the color of her eyes was not even mentioned
in Salomé's version). She succeeds in fending off the master's sexual
assaults, for which she pays dearly. She is saved in the end, but by
whom remains unclear. What forges her power in death is her suffering in life, which has purified her soul.

In 1986, Milton Gonçalves, television actor and then director of the
National Radio Company, commissioned a one-hundred-part radio
dramatization of Anastácia's life, to be written by a white spiritist
named Marizete Kuhn. This series was heard by thousands of listeners
throughout the country. In this version, Anastácia is the daughter of the
master who owns her, who had fallen in love with her mother. The mas-

ter's wife, suspecting that her husband's tender treatment of Anastácia is due to his paternity of her, tries to banish the young slave from the plantation, but fails. Anastácia having inherited from her white father a strong sense of dignity, fails to recognize herself as a slave, and speaks to everyone with the calm and tranquillity of a freed person. This behavior enrages the master's wife, who, along with her biological daughter, makes the owner believe that Anastácia is planning to lead a general slave revolt. This is too much even for Anastácia's father to bear. She is seized and tortured to death. Only after she dies does her father learn of the lie. He repents and asks the spirit of Anastácia for forgiveness, which she grants. This was the first version of Anastácia's life that made her out to be a voice against slavery, albeit a voice qualified by an unwillingness to lead an all-out uprising, and by the final act of forgiveness.

In the wake of the media blitz, members of whole new social categories were becoming followers. Anastácia became known among nurses, who saw in her an exemplar of selfless healing. Prisoners became devotees, seeing in her an inspiration to patience in captivity. Her image began to proliferate in black beauty salons, as a model of the beautiful black woman. The popular Afro-Brazilian religion of *umbanda* seized upon her image, and offerings to her became incorporated into the cult of the *pretos velhos* (old black slaves) in *umbanda* centers throughout the city. Various marginal populations, from street children to gays, saw in her not only someone who understood suffering, but who was endowed with the power of an official saint, with none of an official saint's off-putting formality and distance.

When the petition was sent to the Vatican—in blatant defiance of protocol, which required that the petition be routed through the archdiocese—the story received full coverage from the single most watched television show in Brazil, *O Fantástico*, on the largest TV network, Globo. The national press quickly followed suit. Within days of the broadcast a craze set in that had impact upon all social classes. Several famous soap opera actresses publicly declared their devotion to the saint. One of them told me: "When I gave an interview in 1984 that I was a devotee, that became the big story in all the papers. Then I got the producers of the soap to include Anastácia's name in the script as background to my character."

By the mid-1980s, devotees to Anastácia were proliferating in virtually every corner of Brazil. Those who received blessings began recounting their miraculous stories by calling in to any of a dozen national radio shows. Soon there were reports of Anastácia worship in São

Paulo, Minas Gerais, Espirito Santo, Bahia, Pará, and others states. "Almost overnight," Ubirajá remembered, "Anastácia went from a Rio thing to a Brazilian thing; from the thousands to the millions."

By 1985, Nilton was spending more and more time on his spiritualist "mentalizations" in public squares, and in 1986 he founded the "Universal Order of Escrava Anastácia," centered in a house in Madureira, in the Zona Norte, located near one of the largest shopping centers in the city. By 1987, two hundred people were squeezing daily through the center's doors. In 1988, the centennial year of abolition, the house at Madureira became a pilgrimage site for devotees of all social classes and colors, as people of the Zona Norte mixed with the rich and famous who came from the Zona Sul to make their offerings at the slave saint's shrine. During the Carnaval of 1988, two different *escolas de samba* incorporated Anastácia into their sambas. That year, between five hundred and a thousand people were visiting the Madureira shrine each day.

The Catholic Church could not remain indifferent to this situation for long. During the 1970s, when the bishops were preoccupied with liberation theology and human rights, they had not had much time to worry about an obscure slave worshiped in a church annex. In the mid-1980s, with the dangers of liberation theology and state repression receding, the threat to Church authority posed by the Anastácia devotion had become a matter of consequence. While Anastácia's association with *umbanda* might have been tolerable on a small scale, it was rather less so now that the devotion was fast becoming a mass movement. Cardinal Dom Eugênio had, moreover, been infuriated by the Silvas' disregard for Church protocol. It is clear from the angry letter he addressed to them in 1984[21] that he had already made up his mind that Anastácia was a noxious superstition. Closing down her devotion at the Church of Rosário had become for him a matter of personal honor.

In the mid-1980s Dom Eugênio asked Monseigneur Guilherme Schubert, a historian, to find out whether Anastácia had in fact ever existed. Through two years of research, Schubert never hid his contempt for the devotion; it is thus not surprising that he arrived at the "conclusion," in 1987, that Anastácia had never existed.[22] Immediately the cardinal ruled that the Brotherhood would have one year to sell off its remaining Anastácia paraphernalia, and then would be required to remove any vestige of the slave saint from its premises.

The popular reaction to this news was strong and widespread. Some public figures, like Wilson Prudentes of the Workers' Party, wrote in the pages of *O Dia* that the attitude of the Church was "authoritarian and racist," recalling the "days of the Inquisition."[23] Others, like the singer Gilbero Gil, called the prohibition a case of "deep insensitivity to the faith of the people." On the other side of the polemic, Dom Marcos Barbosa wrote in the pages of the *Jornal do Brasil* that "The Church cannot accept this devotion, not because of the slave's social condition nor color, but because she never existed."[24]

The reaction of the black movement was ambivalent. Many in the movement made gestures of support for Anastácia, but they were half-hearted. Movement militants were not especially fond of the slave saint. They had a general mistrust of anything to do with the Catholic Church, the historic oppressor of the slaves. Based on what they knew of her story, they gathered that Anastácia had not been a rebel against the slave regime. Thus they were, if anything, relieved to have an argument from historical realism—that "she never existed"—on the side of trying to have as little to do with her as possible.[25]

As for the mass of her devotees, after initial bewilderment about the Church's stance, most simply retained their devotion and respected the Church that much less. As one of them told me, "The Church is made up of men. Anastácia's miracles come from God. The Church cannot change that." Some continued to visit the museum, even without Anastácia's image. Others started visiting the center at Madureira, which saw its visitors' books fill rapidly.

The television network Manchete cashed in on the controversy surrounding Anastácia's prohibition. The producers of the series "The Frontiers of the Unknown" bought a script on the slave saint's life in 1989, and proceeded to make one of the costliest miniseries in Brazilian television history. The three-part, three-hour production aired in mid-1990, and captured one of the largest audiences ever for a miniseries.

The television version portrayed Anastácia as a Nigerian princess, of pure African blood. Her eyes are blue, as a sign that she has been endowed by the spirit of the rivers (Oxum) with miraculous healing power, and assigned the mission to bring spiritual liberation to her people in bondage in Brazil. She has just married in Africa, and lost her virginity, when she is kidnapped by slavers and dragged to Brazil, where she is sold to an evil master and a jealous mistress. The master falls in love with her, and pleads with her to cede her body to him. She refuses, and he bides his time. Meanwhile she cares for his children, who love her, and she lays her hands' healing power upon the whipping wounds of the other slaves. Anastácia is tranquil, serene, and immune to vindictiveness. At one point another slave, embittered about nursing the master's child, sets fire to its crib, but Anastácia arrives and miraculously douses the flames with the gaze of her crystalline blue eyes.

Finally, the master can resist temptation no longer: he tries to rape her, but, in her one bodily act of resistance, she pushes him away and runs to the plantation's front gate, which she flings open for a group of runaways. She, however, insists on staying on the plantation and facing her destiny. For the crime of letting out the slaves, and, implicitly, for having refused the master, she is tortured and confined to a facemask. But her inner freedom is so great that she need only meet the looks of the other slaves to evoke their love of freedom.

As she lies dying from the gangrene that has set in around her facemask, she heals all those who come to her. Then, in what was for many viewers the most memorable moment of the series, the master and mistress come to Anastácia with their son, who is dying of pneumonia. Without hesitation, in an act of monumental dignity and forgiveness, she cures him. As she does so, she dies. The final scene is a view from the kitchen, as one of the cooks looks through the window and sees a white dove flying away from the plantation.

Today there are numerous devotees who date their devotion from having watched this program. Parts of this version of Anastácia's life became enormously influential, and certain elements remain imbedded in the popular culture surrounding the slave saint. In one popular black women's group named after the slave saint (to be discussed later), every new visitor to the group is regaled with a viewing of at least one episode from the videotaped miniseries.

By the mid-1990s, Anastácia had four main sites of worship and pilgrimage in Rio de Janeiro. At the old museum of the Negro, attached to the Rosário Church, at least a hundred devotees visit each day. The shrine in Madureira moved to Vaz Lobo in 1994, and attracts several hundred visitors each day. In 1995, following the death of Nilton da Silva, a faction split off from Vaz Lobo, and founded a separate Anastácia shrine in Olaria, which now recives about two hundred faithful per day. A bust of Anastácia in the Praça Padre Sousa in Benfica has received, since its installation in 1981, at least a hundred devotees per week.

The number of Anastácia's devotees is impossible to determine, but her penetration into every nook and cranny of popular Brazilian culture testifies to her widespread appeal. Although the image of Anastácia can no longer be obtained through the Museum of the Negro, thousands of Anastácia busts and statuettes, crosses, rosary beads, prayer sheets and cards, candles, matches, keychains, placemats, calendars, earrings, medallions, rings, and T-shirts may be bought at the pilgrimage sites in Olaria, Vaz Lobo, and Benfica. It is common for devotees to fulfill promises made to Anastácia by distributing thousands of her prayer sheets.

In Rio de Janeiro, Anastácia seems at first glance to be nowhere; but in fact she is everywhere. Her image is present in the form of prayer cards inserted into wallets; of medallions stuffed underneath shirts; of lockets kept in glove compartments; of prayer ribbons tied to rearview mirrors; of portraits on walls inside homes; of statuettes placed carefully alongside other saints in bedroom sanctuaries. One popular practice is for devotees with businesses to fulfill promises to Anastácia by naming their enterprises after her. If one pays attention to the names of commercial establishments, her ubiquity becomes clear. There are "Anastácia" bars, snackshops, apartment houses, clothing stores, even an "Anastácia Bikini" located in the heart of Copacabana, not to mention at least four hair salons named after her, and at least three poor private schools emblazoned with her name. One cabdriver I got to know assured me: all Brazilians were devotees of Anastácia!

Anastácia's name is also present in popular music. Aside from the musical incantations sung to her in some *umbanda* centers, the slave saint has been praised in the winning sambas of two consecutive Carnavals (1988 and 1989); the singer Leci Brandão has immortalized the shrine of Anastácia in her samba *Ei, Madureira*; a popular composer who lives in the *favela* of Cantagalo has written hymns of praise to Anastácia, to the beat of reggae; a composer of repentismo (a popular musical genre from the Brazilian Northeast) has composed a ten-page song-poem to the slave saint; and in Salvador, a black women's dancing troupe called Didá Banda has made Anastácia their patron saint, which they symbolize in concert by wearing leather face-masks just like hers.

Ritual Relations with Anastácia[26]

Like other popular Catholic devotions, Anastácia is worshiped in two main ways: through an intensely personal relationship directly with her spirit, mediated by small movable images such as prayer cards or medallions; and through pilgrimages to a shrine where one of her life-sized statues is preserved behind glass. (Because of limits of space and the nature of my sample of devotees, I will not treat here how Anastácia is worshiped in *umbanda* or spiritism, where she is also extremely popular.)

Dona Lucia, a devout Catholic in her sixties, has been a devotee of the slave saint for almost twenty years. In her living room hangs a simple wood bas-relief of Anastácia, and a small bust of Anastácia rests upon a small table in her bedoom, next to figurines of Nossa Senhora, Santa Luzia, Santa Rita, and São Lazaro. Although she prays to all of these saints, her relationship to Anastácia is, she says, special. Every morning, soon after she wakes, Luzia takes a moment to look at Anastácia and speak with her. "Oh, Anastácia," she says, "you who know patience so well, give me the strength today to meet all troubles with peace, patience, and love." If she knows that a particular vexation awaits her, she will speak of it in detail to Anastácia, and that "gives me peace of mind."

"A Typical Statuette of the Slave Saint."

If it is a Monday, the day of the blessed dead, Luzia lights a candle in front of the small statue. The candle is supposed to burn for seven days, but rarely does. While for other souls this would represent a divine light to help the soul find its way out of purgatory and toward heaven, for Anastácia, who is already in heaven, the candle is a simple offering of respect and love, which, by gratifying her ensures her positive energy and protection all week long. Once a year, on Anastácia's feast day (May 12), Luzia places a white rose and a glass of water in front of the image. Both become drenched in Anastácia's spiritual power on that day. Luzia presses the rose, which she carries with her in her purse to protect her against mishap in the street; and she applies the water to her forehead to alleviate headache.

The relationship between devotee and Anastácia is governed by what anthropologists call generalized reciprocity. That is, exchanges with Anastácia take place in the context of a relationship suffused with warmth, love, trust, and beneficence. Luzia makes requests of Anastácia all the time, because she believes Anastácia is "very miraculous," but also because she knows that Anastácia will not let her down. "I ask of her, and I receive," she says. " It may take a little while, but she always gives me what I ask for."

Usually Luzia requests help in arriving at and maintaining positive emotional states—such as courage, faith, hope, patience, love, and understanding—for herself and her family. She also asks on a regular basis for material blessings such as protection against intruders, thieves, and violent crime; for good health; and for financial security. When she is facing a specific crisis of health or safety, she calls upon Anastácia with a profusion of prayers.

Recently, Luzia faced a crisis: her daughter, a twenty-year-old married woman, became grievously ill. "I immediately spoke to Anastácia," she told me. "I said to her: "Ah, Anastácia, you who have suffered so much, you know what it is to suffer. Please, my darling Anastácia, do not let my daughter suffer. Give her the strength to overcome this. If she is cured, I will go to your shrine and place three roses there for you, and I will distribute one hundred prayer sheets in the street."

Let us follow Luzia to Anastácia's shrine at Olaria. She arrives on a Tuesday morning, and the place is thronged; about fifty people are crowding the anteroom, waiting to approach the image of the slave saint. Here, as in the other pilgrimage sites, the majority of pilgrims are women, on the order of eight to every man. While most are middle-aged and elderly, there is a sizable contingent of young and unmarried women as well. All the colors of Brazil are represented. It is impossible to say whether Anastácia's followers are preponderantly *preta, morena, mulata,* or white. Here in Olaria, most of the visitors are poor, working-class and lower-middle-class.

Crossing the church's threshold and glancing immediately to the right, we see a low table upon which sit a large Bible, open to the Psalms, and a life-size painted ceramic bust of the slave saint. On most days, but especially on Mondays, the bust is surrounded by dozens of flickering candles, offered as tokens of love and respect, and in hope of receiving peace, positive energies, protection from maleficent forces, or tangible blessings. Some are tokens of gratitude for blessings already received.

The Statue of Anastácia at Her Shrine in Vaz Lobo.

Turning to face the opposite wall, we see one of the church's two full life-size statues of Anastácia. The priest had this one commissioned in 1995, following Nilton's death. It is an impressive sight. Anastácia stands in a full-length white silk dress, which for many devotees symbolizes the purity of her spirit, and for some the chastity of her body. Her hands are outstretched palms up, in the classic Catholic gesture of saintly benediction. Her fingers are weighed down by gold, silver, and pearl rings, offered to her by grateful devotees. Some devotees say the offering of expensive rings show the depth of their feeling for the slave saint, symbolizing their lifelong bond with her. Others say the rings symbolize Anastácia's eternal bond with God. In practice, the rings represent a compromise reached by the priest with the devotees, who used to bring in fancy necklaces and brooches: the rings allow devotees to offer jewelry—for many, a powerful expression of sacrifice—while preserving the slave saint's image of virtuous simplicity.

Anastácia's neck is encircled by a single gold necklace with a pentagram pendant, the symbol of balance and equanimity. Upon her head rests an imitation-pearl tiara, a sign not only of her earthly status as a princess, but, for many devotees, the equivalent of a halo. Her skin is dark brown, her hair black, her eyes blue, and her mouth hidden behind a silver-colored mask.

The statue stands inside a locked glass case adorned by white carnations and abundantly surrounded by daisies and jonquils as well as a profusion of white, pink, and yellow roses—all offered by devotees, and symbolizing, one of them told me, the beauty of Anastácia's spirit. At eye level, through a round opening in the glass, some devotees push slips of paper upon which they have written requests for blessings, while others place flowers, prayer cards, or medallions. Once every two months the presiding Orthodox priest opens the case, and burns the accumulated slips of paper in a small ritual that, he says, shows his respect for the devotees. "I would never think of simply throwing the papers away," he says.

Finally Luzia approaches the image and lays her right hand on the glass case. She stands, her head slightly tilted back. The blood is rising to her head, as she remembers the miracle that Anastácia has bestowed on her, as she sees her daughter, healthy and whole, before her mind's eye. She is whispering loudly. "Ah, Anastácia, thank you, my dearest sweetheart, for what you have done. I have brought something for you."

She reaches into her bag and draws out three roses—one red, for love, one white, for peace, and one yellow, for hope. She places them tenderly in the great vase of flowers at the foot of the glass case. Then she kisses the case, makes a sign of the cross, and sighs deeply.

The interaction is over, but she stands a few more minutres gazing at Anastácia, looking into her eyes. "That gives me so much peace, just to look at her," she tells me later.

THE POWERS OF THE HOLY SPIRIT

Although we spent equal portions of our time with the Renovated Baptist, Assembly of God, and the Jesus is the Truth Churches, I have chosen to focus here on the history and practice of only one of these—the Assembly of God—which (despite the arrival of the Universal Church on the scene[27]) continues to be the single most important and influential pentecostal church in Brazil.

The Origins of Brazilian Pentecostalism

The pentecostal movement was forged in the struggle to project an ideal of universal egalitarianism over the reality of the profoundly unequal race relations of North America. The movement formed in Los Angeles in 1906 around the certainty of a black preacher named William Joseph Seymour, the child of former Louisiana slaves, that the Holy Spirit was at long last raining down from heaven, as it had done upon the apostles in the second book of Acts. There, in Jerusalem, shortly after Jesus' death and resurrection, his followers from many nations had joined to celebrate the fiftieth day after Passover (the Pentecost), when "suddenly a sound came from heaven like the rush of a mighty wind, and it filled all the house where they were sitting. And there appeared to them tongues as of fire, distributed and resting on each one of them" (Acts 2:1–3).

On the first Pentecost, men and women of all nations had transcended the human barriers that divided them and spoke the single language of the angels. So too, in Seymour's vision, the power of the Holy Spirit arriving in the new Pentecost would dissolve all human divisions.

Seymour's vision was nothing short of revolutionary: to imagine interracial churches in the heyday of Jim Crow. It was a vision in which "true Christians should leave the existing denominations—both black and white—in order to become part of the purified and racially inclusive church."[28] At first locked out of all-white churches in Los Angeles, Seymour organized prayer meetings in the black section of town, in the homes of black domestic servants and washerwomen. The first spiritual gift was that of vision, given to Edward Lee, a black janitor, who foresaw the spread of speaking in tongues. The first service was held on

Azusa Street, in a house that had once been occupied by the African Methodist Episcopal Church.

Within days, the Azusa Street mission was attracting men and women across the racial divide. As Cox has noted, "in a segregated America, God was now assembling a new and racially inclusive people to glorify his name and to save a Jim Crow nation lost in sin."[29] The most striking thing about the pentecostal movement, at its point of origin, was that "blacks and whites, men and women, embraced each other at the tiny altar as they wept and prayed. A southern white preacher later jotted in his diary that at first he was offended and startled, then inspired, by the fact that, as he put it, 'the color line was washed away by the blood.'"[30]

This racial harmony did not last long. The whites who had been ordained in the mainly black Church of God in Christ left and started the mainly white Assembles of God in 1914, in Hot Springs, Arkansas, in an effort to avoid nonwhite leadership.[31] Chicago, meanwhile, had become a center of small pentecostal churches, with a sizable membership of poor Swedish immigrants who were running away from the stuffiness of their home society's monochromatic Lutheranism. Among these were Gunnar Vingren and Daniel Berg, who were informed by a prophet that they should go to a place called Pará to be missionaries. So they went to Belém (Bethlehem), the capital of Pará state, in Brazil, in 1913, and officially established the Assembly of God there in 1917. That was the first pentecostal church on Brazilian soil.

The church expanded mainly in the north of the country until 1930; until the 1960s, the church was led mainly by rural Northeasterners. Contrary to a widespread misconception, the Assembly of God in Brazil never derived major benefits from its international ties. Very few North American Assembly of God missionaries ever arrived in Brazil, the largest number being no more than twenty for all of Brazil, in the 1970s. Furthermore, local congregations are largely self-supporting, depending little on outside financial help. By 1990, Freston[32] estimated that the Assemblies of God in Brazil numbered some seven million members, accounting for more than half of all the pentecostals in Brazil.

Growing in the Spirit

I want now to give the reader a sense of what it is like to become a pentecostal believer, to "grow in the Spirit."

I first met Laise ten years ago, in the *sala* of her mother's house in São Jorge, a semirural town about an hour to the north of Rio de Janeiro. I was interviewing her mother, an elderly woman named Carolina, a long-standing lay leader of the local Catholic church. Suddenly Laise appeared at the door, tall and lanky, powerfully built, with muscular arms. She was breathless from the walk up the hill from the public school where she worked as a cook in the mornings. Like her mother, she was very dark-skinned; later I would learn that she called herself *negra*. When Carolina introduced us, however, what struck me was how different this person was from her small, frail mother.

The air was filled with tension. What was I doing there, Laise wanted to know, speaking to her mother and averting her eyes from me. Carolina said I was an "American," who had come to Brazil with his wife to study religion. This made her stiffen even more. Without looking at me, she said, "Religion? Why did he need to come all the way to Brazil to learn about that?"

I intervened. "Well, I can't learn too much about Brazil's religions if I stay in the United States."

Laise could no longer avoid looking at me. She eyed me suspiciously. "Are you a missionary?"

"No, I'm an anthropologist." I mumbled something about trying to understand different cultures. Laise was not impressed. But she was willing to lay down a challenge.

"If you are not one of those *crente* missionaries, come by my house and I'll tell you some things you don't know about religion." She looked again at her mother, who broke into a smile.

As it turned out, Laise became an extraordinarily helpful informant about her own religion, which was *umbanda*. In her late twenties at the time, the mother of two children in elementary school, and married more or less happily to a man who had steady work as a construction worker, she was a fount of detailed commentary on the various spirits in the *umbanda* pantheon. We ended up spending many afternoons together, in interviews about her religion, as well as in more general informal chatter.

Laise's husband was a medium at the *terreiro* (ritual center), and they shared their religion intensely. I visited the *terreiro* with her several times. The sprits of *umbanda* had treated her well: her family was healthy; both she and her husband were employed; her mother was alive; and they all had roofs over their heads. In those days, Laise saw the Protestants quite clearly as the enemy. She despised their arrogance, how they demanded attention when you didn't want to give it; and how they were dead set on destroying the religion she identified as her own.

Then the disasters started to occur. Her husband was diagnosed with a fatal illness. Her mother became ill, and had to be hospitalized. The state started to threaten to pull funding from the school where she worked. Her own children began to talk back to her. Her world was falling apart. I recall a conversation we had on her porch in the midst of it all. She was depressed.

"You know, John, I have stopped going to the *terreiro*," she said.

"Why?"

She shooed away the dog. "Because Jorge is dying. He can no longer be a medium. And I blame them there: for how they have treated him. I believe it was a *coisa feita* [an act of sorcery]. There is a lot of jealousy there. I know the one who did this."

Unfortunately, her husband did not improve. When he died, Laise was in dire need of spiritual support, but she could no longer turn to *umbanda* for this. She had lost her faith in the spirits; she now saw them as adversaries, as the servants of her enemies.

It was in this context that she first visited the local pentecostal church, a small congregation of the Assembly of God. She did so, well aware of the irony that she had recently denounced the very church where she was now setting foot. But she was desperate. The first time she went, she converted, raising her hand for Jesus.

I asked her to tell me how this happened, and what it was like.

"I couldn't rightly believe it was happening," she said shaking her head. "Here I am, a *macumbeira* in a *crente* church. But I tell you, when I heard those hymns being sung, I felt it deep down. I realized that the only way I was going to escape those demons was through the power of the Holy Spirit."

Toward the end of every pentecostal service there is a moment when the pastor asks if any of the unconverted who are present are prepared to raise their hand for Jesus and be written into the Book of Life.

"When the pastor got to that point, I was already thinking, I had already made up my mind. I thought, if the demons have killed Jorge, and they are killing my mother, won't I be next? And then I thought: 'This is God revealing all of this to me right now.' And when I thought that, I said, well, there's nothing left to be done but to raise my hand."

"How did that feel?"

"Ah, John, it was the greatest moment of my life. The feeling, well, it's hard to describe. Like a great joy, a huge weight lifted up off your heart. When I walked down that aisle to the pastor, he was smiling, and I could hardly see because the tears were coming down. And everyone extended their hands over me and prayed, and said 'hallelujah.' And hallelujah it is, glory be to Jesus."

Raising one's hand in church does not, by itself, mean that one is saved. In the theology of pentecostal churches, salvation is by faith, but faith must be tested and proved. Laise could have simply been moved by the hymns, or had a moment of emotional overflow. Pentecostal pastors are all too aware of their flock's proclivities to feel the emotion of the moment. This is why the new convert must usually wait at least three months before being baptized into the church. During this time, she receives biblical and doctrinal instruction. If she is able to understand the basic elements of God's law and to incorporate them into her own life in a convincng manner, then she is ready for baptism.

> Laise recalled this period with feeling. "I had to kill my old self and allow the new Laise to be born," she said. The "old Laise" was someone who listened to samba and the music of the "world," liked a bawdy joke, enjoyed smoking, drank a beer from time to time, and wore makeup, shorts, and revealing clothing. All of these had to go. "At first it was a real trial," she said. "You know, it's not easy to give up smoking. I was addicted. But with a lot of prayer, and knowing that this really is against the will of God, I let that go, and the other things besides." For five long months Laise attended Sunday school and another Bible course for new converts, and had almost daily conversations with a woman who had been assigned to guide her through the trial period.

The change in Laise's appearance has been dramatic. I knew her for years when she wore tank tops and cutoff jeans, and now she wears long dresses with mid-length sleeves. Her congregation is quite traditional on these matters of doctrine. There are other Assemblies of God that are more "liberal," where women may wear sleeveless dresses and even a little makeup.

What has not changed is Laise's forceful, outgoing personality. Here, it is important to point out that Laise participates actively in her neighborhood association and is an active campaigner for the Workers' Party. Recent research[33] has gone a long way toward problematizing older views about the natural or inevitable apathy and depoliticization of pentecostals. A major finding of the Instituto de Estudos de Religião's 1994 survey of Protestants throughout the metropolitan Rio area[34] is that Protestants with spiritual gifts tend to be more involved in their neighborhood's social activism rather than less.

Laise has not insisted that her two sons come to the church. She recognizes that this is a highly individual matter, one that each soul, including those of her own children, must determine for itself. "Of course I would be very happy if one of them, or, God willing, both of them, would accept Jesus into their hearts," said Laise. "But who am I to say this? That is between them and God."

After five months of preparation, Laise was finally ready for baptism. This would be the moment of her true transition from the damned to the saved. Raising her hand for Jesus had been a sign of her intention to be saved; baptism was to be her salvation's public consecration.

"It was very emotional for me," said Laise. "We were dressed all in white, in long flowing white gowns, because they say that it is like becoming a baby, pure as a baby all over again." Joining a half dozen other new converts in a joyful march up the São Jorge foothills to where the river rushes clear and clean, Laise was immersed in the waters and emerged from them a new woman, born again in Jesus Christ.

But then began a new phase of her odyssey. "I wanted so badly to have the second baptism," she said. By this, she meant the baptism in the fire of the Holy Spirit. Laise wanted what most pentecostals crave: the direct experience of the power of God in their bodies. This is not a distant, abstract matter: *crentes* see the power of God at work among their co-religionists every day, in the various spiritual gifts—of healing, of vision, of tongues, or, most dramatically, of prophecy.

In the view of the *crentes,* God chooses people to be vessels of His Spirit according to His own plan and design, which is often obscure to the small, limited human mind. It is not always the most righteous or faithful who are chosen. Still, because the power of the Spirit can come as a major shock to the physical body, *crentes* tend to believe that God chooses stronger, more robust, more vigorous, even more youthful bodies to receive that most awesome of spiritual gifts, the gift of prophecy. But robustness of body will be of no avail if the soul within is not pure, which is why pentecostals have so many all-night prayer vigils, and why they value fasting. "A person has to be walking right by God," said Laise. "You must purify your heart and soul. You must have all your energies focused on God." Only then will God reciprocate with the pouring out of His holy fire.

"This is how it happened to me," said Laise. "I was at a prayer vigil, and we were there, praying and praying. And I started to get tired, I tell you it is not easy. But I had been searching for the gifts for so long, praying every day, asking God to have mercy on me and to let me see a way toward receiving the gifts. Hallelujah. And it must have been late, very late, maybe three in the morning. And all of us bleary-eyed, but staying awake to sing the praises of the Lord. And that's when it happened. I had been looking so hard for the gifts, praying, and fasting, and reading my Bible, and searching. And all of a sudden, this feeling comes over me, like, 'I don't need to search. I will never deserve the gifts. I am a sinner, and sinners cannot deserve these things.' And as soon as I felt that. . . . It was like an onrushing train. It fell down right upon me, I felt the spirit like a warmth entering into my head, then through my head and into my body, my chest, my heart. And when it did that, it was like I was standing alongside myself, watching, because I started to prophesy right then and there, started to speak the words and listening to myself, I couldn't believe it."

Now Laise has grown in the Spirit, and receives the gift of prophecy often. With this gift, she can stand forth and feel the voice of God speaking through her, using her to edify and discipline His church. She knows that not everyone who claims to have the gift of prophecy is a real prophet. "Some kids," she said, "just get carried away. That is their flesh talking, not the voice of God." She knows that, according to the Apostle Paul, the true prophet must always remain standing, cannot fall down, nor bring scandal into the church. According to these standards, Laise is sure that what moves her is the Holy Spirit indeed, and no mere illusion of the flesh or the devil.

"Ah, John, to be with the Lord is so sweet," said Laise.

THREE

The Politics of Mystical Substance

Black Women and the Catholic Inculturated Mass

THE INCULTURATED MASS AS A CONTRADICTORY SPACE

According to its most impassioned theoretician, the inculturated Mass has the potential to stir the consciousness of more people than any other activity of the black pastoral. By challenging the Catholic Church to open the most sacred of its rites to African cultural influence, the inculturated Mass promises, according to Frei David, to transform the Church itself. "We are initiating a whole new stage of the Church in Brazil," he declared in his office in the center of São João de Meriti, a city in the great sprawl of the Baixada Fluminense. "I think none of us is fully aware of the revolution we are starting. But I assure you: this work is going to revolutionize the Church. Of that I am sure."

Frei David had been leaning forward on his elbows, looking at me intently across his desk piled high with papers and books and ideas. He is in his mid-forties. He stroked his little beard as he spoke, as usual, in whole, succinct sentences. When he finished a paragraph, you knew it. He hadn't finished this one.

"And then there is going to be a world revolution. I have no doubt about it. The Brazilian Chuch and the global Church are going to change radically due to the simple and sincere experiment that is occurring here."

Whether or not the inculturated Mass is headed toward this particular destiny, there is no question that the rite, which was born in 1988 and has since established a generous following in Rio de Janeiro and a half dozen of Brazil's principal cities[1] has garnered among activists in the black consciousness movements greater respect than any other Christian initiative. A leading black activist told me that despite his misgivings about the Church in general, he believed that the inculturated Mass "has the greatest potential to bring together the Christian tradition with the agenda of black politics." In the black women's movement, several leaders expressed the opinion that the inculturated Mass was precisely the link that would allow the ideas of the movement to filter into the Christian arena. A leader at Criola said: "I was skeptical at first, because you never know with the Catholic Church. But when I actually witnessed it, saw how respectful it is of Afro-religion, I realized that this was a cultural activity, it wasn't trying to take over *candomblé*. Frei David really is trying to build respect for the value of African culture."

A closer look at how Catholics at the neighborhood level respond to and feel about the rite suggests that it may be premature to expect it to announce a revolution in values. We would do better to regard the inculturated Mass as a set of practices, symbols, and ideas that has carved out a space in which stereotypes coexist with new ways to conceive of *negro* identity. This coexistence is problematic. The rite does help some people to articulate the unarticulated, and to think in new ways, but at a price. The Mass authorizes some experiences and desires, and marginalizes others. It thus restricts the space in which people can evolve as whole persons and alienates many who might otherwise contribute to the evolution of the Catholic Church's struggle against racism.

My approach in this chapter will be to examine how the ritual of the inculturated Mass, and its theology, construct the ideal of *negra* womanhood, and how *negra* women in turn respond to, negotiate, and sometimes reject that construction.[2] I thus will be paying attention both to *negras* who participate in the movement, and to those who have left it, refused to enter, or, in some cases, have remained indifferent to it. I will argue that when we pay close attention to the range of variation that exists among these women, the ideological power of the inculturated Mass in relation to Brazilian black women's experiences begins to emerge, but so too does its considerable ideological limitations in articulating those experiences.

Women's Responses to *Ginga* and the *Atabaque*

Theologians of the *pastoral negro* say that black women's bodies are so full of *axé*, the African life force, that this fullness must "overflow into the world."[3] This overflow, manifested "not by intellect, but by women's body, gestures, music, and dance"[4] is known as *ginga*. Its most tangible manifestation is in *negras'* proclivity to sway to the beat of drums. While black men have *ginga* too, they are better able to repress it, while for *negras* its bubbling up is irrepressible. Helena Theodoro and Muniz Sodré, whose work has lent intellectual respectability to the claims of the *pastoral*, insist that *negras*, "by virtue of being possessors of *axé*," express themselves through movement.[5]

Because *negras* are supposed to be naturally privileged sites for the manifestation of *ginga*, the dancers in the inculturated Mass are always young black women. They are at the performative core of the Mass, their movements accompanying the ritual at every point. Between six and twelve of them, dressed in colorful "African" garb, appear at the start of the rite, and move in unison through a series of movements choreographed around sweeping arm gestures and samba-like footwork. They remain in full view throughout the ceremony, and always in close proximity to the altar.

The association in the inculturated Mass of *axé* and *ginga* with black women belongs to the tendency of ethnic movements in general to invest women with the power to signify ethnic difference. Anthias and Yuval-Davis point out that women frequently become "a focus and symbol in ideological discourses used in the construction, reproduction and transformation of ethnic/national categories."[6] In the case of the black movement in Brazil, this tendency emerges from the notion that women are more in touch than men are with their natural environment, the heavens, the moon, and their own inner rhythms, and are thus less able than men to repress the *axé* within them.

What do black women with personal experience of the inculturated Mass have to say about *ginga* and its relation to them?

About a third of the women we spoke with told us that the inculturated Mass did in fact touch and draw out something deeply physical in their bodies. "The first time I witnessed an inculturated Mass," said Benta, a *negra* schoolteacher in her forties, "the body movements were contagious. It touched my whole body—and still does!—not just the voice and the head, not just the mind. Here we move our legs and arms as well."

Benta was deeply involved in the preparation and coordination of her community's inculturated Mass. She had been a lay leader for more than twenty years, and had grown up surrounded by the institutional Church. But like many other women of her color, she had burning childhood memories of the humiliation of being passed over when the time came to choose little girls to coronate the image of Mary in the

June festivities. She had never doubted that she was *negra*, she said, and had never been under the illusion that the way she had been treated was due to anything but her color. "I mean, I was only ten years old. At that age you know why you are being passed over. I didn't have the hair, I didn't have the skin."

But now the Church was finally opening its ritual arms to her, proclaiming her to be valuable and beautiful. She went further: the inculturated Mass allowed her to realize the deep bodily longings of *negritude* that had been long "repressed by the traditional Mass." She described the longings as a desire to be "whole":

> In the regular Mass, I cannot be whole, it is good there, but something is missing. It is cold, the body is not permitted to move and express that joy we feel. Because we *negros* are a happy people, we have that joy within us, we are more in tune with the rhythms of nature. That is why there is so much water, and the plants we use in the inculturated Mass. We like being surrounded by nature.

Her voice grew husky.

"And so too with the drums: that touches our natures. In the European mass, you are still: the more still you are, the more you are in . . . plenitude. But in the inculturated Mass, it is the opposite. In the inculturated Mass I can finally worship God in my way; it is the place I have to worship God while dancing."

But Benta's was not the only kind of experience evoked by the ritual. Indeed, other black women felt impatience with the expectation that their bodies should resonate to the rhythms of the *atabaque*.

᾿Yvonne is an educated, unmarried woman in her twenties who works as a clerk in a clothing store. She is proud to call herself *negra*, and, she says, she has suffered personally from racial discrimination. "When I looked for a job, I was turned down again and again because they only wanted someone with 'good appearance.'" She wears her hair in the natural style, and has no interest in straightening it.

Two years ago Yvonne started participating in the *Quilombo*, the Catholic group in São João de Meriti made up of black laity that coordinates the parish's inculturated Mass. After participating for several months, she began to have second thoughts. She now attends meetings from time to time, but prefers to keep her distance. She does not, she assured me, feel hostile to the group, and remains sympathetic to the group's agenda of combating racism and building black self-esteem. Her reservations have to do with the inculturated Mass.

⅋ "It is very pretty," she said. "And it is very good to have a Mass that shows us that we must valorize ourselves, our culture." The problem, she said, was that contrary to what she knew other participants expected of her, she personally did not feel the deepest level of her being touched by the rhythms, gestures, and sounds of the inculturated Mass.

She slowed down so that I could register every word:

> Look, it just doesn't speak to me. I don't feel any more at ease, any more 'myself' there in the inculturated Mass than in the traditional one. How many times have I gone to a traditional Mass and felt moved, so moved? And if I go to an inculturated Mass, sometimes I feel moved, sometimes I don't, depending on how I am with Christ. It is Christ that moves me, not because there is an *atabaque* there, or dancing. I could see that I was not having that rush that the others were having. I felt different. I am *negra*, but I felt like I didn't belong with the other *negra*s, if that is what I am supposed to feel. . . . I like the *atabaque*. I really do. It is a beautiful instrument. But does it speak to some hidden part of me? I just don't feel it. I also like classical music. And piano. Does that make me any less *negra*? Does this mean I am trying to escape my race? Don't I have a right to like classical music? Should I not like classical music just because it is European?

Her voice was strained, pleading.

"I like having a few quiet moments during a Mass, to reflect and concentrate. I like to be able to hear myself think. But with those drums constantly beating, it is hard to do that. Does that mean I am denying my race? Does being *negra* mean not wanting to hear your thoughts?"

"Yvonne," I asked, "who thinks anything different from this?"

Her face tensed. "The people in the *Quilombo* say I have whitened, that if I were an authentic *negra* I would vibrate more to the *atabaque* than to other instruments. That I would sing and dance for three hours [the normal length of the inculturated Mass]. I guess I am not an authentic *negra*. So I shouldn't participate with them."

Yvonne shifted registers, from the language of personal experience to that of judgment. "I think," she said, "that this is discrimination, to say that the *negro* is more this or that. I feel what I feel: I don't want to be locked into a single *jeito de ser* [way of being]. I like and enjoy various things. For me, the inculturated Mass doesn't correspond to me."

"But what do you think should be done? Should the inculturated Mass be abandoned, and everyone return to the traditional one?"

Yvonne was looking at her hands. "No. I think we need a Mass which encourages the *negro* to be any way he wants, not take him out of one box and put him into another."

She was saying things that several other informants had hinted at, but none had articulated with her acuity. My first impulse was to draw a division in my mind between "those women who are stirred by the Mass, and those who are not." My task would then be to find some neat variables permitting me to distinguish between the two groups. But each time I thought I had isolated one—the "non-stirred" had not faced the same degree of color prejudice as the "stirred"; the "non-stirred" were younger; the "stirred" had been exposed in a more sustained fashion to the discourse of the black movement—I was quickly proved wrong. I still believe, in good sociological fashion, that if the sample were large enough and enough variables were taken into account, some experiential pattern differentiating the two groups might appear.

But after a while, the hope of finding the magic sociological variable began to fade, and recognizing the importance of the contrast itself began to become more central. I began to wonder whether I might be presuming too stark a contrast. To what extent, for example, did women who spoke in near mystical terms of bodily response have other feelings that were being left unsaid?

With this question in mind, Ruth, Marcia, and I returned to ask the black women most involved in the inculturated Mass whether someone who felt as Yvonne did (without naming her) was therefore denying her *negritude*. The answers we received were surprising.

What we heard was, in effect, two registers. First, we heard a judgmental response, which identified experiences and feelings like those of Yvonne as indeed indicating a weakening of *negra* identity. But we also heard something else. Once we had stated that the person who had spoken to us in this way also proudly called herself *negra*, various previously unarticulated ideas and experiences started to surface.

"Well, the European Mass is very slow," said Dona Ana, who had earlier told me that liveliness of the inculturated Mass resonated with her own *axé*. "But it's true, when you read the Bible, you see that when Jesus created that moment, he was sitting there quietly, at the table of the Last Supper. Every one was sitting there, gesturing, but still."

"But isn't that just a European way of understanding the Bible?"

"I don't know, I don't know. If this thing of being still is just a European thing, no. I don't know that."

"Well," I asked, "one of the reasons the inculturated Mass was created, if I understand it correctly, was so that *negros* could feel comfortable expressing their *jeito de ser*. Do you feel more comfortable in an inculturated Mass than in a traditional one?"

Earlier, Dona Ana herself had said: "The traditional Mass has nothing to do with the *negro* race. The *negro* race is happier, looser. And European culture is not that way: it is more withdrawn."

Now she was thinking once again, and more directly, about her own experience of the Mass. "To tell you the truth," she replied, "not really. For me there is no difference. For me any Mass has one main goal, one main value: to meet God. So I can be fortified spiritually in either, equally. In any Mass I attend, European or inculturated, the important thing is for me to stop there, and receive that light of God, and feel strengthened by it." She thought some more. "In the traditional Mass, there are many strong moments. Like when the Bible is read; and the consecration of the host. I experience this moment in my heart, with love and all my energy."

"But this is a quiet moment, a moment of silence."

"Yes! That is lovely, the European Mass has that, it offers that. Because you realize yourself in the quiet too."

Dona Ana's testimony did not make me doubt the depth of her existential response to the inculturated Mass. Nor did I assume that she was speaking for anyone other than herself. But I did begin to think of Paul Gilroy's argument that what characterizes a large swath of popular black consciousness is not the either/or of European inauthenticity versus African authenticity. I thought that perhaps here I was witnessing what Gilroy has called "double consciousness," in which the two (at least!) cultural/experiential legacies have become so fused and sedimented that to seek the grail of authenticity is pointless.[7] What was being lost in failing to find a way to allow this doubleness its own expression? Was Dona Ana destined to live in a split ritual world, in which she alternated between the two Masses, only allowing one side of herself to be expressed in each? What would happen if one day she were obliged to choose?

Constructing an Alternative Aesthetic

The inculturated Mass is, among other things, a celebration and display of the *negra's* beauty and sensuality. The dancers whose presence and movements form the performative core of the inculturated Mass are not just women: they are young women, whose facial beauty is emphasized, and whose bodily self-presentation and movements have an unmistakeable sensuality about them. They wear makeup for the occasion. Their shoulders, arms, and calves are bare, they actively deploy their hips, and occasionally flash their thighs. And they remain plainly in view for the duration of the Mass.

The projection here of female beauty and sensuality is anything but unconscious. When I asked several dancers why the dance was always performed by women, I heard one or both of the following: "Because women are beautiful, and we want to make something beautiful. Something to be seen and enjoyed." And: "Because *negras* are beautiful, and we want to valorize *negras'* beauty." Or, most synthetically, as a published text of the black pastoral movement declares: "The *negra*, with her feminine gifts and beauty, makes it possible for us to visualize more clearly this love of life, of this permanent *festa* that exists in heaven."[8] The inculturated Mass's practices remind *negras* of the importance of rejecting the dominant European aesthetic model and of thinking of themselves as beautiful in a new way. Women chosen for their dramatically long braids and dark skin often stand on either side of the priest. A popular song of the rite avows: "Little *negra* girl, with hard hair / You are so beautiful, from head to foot," and another intones: "*Negra*, what beauty!" In an inculturated Mass performed in Espirito Santo, the priest made clear in his homily that the display of black female beauty was crucial to the ritual: "There are still people in the church," he said, "who do not look kindly upon what we are doing here today. People who don't like us saying that the *mulher negra* is beautiful. That we want our little girls to learn that it is beautiful to be a *negra*. That they do not need any longer to pass a hot iron through their hair."

A casual observer might find in the dancers' movements—and in the occasional flash of an exposed thigh—an erotic sensuality hard to distinguish in the Brazilian context from that of the *mulata*. But the *mulata*'s sensuality is directed toward the white male gaze, toward a man who has no intention of marrying her, or having children with her, or contributing to the future of a people with her.[9] In contrast, the bodies of the *negras* on display in the inculturated Mass are the visible accompaniment to the hymn, "I will make my offering to you: *Negra*, beautiful root of this happy people." These are not bodies to be consumed or exchanged like commodities. They are sacred bodies, that ask of their onlookers commitment and seriousness. The *negra* sensuality on display here is directed toward marriageability and the production of children, not promiscuous, childless sexuality.[10]

Still, it is an outwardly directed sensuality that depends upon performance and display in order to be reassured of its value. The young *negra* body in the inculturated Mass still takes form primarily through the eyes of others: hers is a body meant to be watched. But by whom?

The watchers here are, first, the *negro* men who have been lost to white women. "The ideal," said Gegê, "would be for the *negro* man who sees this to say: 'Wow, *negras* are not so bad after all,' to revalorize the *negra* woman's beauty, and cease the racism which he has against her." But the watchers are also white men and women, to whom it must be proved that *negras* can be beautiful and sensual in a modest, respectable way. "Brazilians are used to seeing the writhing, naked bodies of *mulatas* on television," said Marisa, one of the dancers. "But we are different. We are not *mulatas*. We are *negra*s. We are not naked." Or, as Gegê also said: "When the Brazilian thinks of the *negra*, he automatically thinks of her as a slut, a prostitute. But these girls are not prostitutes: just the opposite."

At perhaps the deepest level, the ritual dance is directed at *morenas*. I got a sense of this meaning when I spoke with Carolina, a young *negra* dancer. "Only girls with nice, pretty hair think that they can do anything that is pretty," she said. "They are always the dancers, the ones up front. What I like about the group in the inculturated Mass is that we don't think this way. The pretty *morena*, or the one who calls herself that, will have to watch us and say, 'They are not ugly, they are beautiful!'"

Certainly the presentation of *negras* dancing in a way that transcends media representations, who wear braids and African dress, is at odds with dominant European aesthetics. But there are ways in which the faces and bodies presented here break not at all from dominant aesthetic norms.

First, there is the ritual's preoccupation with female surfaces: that valorizing the external beauty of the bodies and faces of *negras* is an important enterprise. The principle is that female self-esteem is properly and inevitably bound up with appearance. There is the sense that it is not enough for *negras* to feel satisfied on their own appearance; it must be turned into a performance whose value emerges from the pleasure they produce through the gaze of others. The image of the *negra* in the inculturated Mass thus depends, to some extent at least, on making a spectacle of her.[11]

How did participants respond to this spectacularization? Several *negra*s felt that the spectacle of *negra* beauty had altered their self-perceptions. With much feeling, Carolina said:

I look much more at *negra* beauty now. The inculturated Mass really taught me to think about this in a new way. To believe that I am beautiful. That my color is a beautiful color. That I don't have to approximate lighter skin tones, or straighten my hair in order to be beautiful.

Because in the regular Catholic ritual, it is unusual for a really *negra* girl to ascend the altar and crown the image of Our Lady. And even I, before the inculturated Mass, didn't think it would be pretty for a girl with nappy hair to be an angel. You see how this had entered into my own head! So the inculturated Mass really did help me in this.

We even heard from two young black women that exposing young men and women to this aesthetic might have an impact on the dating market. She had not seen it occur yet, but Cléa, an eighteen-year-old black, said she felt confident that "if *negros* see these things, and think about them, they will stop avoiding *negra* girls."

There can be no doubt that the effects of Brazilian aesthetics continue to make themselves felt among dark-skinned *negras* as well. One young *negra* named Cleonilda, found herself caught between the inculturated Mass's summons to her to valorize herself aesthetically, and the images she encountered daily on television. Although several of her companions in church criticized her for it, she continued to straighten her hair. Her defense: "I don't think anyone can tell me what to do with my hair. I am *negra*, and proud of it.There in the inculturated Mass they say that *negras* should learn to valorize themselves. Well I *am* valorizing myself. I am taking care of my looks. And this is what I like."

It was clear that her choice, however, was creating some strain. Her voice rose, and she launched into an argument with an invisible interlocutor. "You know, I think it is hypocritical," she said. "Because this is supposed to be about freedom. And this is what I choose to do. Free, I am free to choose to do this. If they want to let their hair go, that's up to them. This is what I think is beautiful. Do they want me to leave my nails uncut or to stop taking baths?"

The irritation expressed by Cleonilda here was not inconsistent with her continued participation in the inculturated Mass and the *pastoral negro*. "No, I will not stop participating just because of this," she said. "Because I have a strong commitment to my race, to valorizing our culture, to remembering our history." She felt the overweening emphasis on appearance was a distraction from these more important goals. She compared herself to black women in the United States. "If you look at the black women in the videos, or in the movies by Spike Lee—no one can say they don't assume their blackness just because they straighten their hair! I mean, it's ridiculous."

Cleonilda is touching on a delicate issue. She is not alone among black Brazilian women who pride themselves on their *negra* identity, insist on being able to continue to straighten their hair, and point to U.S. models to justify themselves. I presented this response to the criticism leveled at them to another *negra*—Rosana, in her thirties, who does not straighten. "Yes," she said, "I know that some women will say that. It is a matter of consciousness. The problem with comparing *negras* in Brazil to Americans is that in America they cannot say they are something they are not. There are no *mulatas* or *morenas* there. But here, if you straighten, pretty soon you'll start saying you are *morena*."

"But the woman who told me about this says that she is *negra* and proud of it."

Rosana thought about this. "Maybe she says that," she concluded. "But if she really assumed her *negritude,* how could she want to straighten her hair? Sooner or later her whole identity is going to fall apart. She cannot sustain that for long."

Whether Rosana is right or not, Cleonilda has refused to give up on the inculturated Mass (although, as I left the field, her resolve was wavering). Marthe, a *negra* in her thirties, lacked Cleonilda's commitment. She had attended one or two meetings of the *pastoral negro* in her community, and refused to participate any more, in part because of what she saw as a high-handed stance about women's appearance. She was terse on the subject, but her feelings came through. "I went there and saw that I wouldn't fit in. Those women. I use products on my hair. I'm not going to give that up."

What is significant here is that Marthe identifies herself not as *morena* or *mulata*, but quite squarely as a *negra*. She did not need the movement to teach her this. The darkness of her skin, and the fact that she needed to apply products to her "hard" hair, were all she needed to know in order to assign herself to this category. What she felt she didn't need was other women criticizing her about what to do with her hair.

Two other women reacted negatively to what they regarded as the inculturated Mass's overall preoccupation with female appearance. One of them, a middle-aged *negra* named Maristela, continued to participate in the Mass, but did not like the dancing. "Sometimes I will say something, but everyone jumps and says, No, you don't understand. Maybe I don't understand. But I don't like it, and I won't say anything more to them about it."

"What don't you like?"

"It's not just the dancing. This is a church, this is a Mass, a religious thing. It is not a beauty pageant, or a fashion show, or a rock show. This has nothing to do with that. I feel that sometimes people get these things mixed up."

Maristela's concern that the inculturated Mass turns into a "show" was echoed by Lurdes, a elderly *negra* who has refused to attend any more inculturated Masses. "I went to one," she told me, "and I was shocked. What I saw there. It is not decent. We are in the house of God. If young people want to see those things, they can go to a show. This is not a show. But they are turning it into one."

I raised this concern—that is, that the focus on black women's appearance and sensuality during the Mass might offend some women's sensibilities—to one of the leading priests of the movement. His response was thoughtful, but unequivocal in his delegitimation of the concern.

> It's an interesting concern. But it is exactly this that is the discourse of the oppressing classes in Brazil. They say that this way of being inculturated is a way of being profane. They say that this happiness, this dance, is brought in by worldly things. And they question the valorization of *negra* beauty: for that is what is happening there. What could be more divine? And those who say this is a show: if the people have become used to this kind of dance in the civil space, because the Church was unwilling to let it into its precincts for five hundred years, that is not the fault of the people. It is the fault of the priests.

This priest's views are influential in the communities that practice the inculturated Mass. I should therefore not have been surprised when I witnessed in a preparatory meeting for a Mass the following exchange: a *negra* was expressing reservations about the the style of dance that would be performed. "This is not a show," she said. The coordinator of the group replied, politely but firmly, "We must be careful to think about who thinks such things are a 'show.' Is it European or African?" The woman raising the objection said nothing more.

The Black Woman's Combativeness

A common adjective used in the *pastoral negro* and inculturated Mass to characterize the *negra*, in song and prayer, is "*guerreira*" (warrior); among the most common qualities of the *negra* is that she possesses "*garra*" (guts). In a hymn of praise to Nossa Senhora de Aparecida, the lyrics proclaim "In sharing love and *axé* / Comrade, warrior, mother, woman." In another popular song, there is a stanza that affirms, "I am a *negra*, I am a warrior / From the north to the south of Brazil / Maria, any other, I am woman." In the "Psalm of the Martyrs," alongside the names of Henrique Dias, Zumbi, and Martin Luther King Jr., are listed the names of Dandara, the wife of Zumbi, Luiza Mahin, the heroine of the 1835 Males revolt in Salvador, and Margarida, a twentieth-century freedom fighter. One of the key acts of the gutsy woman is to "shout," to make her voice heard, crying out for justice and liberty. "Consciousness is our struggle," intones the song "Negro Nagô": "Because history has stolen our memory / The blood of many has been shed / Cries out the *negro nagô*." The visual image of *negras* used in the inculturated Mass's pamphlets, songsheets, and posters emphasizes freedom, joy, and the "shout." In one image, a *negra* woman is lovingly embracing another person; in another she is breaking her chains; in another she is joyfully dancing; in yet another, she joins other smiling women dressed in African garb, one with a baby on her hip. Indeed, throughout, there is the constant visual refrain of the woman with a baby in her ams, smiling contentedly, or surrounded by her family, happily ensconced in domesticity.

What these musical and visual images marginalize is the representation of the suffering female body, of women in pain. Absent are images of women who are suffering, tortured, or silenced.

I asked several women involved in the Mass about why there seemed to be no images of women suffering any of the brutalities of slavery or oppression. My question was met with a thoughtful reply by a *negra* named Dona Madalena. "Everyone knows that slavery was painful," she said, "so there is no reason to go over that again. We are tired of that. That just makes us feel all the more inferior, that we took all that pain for so long. How could that have happened? Why didn't we break the chains earlier? So this is very depressing to us. What we want to recall are the positive things: that we did break the chains in Palmares, that in spite of all of this we can be self-respecting and happy, and that we now can send this positive message. There is no reason to have heavy images of suffering here." Or, as a priest declared while performing an inculturated baptism: "We have not come here to cry. We have come to celebrate our beauty and hope as a people."

Images of being a "*guerreira*" and having "*garra*" have a definite appeal for some *negras*. Janainha, a black woman who works in a textile factory and has three children, told me that all the talk of *garra* had been very important to her. "I have never been a pushover. I have always struggled in life," she said. "It's just that, you don't hear this being valorized. This is just expected of us. Yes, women are warriors. I am a warrior. I feel that this gives me the respect I deserve."

This desire to move beyond "crying," to set aside the images of torture and pain, may be one of the reasons that the image of the slave saint Anastácia is not more emphasized in the *pastoral negro*. As I will discuss in a later chapter, among black activists there seems to be a general discomfort with Anastacía's face-mask as too focused on the silencing of black women. The face-mask may be seen as the imagistic opposite to the inculturated Mass's focus on the "shout." I heard from some laypeople in the *pastoral negro* that if the image of Anastácia were to be used in their rituals, they would like to see her mask taken off. The one large image of her that I saw in connection to the *pastoral negro*, at the headquarters of the *Quilombo* in São João, was placed over the caption, "We will never be silenced again." In a strange way, this caption conveyed the message that one should not focus on the image itself, on its intrinsic association with torture, but rather immediately set one's mind's eye elsewhere, to the future, to a place where there was no face-iron to silence anyone.

While this focus on black women's everyday heroism and the call to them to "shout" resonates deeply for some women, it also calls upon them to look down upon their own feelings of uncertainty and trepidation, and to think about their pain not by looking at it, but by looking away and beyond it. Again, this emotional strategy works for some. But Agostina, a dark-black woman in her forties, mother of four and sometime domestic servant, has some difficulty locating herself inside the heroic image of a woman shouting and breaking her chains. It was not that she disliked or disapproved of the image: it was just that, as the only image available in the inculturated Mass, it felt unrealistic to her.

Agostina has called herself *preta* since she was a little girl. She has done her share of struggling, of coping with children's illnesses, dealing with two abusive spouses, coming close to death in one violent relationship. She has overcome one adversity after another. She certainly understands what it means to have guts and to be a warrior. But she is once again faced with a troubled spousal relationship at home. And in connection to this, she feels the image of the "gutsy" black woman has little to say.

"I was having a conversation with [someone] in the pastoral last week. . . . And I said, well, I started to talk about what was happening with the man. And she said to me: 'All of us women have this to bear. A black woman doesn't let these things get her down.' Can you believe it? So if I get down because of these things I am not a black woman?"

I do not know how typical Agostina's experience is. That it can happen at all, however, is, once again, a useful reminder that every ideological position is simultanoeusly an articulation and a marginalization. But Agostina's account actually points to a more troubling issue: the inculturated Mass's marginalization of discourse that might be construed as critical of black men.

Motherhood and Domesticity

In the last section I mentioned the pervasiveness in the inculturated Mass of imagery highlighting motherhood and domesticity. Let us take a more careful look at this imagery, which is involved in a tense interaction with the images hailing women's warriorhood.

Let us begin with an iconographic point: no woman occupies a heroic status in the *pastoral negro*'s pantheon commensurate with that of Zumbi. While several heroines are regularly invoked during the recitation of lists—including Luiza Mahin and Dandara—none of these has a prayer or song devoted exclusively to her, in which her story is told. I asked all the women I met who were involved in the *pastoral negro* if they knew anything specific about either Luiza Mahin or Dandara, and they all drew a blank. When I asked whether any of the female warriors might have used weapons in physical combat, I was met by shrugging shoulders and shaking heads.

Confronted with the implications of female warriorhood, at least one informant declared that the priority was not, in the end, to develop a roster of female heroines, but rather to focus on the heroism of black men. "We do not really need heroines," she said. "It is the black man, not the black woman, who lost his identity. We have always retained our identity, as mothers. Slavery did not take this away from us. But slavery took away from men the ability to be leaders, warriors, kings. So the suffering was much worse for them. We need to help build up men's egos, we don't have to worry about ours. We want men to feel more confident, so they will return to us and help us raise our families."

The image of ideal womanhood projected in the inculturated Mass does not require that *negras* stay at home. In songs and prayers it is readily and proudly recognized that black women have long worked outside the home, and that they have struggled in popular movements, with great *garra*. But this is only one part of the image. The full image is conveyed by the position that "we can see [the *negra*'s] liberating action in the history of the *negra* people, among women who suffered, struggled, resisted, and had faith, all the while keeping their beauty, tenderness, and grace."[12]

One way of reading this message is: by all means, go out and struggle and be heroic, but be back in time to fix supper and bathe the children. The sincerest and most poignant prayers and hymns of the inculturated Mass are reserved for the *negra* as mother. "Long live all the *negra* mothers," goes one especially well-liked hymn. "All the *negra* mothers / All the girl mothers / All the mother girls." An important prayer goes: "We believe in a mother God, who is alive, fecund, of great fertility, a God who, as a woman, knows what it means to bleed in order to give life."[13]

The theology of the *pastoral negro* is quite clear on this point. As one theologian writes: "the *negra* is the center of gravity of the *negra* family, being the decisive factor in the education of children and the defense of the family. The great value of the black family is that the mother has total responsibility for her children inside the house: in the woman resides the security—emotional and personal—of the entire family. Her importance is marked by her constant welcome, sacrifice, and tenderness."[14] "Our spirituality," declares another text, "is that of the mother: the *negra* mother. The one who braids her daughter's hair, takes care of the children, in God who takes care, takes care with tenderness of the weakest, just as we do with our children."[15] Put another way, the black nation needs you working, not one, but two heroic shifts.[16]

In one songbook, we see an image of the ideal *negra* family: under the caption "The *negro*, and his cry for justice" we see a bearded black man looking up to the sky, while placing a hand on the shoulder of his wife, who looks open-eyed and smiling at their child. Given such imagery, it is clear that the ideal *mulher negra*—according to the inculturated Mass— is not fundamentally different from her European counterpart: the Virgin Mary, albeit in her embodiment as the dark-skinned Aparecida.

It should be apparent that the inculturated Mass is hardly suited to the articulation of issues having to do with male dominance, the division of household labor, gender inequality, or male violence against women. The focus is on the fantasy image of the man as warrior and leader, and on the need to attract the successful black man back from white women in order to reconstitute the ideal black family. Reflections on machismo, sexism, patriarchy, male violence, abuse, or rape would in effect be distractions from this agenda.

I asked a black lay leader why these themes were never touched upon. "That is not the point of the inculturated Mass," she said, impatiently. "We are there to celebrate, not cry. We are there to talk about our victories, not to accuse anyone." And another informant said: "The black man does not need *negras* to be accusing him. Watch what happens if a *negra* criticizes a black man: he becomes defensive, he will simply look the other way and find himself a white woman."

The issue of division of labor in the household is also taboo. At one meeting of the *pastoral negro* I witnessed a black woman raise the question of how, as women, they were socializing their children: Could it be that they should teach their sons to cook and clean too? Although the suggestion was met with some laughter and smiles, it was not taken up, but simply left to one side. These themes are left untouched, at least in the context of spiritual work. The priority of the ethnic struggle—to help men become more powerful in society, to get them to appreciate black female beauty in order to return and build strong black families—requires leaving such issues alone.

I have already mentioned the story of Agostina. But she is not alone. I met several black women who, while participating in the Mass, knew that any effort to deal with their domestic problems there would be awkward and unwelcome. One of these women, Dona Lurdes, a woman in her forties, spoke directly to what she regarded as the incompatibility of such complaints with the image of ideal black womanhood being projected by the Mass. "I will not mention these things to Dona Benta or Dona Carolina," she said.

"Why not?"

"Because they will say that what our husbands need from us are not complaints but support."

It is common, and often useful, to declare that in non-European contexts allusion to the issues of the sexual division of labor, sexism, and domestic violence are impositions from white middle-class Euro-American feminist concerns. This may be so in many situations. Yet I have been struck in my conversations with women in the privacy of their homes by how often they talk of anger at men's unwillingness to help at home, their irresponsibility with the household budget, their profligacy, their alcoholism, their violence. It neither dishonors those men with whom women find a measure of peace and tranquility, nor those women who regard talking about such problems in the context of the black pastoral as unwelcome, to suggest that wherever their feelings and views come from, there do exist women who undergo these things and want to change them. In the inculturated Mass, at least, the symbolic or social resources with which they might do so are less than robust.

The Problem of Afro-Religiosity

While the inculturated Mass's embrace of "Afro" spirituality challenges the devalorization of this spirituality, it also reinforces the dominant view that *negras* are the semi-unconscious carriers of this spirituality. In workshops that prepare laypeople for an inculturated Mass, coordinators praise *mães-de-santo* (mothers of the saint) from *candomblé* for keeping alive the traditions and identity of the *negro* people. Their spirituality is figured as an overflow of *axé*. "Faith in religion," writes Theodoro, in a text influential among the black clergy, "is the great support of the *negra*; it is her *axé*. Her activity in the community is made complete through her spiritual force, worked upon in the *terreiros* rooted in the concepts of the *nagô* tradition."[17] Women's spiritual force is realized in their role as spiritual guide to the next generation. "The role of women," writes Theodoro, "in the religions of Black Africa and in Afro-American cults is related to the guardianship and transmission of religious and cultural traditions, they being the axis that connects the Sacred with communal life."[18]

The calls of theologians to de-demonize *candomblé* and *umbanda* are in practice rarely taken to heart among parishioners at the grass roots. This is partly because the priests also set forth a neat division between religion and culture; thus there is no strong motive for local people to worry much about trying to learn respect for a religiosity they have grown up associating with the devil.

The association of the inculturated Mass with "*macumba*" (the pejorative term for the mediumship religions of *umbanda* and *candomblé*) is the most important reason people at large in the communities stay away from it. Thus, when clergy and laity say that locals in general loathe the inculturated Mass because they regard it as opening up the Church to diabolical forces, they are mainly right. Advocates of the new Mass call anyone holding this opinion guilty of perpetuating the stigma of Afro-religiosity, or, at best, these critics are seen as simply ignorant, failing to see that elements in the new Mass that resemble *candomblé* and *umbanda*—the drums, the music, the offerings on the ground—are cultural, not religious things. Then they brook no further criticism.

Certainly in the struggle to valorize Afro-religion there is no reason to compromise on matters of principle with people who simply will not listen. To this extent the clergy and laity who insist on maintaining the centrality of Afro elements in the Mass are certainly justified in standing their ground. Yet I want to suggest that there are many other more complicated popularly held reservations and concerns about Afro-religiosity that are not easily reduced to simple prejudice or ignorance.

A few women have taken the leap and striven to overcome their own preconceptions. Those with the nerve to follow this path tend to have the most highly politicized views about their own black identities, and tend also to be the best educated. They also prefer to respect the "more

African" *candomblé* to the impure, syncretized *umbanda*. *Umbanda*, in their view, is a place in which *negra* identity becomes diluted and lost, while in *candomblé* it is strengthened.[19] "There are more charlatans in *umbanda*," says Gegê. "*Umbanda* has more of that stuff of the low spirits, the spirits of evil, these scary things."

Still, women like Gegê have an uphill battle to reach a comfort zone even with *candomblé*. "There are simply many practices there that I do not understand," she said. "I try; and the *pai-de-santo* that Frei David invited to talk with us helps take away that fear that we have. But not everything is very clear to me."

I asked her to give me an example.

"Like sacrifice, the sacrifice of animals. The *pai-de-santo* told us to think about the lamb that Abraham sacrificed in place of his son. That helps a little. But I confess I do not understand the meaning of the '*despachos*' [deeds of sorcery] that are put out."

Camila, too, a young *negra* schoolteacher and theology student, with a resolute, lucid consciousness of racial injustice, regards it as her duty to strive to build her understanding of Afro-religion. Thus, for instance, she can speak insightfully about the sacredness of the drums in *candomblé*. Yet she too, like Gegê, finds herself faced by gulfs in comprehension. She struggles to speak of her limits of empathy, which usually are set by Christian theology. "When I see a sacrifice of animals," she says, "I can't really understand or accept that. I also cannot accept this vision in which you have to give to the entity, because if you fail to do so it will punish you. Because for me God gives full grace for free."

Gegê's and Camilia's efforts to respect *candomblé* are uncommon. Far more widespread among the black women who participate in the inculturated Mass is a resolute hostility to any suggestion that they should respect or valorize Afro-religiosity. The logic is well-illustrated by Dona Donata, a dark *negra* in her sixties, and one of the chief coordinators of the inculturated Mass in her community. Dona Donata loves the inculturated Mass as an expression of her ancestral culture; but she feels that this in no way requires her to respect *candomblé* or *umbanda*. "They have nothing at all to do with the Mass," she says.

Donata was raised a strict Catholic, and never frequented any religion or church outside the Roman faith. Her views of Afro-religion are thus almost entirely shaped by its external aspect. "Look," she says, "I know people who have been there, who know it, and they have warned me: never go there. Because there are many bad things there. They enslave you there: I have a friend who was involved as a *mãe-de-santo*, and she said that she was caught there, even after she wanted to leave, they wouldn't let her go." And then there is the theology of moral purity: "We Christians only believe in doing good. They believe you can do either good or bad. Look, doing evil unto others—isn't that a work of the devil? Everyone knows they do that; it's no secret."

It is true that Afro-religion often involves intense competition between *pais* and *mães de santo*, which can end up in costly battles for power and self-interest; and that the powers of *candomblé* and *umbanda* are indeed usable for antisocial and self-interested ends. These realities are part of the reason some ex-practitioners of these religions are uncomfortable with any hint of their reappearance inside the Catholic Church.

Donata has been able to accept the drums; she has never been directly involved with mediumship, and she can separate the drums from the arrival of spirits. Women with direct experience of mediumship, however, have more difficulty making this separation. Such women, if they feel drawn to the inculturated Mass, are usually haunted by ambivalence toward the drums. Marisa, a married *negra* in her late thirties, has taken part in the inculturated Mass off and on for several years. "The inculturated Mass made me look within myself," she said. "Before I started going to it, I called myself *preta*. I didn't know. And so from then on I started using the word '*negra*.' And when people said, 'Ah, you are *marrom* [brown],' and others say '*morena*,' I say, 'No, I am *negra*.'"

Participating in the new Mass has also clarified for her the importance of valorizing her African cultural heritage. "Before participating in the inculturated Mass I didn't understand any of this. The Mass showed me," she says firmly, "that it is necessary for us to increase our consciousness, to remember our culture, because we so often forget our origin, which is Africa."

Yet despite all these compelling changes, Marisa continues to feel deeply ambivalent about the Mass. "Sometimes I go, and then I say, 'No, I'm not going to go again for awhile,' and then I stop. But I go back." The root of Marisa's ambivalence is this: while she has learned to regard the *atabaque*s intellectually as an example of "African culture," at a deeper, emotional level she still associates them with her personal tortured experience in *candomblé*.

"I didn't want to follow that religion," she says. "I didn't want it." Talking to my research assistant Marcia, her voice was somber. "I was in it for years, but I didn't like it. After I graduated high school, and felt I was an adult, and I finally left it. My family continued in the *terreiro*, and I tried other churches, to get away."

It was her background in *candomblé* that led Marisa to be terrified by her first encounter with the Mass. "When I went to my first inculturated Mass, I was frightened," she said. "I found it totally different. I was raised in *candomblé*, right? All of a sudden here were the *atabaques*! I thought I was entering a *terreiro* of *macumba*. So I was frightened."

It was a fear, she says, that passed, at least a little. The explanations given by Frei David helped her to stop, at least for a time, to think of the rhythms of the drums not as the call of the *terreiro*, and instead to think of them as the expression of the "festiveness" and "blood" of her people. "In Africa . . . well, I have never had a chance to visit Mother Africa, but in the movies, those drums, everything there is done through dance and song. Where *negros* are, there too you'll find happiness, because it comes from Africa. Because even the quietest *negro* will start dancing at the slightest thing. It's the race."

She also understood the cultural argument. "I learned, too, that the things in *candomblé* are African, from African culture. The instruments, the music, the dance. So when we see these things in the inculturated Mass, it is not religious, it is from African culture. And when I understood that, I started to be calmer about it."

Still, Marisa continues to have doubts. The drums and dancing, for all her new understanding, continue in her opinion to have deadly objective powers.

> The *atabaque* is used to call down the entities. And when you hear the drumming on the *atabaque*s, we who have seen these things know that the spirits really are attracted, and that worries me. So I remain in doubt about that. I have seen a lot of bad things in *candomblé*. The way they make people pay through the nose for nothing. The way they set one person against another. . . . It is for that reason that I don't participate any more in the inculturated Mass: because I am not well decided on that point.

Sonia, a *negra*, stopped attending altogether because she couldn't handle the drums. She said:

> The problem is that the way people move there, that invites the spirits. They may say that it is culture, but it is not. The food they put on the ground is a problem too, because it's the same food people place at crossroads: so that too will attract the spirits. The spirits will take advantage of the situation. Don't you see? They are waiting for this,

this is a weakening. There are no two ways about it. The Catholic Church becomes a spiritist center. It opens a path for them.[20]

⸂ While an outside observer might suppose that *negra*s who are practitioners of Afro-religions would respond positively to the inculturated Mass, in reality they have kept their distance, looking on it and its enthusiasts with feelings ranging from indifference, to watchful cooperation, to mistrust, to angry indignation.

I met a few *negra filhas-de-santo* (daughters of the saint) who knew of the inculturated Mass, but said they cared little about it. They claimed it was simply a matter of no concern to them, the internal affair of a foreign religion. A *mãe-de-santo* in *candomblé* put the view succinctly. "Whether the Mass is inculturated or not," she said, "is entirely irrelevant for us. It is important only for the Catholic *negro*, who is already there in church. Afro-religions have our own concerns, our own law, our own beliefs."

The rugged independence of this view probably includes a dose of disingenuousness. It is not easy to remain entirely uninterested in the goings-on of the most powerful church in the world, the one all good *candomblecistas* must take communion from before they can be initiated. And indeed, most of the *negra* female practitioners of Afro-religion with whom I spoke had opinions—some of them quite strong—about the Roman Church's most recent attempt at liberality.

The most positive views I heard were from a middle-aged black *mãe* in *umbanda* named Tatiana, who thought that the new Mass represented the possibility of gaining some protection under the wing of the Church against the onslaught of the Protestants. As we sat in her *terreiro* one weekday evening, after the stream of her petitioners had thinned, she told me she knew that there was a lot of self-interest in the Catholic Church's embrace of Afro-religions, but she said: "I don't care. The Catholic Church is very powerful, and maybe this way we will survive. If they didn't start doing this, the *crentes* would destroy us in a second."

This motivation may be part of why other *mães-de-santo* have decided to cooperate, at least in small ways and at least temporarily, with Frei David and the *pastoral negro*: not out of a belief that the inculturated Mass represents a sincere opening up to them, but as a strategic decision. One *mãe* who periodically visited the black pastoral to lecture said that she was happy to cooperate, but that she would need to see some reciprocity soon, in order for her to continue. "When," she asked rhetorically, "will they start helping us to fight the Protestants?"

Most serious practitioners of the Afro-religions are deeply suspicious of the Church's initiative. There is simply too much bad water under the bridge. Hadn't the Church striven in centuries gone by to repress their ancestors' religion, and then alternated, in this century, between periods of neglect and frontal assault against them? Hadn't their beliefs been stigmatized as diabolical, and didn't they even now still have to pretend in church that they did not hold them? Should it then come as a surprise that they were skeptical about the motives of the Church's most recent overtures toward them?

Most commonly, the *mães* and *filhas-de-santo* with whom I spoke intepreted these overtures as resulting from a crisis in the Church: the inculturated Mass in particular, they said, was a way to stanch the hemorrhage of the faithful to Protestant churches. "They are losing a lot of people," Marinete, an *umbanda mãe-de-santo*, commented. "This is a way for them to take from *umbanda* the things that will help them, that will attract people: the drums, clothing, and so on."

"But why," I asked, "don't you simply take this at face value, as a show of respect for Afro-religion?"

Marinete thought about this for a moment, then answered gently. "In the old days," she said, "if you entered the church wearing your white [*umbanda*] apparel, the priest would not give you communion. Until the day comes when they will do that [give communion to an identifiable *mãe-de-santo*], it cannot be for anything other than self-interest."

That the Church was acting more from self-interest than from genuine respect could be seen, in the eyes of *candomblecistas*, in its practice of choosing to valorize only parts, never the whole, of Afro-religion. "The problem," Marinete explained, "is that they only want to respect those things that already suit them. So they talk about how pretty the music is, but they criticize us for sacrificing chickens. Is that respect?"

Those parts that they did choose to valorize they had mistranslated or distorted. "When they say that Oxalá is like Jesus," explained one *filha-de-santo*, "that is wrong. It simply isn't true. Oxalá is not Jesus. And Olorum is not the Christian God. Olorum did not give Moses anything. These are not simple translations, like they claim: they are totally different ideas, different entities." A *filha-de-santo* in *candomblé*, who identifies herself as *negra*, says that "I don't understand how the inculturated Mass takes symbols from *candomblé*, and places them in Christianity. For example, he takes a bunch of dirt—as we do in *candomblé*, because in *candomblé* this is the material from which we came, and to which we will return—when they use that dirt in Catholicism, and talk about the ancestors. But they have a view of the dead which is totally incompatible with ours! We don't have the theology of salvation. Totally different. So they are negating the original meaning of the dirt!"

Some of the practitioners I spoke with were especially taken aback by the presence in the inculturated Mass of the half-naked dances of *capoeira*. Listen to Rosalia, *mãe-de-santo* of *candomblé*: "For them the *negra* must be the primitive without clothing. I understand that. But this isn't the African spirit, it certainly goes against the cultural values of *candomblé*. You would never see anyone naked in *candomblé*! That is profane. Our belief is that you must remain very well covered, that modesty requires it."[21]

Rosalia's point that "for them" the *negra* must be a certain way is an important insight. Practitioners are highly attuned observers of the Church, and their sense is that the Afro-religion represented by the enthusiasts of the inculturated Mass is mightily stereotyped, locked more into the colonial logic of European desire than the complexity of Afro reality. Perhaps the most telling example of this is the inculturated Mass's insistence that "negro culture" is always filled with "happiness," dance, and song. Yet, much to the contrary, many of the practitioners emphasize their need for moments of silence, concentration, and reflection.

Why then had the inculturated Mass chosen to ignore these things, and had only looked at the singing and dancing? Rosalia was ready with a reply. "Because you know, it is not really about respecting our worldview, it is about taking from us to confirm theirs. So this is what I see: the church wants to paint a picture of the happy *negro,* the one who only knows how to sing and dance. Afro culture is much much more than happiness, *festa*, singing, and dancing. All that is most sacred, most solemn and serious, they don't want that part, because it doesn't go along with the picture they want of Africans."

In the end, the practitioners I spoke with would probably have been able to stomach even this much had they sensed a willingness on the part of the clergy finally to recognize them as equals. But they did not. "Look, a [Catholic] priest who comes to *candomblé*, will be respected as a priest of a religion. But if I go to the inculturated Mass, I will be regarded only as a piece of folklore. There we cannot be who we are, we will be only what others want us to be."

Marginalizing Mestiçagem

In the work of the *pastoral negro* and inculturated Mass, there are only two legitimate ethnic identities (not including the indigenous): *branca* and *negra*. The practice and language of the pastoral systematically stigmatize the intermediate self-identifications of *mestiça, morena,* and *mulata.* The political reason is clear: these terms derive from the ethnocidal ideology of *embranquecimento* (whitening), whose object is to ensure that *negros* will forever devalorize and seek to escape their racial identity. In a recent in-house mimeo, a key theoretician of the pastoral wrote, with customary robustness, of the "psychological misery, due to the enormous incentives, both conscious and unconscious, to deny being *negro*. We must raise up this *negro* citizen who is disarticulated, from passivity and individualism."[22]

The first step, in this view, toward ending this disarticulation is to teach the alienated *negro* to renounce all other terms. Several groups of São João's *pastoral negro* use the booklet "Negro: The Construction of an Identity" in their work. The text, by Conceição Chagas, psychologist and pastoral worker, frontally assaults the term *"mulata"* as a "euphemism that alienates and hides the exploitation and devalorization of race and culture. It is a term that apologizes for turning the *negra* woman into a sexual object."[23] In other pamphlets, mimeos and lectures, the lay leaders of the pastoral drive home the point that the term *"mulato"* is related to the word "mule," the sterile offspring of a mare and a donkey. In fact, I once heard a lay leader correct a recent arrival in church on her use of the term *"mulata"*: "Sorry, my friend," he said. "That is a pejorative term. We must call the *negro* race what it is: *negro*."

The term *moreno* comes in for its share of excoriation. "It is simply another way of helping the *negro* deny who he is," explained Frei David. "It is a way of saying that racial democracy really exists. That all Brazilians are the same, all *moreno*. But this is a lie. White is white, and *negro* is *negro*." In the headquarters of the black pastoral in São João, a newspaper clipping has been approvingly fastened to the bulletin board, in which a light-skinned rap artist declares, "I am the son of a white father and a *negra* mother. Therefore I am *negro*. . . . I am ashamed to know that there are *negros* who call themselves *morenos*. They denigrate our cause."[24]

In the inculturated Mass itself there is no neutral discursive room for a middle term, no legitimacy for any nonwhite identity other than that of *negro*. In the inculturated Mass's songs *"mulata"* appears only once, and then only in order to heap contempt upon it. "Clap your hands," goes the hymn, "move your body / Dance the samba in your feet / Sarará, *roxinho, mulato* / If you're not white, you're *negro*."

The insistence on the exclusivity and totality of *negro* identity has been important and beneficial for some women. For some of them it has put an end to insecurity and low self-esteem. The story of Lourdes, an assumed *negra* in her forties, is important. "I was always struggling to be someone I'm not," she said. "I wanted so badly to be *morena, mulata, marrom bom-bom*. I was embarrassed and ashamed of my features: of my nose, my hair. I would do anything to change these things." What had saved her were Frei David's "talks." "Little by little," she said, "those worked on me and I realized that to the contrary, I must take pride in who I am. I am *negra*. That is all there is to it. So now that is what I say: *negra*, no more of these other things."

Less familiar is the experience of a woman like Sandra, in her twenties. A store clerk, with long wavy hair and a medium complexion, Sandra grew up identifying herself as *morena*. She became involved in the *pastoral negro* through the Church, and was attracted by the message of justice and valorization for *negros*. "I felt that they have been so mistreated for their whole lives, and it is good to come together to help the poor." She herself, however, did not feel a deep ethnic identification with *negros*. "How could I?" she asked. "My skin is lighter, my hair softer, my life has been very different."

Yet she now used the term "*negra*" to identify herself. I asked her why. "It is important to valorize our *negro*, our African ancestry. For so long the *negro* people here have denied this. So this is to revalorize that ancestry." Her willingness to identify herself as *negra* is a political choice rather than a feeling of identification. "I don't think I have gone through anything like what the *negro* has gone through," she said. "I have never suffered discrimination. I have always been treated well. I have nothing to complain about. But Brazil is a terribly racist country that oppresses its *negros*. By saying I am *negra* I join them in their struggle."

This balancing act appears to work fine for Sandra. It is rather more of an uphill battle for Simone, a mother of two in her forties, who works as a seamstress at home. "I am in doubt about this," said Simone. "I say that I am '*negra*,' but I don't feel this. I say it because I am in the group there. I try to avoid saying anything at all."

"Why do you feel doubt?"

"I have ancestors who are *negros*. I never deny that. I am proud of that. I am prouder now than I was. But my mother was white, my father was *negro*. So I feel I have a bit from both sides. So when I say I am *negra*, I feel like I am disowning my mother."

Simone's testimony hints that at least one factor in the shaping of ethnic identity in Brazil is the ethnic identity of the mother. It turns out that Sandra's mother is darker than her father, and it may be that this contributed to the ease with which she adopted the "*negra*" term for herself. Certainly there are other forces at work here, but I was not surprised when another daughter of a white mother and *negro* father complained to me about the totalizing "*negra*" category. "I don't know about it," she said. "I feel I am *mestiça,* you know? In there I may say '*negra,*' but I don't feel it."

I brought this issue to the attention of an influential lay leader. He was sympathetic but unmoved. "If you start using other terms," he said, "you play the game of the oppressor, of the white ruling classes that have for centuries divided black people against themselves. Because if one group can call itself something different, then they expect privileges. It is amazing how this happens: they want to be different from us. And I would ask: Why? What is the interest here? To become more like whites, to get more from them?"

This leader may have been right about many of the women who seek to identify themselves in this way. But the testimony of one forty-two-year-old woman named Janete, a housewife and mother of two, stands out as an important challenge of this view. Janete is a tall, medium-colored woman with very wavy hair. She used to participate in the inculturated Mass, but, she says, she did not feel welcome there. Janete not only acknowledged that racism existed in Brazil, she could think of a range of concrete examples from the experiences of people near and dear to her, and she denounced these manifestations of color prejudice in no uncertain terms. She herself, however, had not suffered from such things.

"What is your color?"

"Me? Oh, I would say I am *mestiça.*"

"*Mestiça?* What does that mean?"

"You know, a mix. Neither one nor the other. Mixed. My mother was very dark, like Dona Agostina. She was *negra,* really. And my father was lighter. And you should see my brothers and sisters: they are of all colors."

"So your mother was *negra?*"

"Yes, exactly. She was descended from slaves. She would tell me about those things, the stories her grandmother used to tell her."

"How do you feel about having slave ancestors?"

"Very proud, very proud. I mean, why shouldn't I be? It's the truth, isn't it? And they worked hard, they suffered. Like this celebration of Zumbi: the slaves' they fought and they died for their piece of land, like anyone."

"But you yourself? Why don't you call yourself *negra*?"

"Because I am not. I am a mixture. My mother was *negra*. If I said I was *negra*, what would that say about my father?"

"Is that why you don't call yourself *negra*? Because of your father?"

"Yes, that, and because the *negra*'s life is very different from what mine has been."

Indeed, Janete's life experience as well as her ancestry were in important ways distinct from those of a woman with much darker skin and curlier hair than hers. Janete was not denigrating her slave ancestors; she was acknowledging and even taking pride in them. She was not denying that racism existed; it was in fact her recognition of racism that partly accounted for her desire to respect the experiential difference between herself and darker-skinned women.

It is a difference that the missionaries of the black pastoral have made it their business to deny. Both in informal conversations, and more formal presentations, clerics like Frei David invoke the statistical studies carried out by Nelson da Silva as "proof" that in fact there is no real socioeconomic difference between *pardos* and *pretos*. The objective merits of the case are not at issue here; my earlier discussion of these studies should, at any rate, have made clear my own views on this matter. The point is that women like Janete strongly perceive in their own lives the differential treatment they have received because of their color.

It was in part this very issue that alienated Janete from the work of the black pastoral. "They say there that you are either black or white. But I am neither one or the other. So I couldn't fit in."

Janete, in identifying herself, did not seize upon the terms "*mulata*" or "*morena*"; she had chosen to say "*mestiça*," which at least so far in Brazil has not accumulated heavy negative connotations. And yet in the orbit of the inculturated Mass, Janete is obliged to give up her seemingly unobjectionable, and to her quite satisfying, ethnic subjectivity, in favor of the leveling term "*negra*." There is simply no room for her particular subjectivity in the articulative space of the *pastoral negro*.

From the point of view of the lay leader who articulated that space for me, if people like Janete refuse to take the terminological leap, they remain forever untrustworthy, a kind of fifth column, enemies within, potential traitors. Given the racial inequality rampant in Brazilian society, the burden would always be upon her to justify why she had failed to do the right thing, get with the program, and adopt the proper term for herself.

Denying the right to identify oneself other than as either white or *negra* makes good political sense, but it also papers over the contradiction between public self-identity and everyday subjectivity. No sophisticated sociological theory of how language structures experience can negate these feelings of discrepancy and contradiction. What political energies get lost by refusing to address and legitimate those feelings? How many women like Janete have given the inculturated Mass wide berth because, although ready and willing to roll up their sleeves in the antiracist struggle, and willing to acknowledge and valorize the presence of slaves in ther own family trees, they were not willing to flatten their ethnic identities into a term that had no resonance for them?

CONCLUSION

In a recent argument, Ron Eyerman and Andrew Jamison have contended that at the heart of any social movement there is always a struggle to reposition existing ideas or to innovate new ones.[25] They call this struggle the movement's "cognitive praxis." In this view, the key parts of Brazil's black consciousness movement's cognitive praxis are to apply the high value placed on beauty and culture to blacks; to declare that the idea that Brazilian society is racially fair is untrue; and to extend the demand for justice, equality, and citizenship to people of African descent.

But if these are the key ideas, a host of ancillary ones accompany them at every turn, largely as means to these ends. They include a variety of ideas about the necessity, for example, of adopting the one-drop rule (to prove how much one values one's black ancestry, and also to forge a large enough base in order to have political impact); about the need for male heroes and the avoidance of criticizing machismo; about the need to return to an essential Africa; and so on. These are all strongly held ideas that have been ladled from the cauldron of the secular black movement into the pot of the Catholic black pastoral.

Because they are up against strong odds, these ideas have tended to rigidify, as if a stiffening were required in order to endure the war of position. Such stiffening and rigidity may in fact be inevitable and even desirable in social movements, and certainly in movements where battles over cultural meaning are so central, as in the struggle for the inculturated Mass.

What kinds of ideological options are available within a given field of action in order to maximize the attaiment of objectives? In posing this question, it may become clearer that ancillary ideas have grown into ends in themselves, or have become so rigid that they crowd out opportunities to think about alternative ways of achieving the same goals more effectively. How does a social movement itself change?

Sometimes there is no need for change, because there is no desire: the goals are being effectively attained. But in any given social movement, there are always different assessments about precisely which goals are actually being attained, and how effectively. Given such differences of opinion, the problem is thus always: What is to be done? What shifts in practice might be undertaken to be more effective? And if one route toward effectiveness promises to harness the emotional and ideational energies of more people with a commitment to the objectives of the struggle, then addressing the question of the internal ideological barriers to harnessing those energies may be of considerable importance.

A key step, then, is to listen, to hear a range of voices of people who could be part of the struggle, but who for one reason or another resist this move.

It may be that in order to achieve the goal of black pride the problem of sexism among black men should remain unarticulated.[26] It may be that African essentialism is a necessary ideological element in the construction of a self-confident black identity.[27] It may be that the privileging of Afro-religiosity is necessary for the revalorization of black culture. And it may be that the dichotomization of the color lexicon is a necessary step in building the antiracist struggle in Brazil.

But then, maybe not.

FOUR

What is the Color of the Holy Spirit?

Racial/Color Meanings in Pentecostalism

THE BLACK MOVEMENT AND PENTECOSTALISM

In early 1996, a remarkable meeting took place in Brasilia. Representatives of black movement organizations from throughout Brazil came together at the invitation of the Movement for African Religious Freedom and Citizenship to discuss how to respond to growing attacks by evangelical Christian churches against the Afro-Brazilian religions of *candomblé* and *umbanda*. The meeting's final document reveals some of the gathering's high emotion. "The violence of the nazi-pentecostal churches against the African world-view," the document affirms, is an "assault against all black people." It continues: "To the extent that Afro-Brazilian religions are blamed for all the social ills that assail this country, an enormous contingent of marginalized blacks are being incited to act against their ethno-racial peers." The meeting resolved to call upon the Minister of Justice to apply the country's antiracism law "to pentecostal churches that practice racism through their publications and other vehicles of communication."[1]

Although yet to elicit a response from the Justice Ministry, this call for legal action suggests the depth of antagonism between the black consciousness movement and pentecostalism, Brazil's most rapidly growing religion. From the point of view of the movement, this antagonism has a variety of sources, of which four stand out as particularly important. First, many black activists reject Christianity in general because of its historical links to slavery.[2] While recent efforts to deal openly with this history on the part of certain segments of the Catholic and Methodist Churches[3] have softened the views of some, the wounds of centuries are not quickly healed. "We can never forget," a black leader told me, "that Christianity was the religion of the masters, shoved down Africans' throats to turn them into docile slaves." Second, Protestantism in particular, with its white North American influences, is regarded by many in the black movement as a religion of ethnic assimilation. What distinguishes Protestant conversion, in this view, is the adoption of a host of white cultural traits, including clothing, gestures, and music. The black who converts to Protestantism passes through "a whole process of self-rejection, of whitening, of self-negation and alienation."[4] Third, pentecostalism's fervent mix of individualism and universalism is viewed as antipathetic to ethnic identity. "They [the pentecostals] are totally closed to the ethnic question, the racial question," explained an activist. "All they care about is the individual, not the group. Or else they say there is no racism for them, because they are all brothers. . . . So they deny the ethnic group dynamic, that the problem even exists." Finally, the black movement's identification of religions of African origin as a fundamental source of black pride is directly offended by pentecostals' attacks on these religions as the work of the devil.[5] The overall assessment is implacable. I was told that, "Unfortunately, when the *negro* becomes a *crente*, he forgets his identity as a *negro*."

While these points undoubtedly have validity, the antagonism toward pentecostalism that they encourage is, at the very least, unfortunate. Pentecostalism is now the single most demographically important religious movement in Brazil,[6] and a major segment of this movement are people who belong to the dark end of Brazil's color continuum. A recent survey of 1,332 evangelicals in the greater Rio area found between 20 percent and 25 percent of all those identified as pentecostal identified themselves as *negro* or *preto*, compared with only 10 percent of those identified as belonging to the historical Protestant churches.[7] A national survey of more than five thousand adults of all religions found that 10 percent of the respondents who called themselves *preto* were pentecostals, while only 3 percent of these were in historical evangelical churches.[8] It would thus be fair to say that people who identify themselves at the dark end of the color continuum are converting to pentecostal churches over historical Protestant denominations at a rate of between two and three to one. Given such numbers, it seems the black movement would do well to inquire into the special appeal pentecostalism holds for blacks, into the potential the religion may hold for the development of ethnic consciousness and commitment to the struggle against racism, and into the extent to which its own portrayal of pentecostalism as irredeemably corrosive of black identity and political struggle is accurate or exhaustive.

Academic opinion has, it is true, tended to reinforce the black movement's negative view. Verger has characterized slaves' conversion to Protestantism as "alienation" from African values,[9] and Bastide has argued that a large part of black Brazilians' motivation in becoming Protestant is to assimilate into white society.[10] Novaes and Floriano have written that Protestant blacks "no longer identify themselves as *negros*. When they develop the *crente* identity, they definitively separate themselves from other blacks, from African cultural traits and from the historical past they have in common."[11] Marcia Contins has recently argued that in Brazilian pentecostalism the issue of black ethnic identity is simply not present.[12] At a more general level, the "universal language" of the Holy Spirit has been characterized as embodying the homogenizing, de-particularizing forces of global capitalism.[13]

While this scholarship no doubt captures the sentiments of many black Protestants, it does not help us make sense of a host of paradoxes. To begin with, what are we to make of *negra* leader Benedita da Silva's unstinting identity as a pentecostal? While the black movement tends to regard her religious identity as an embarrassment (their interviews with her, for example, studiously avoid religious subjects[14]), Benedita sees her religion as central to her ethnic and political consciousness. "I am not any less *negra*," she stated recently, "any less conscious, because I am pentecostal! From my point of view, I am more conscious, I am more *negra*, because I am pentecostal!"[15]

There are other paradoxes. What are we to make of the fact that three times in 1996, the pentecostal Universal Church's newspaper (the largest evangelical publication in Latin America) ran front-page stories on racism in Brazil?[16] How should we think about the various fledgling efforts among black pentecostals to organize around the race/color issue? How do we interpret, for example, efforts such as the "Quilombo Mission" in the *Brasil Para Cristo* Church in São Paulo, or the "Comunidade Martin Luther King Jr." in the Christ in God Church of São Paulo, or the recently founded *Pentecostais Negros do Rio de Janeiro*? How to make sense of the words of Pastor Paulo, of the Pentecostal Wesleyan Methodist Church in Paraná, when he insists in a recent written statement that "there is a large number of new converts who are certain that it is necessary to create a church that is black, pentecostal, and Afro-Brazilian"? How, in the end, are we to understand the clear preference for pentecostal churches of people at the dark end of the color continuum?[17]

The point of these questions is not to imply that pentecostalism in Brazil is a bastion of racial consciousness. The point, rather, is to take such questions as a provocation to inquire more deeply into the complex relationship in Brazil between pentecostal identity, on the one hand, and racial identity, on the other.[18] The sign on pentecostalism's door reads neither "black identity not welcome here" nor "racial solidarity forever." Only by knocking on that door and going through it will we discover whether there is in fact more room for dialogue on this issue than has been assumed.

There can be no doubt that a powerful tendency of pentecostalism is hostility toward racial identity. Yet when we pay attention and listen carefully, we will start to notice discourses and practices that, if not transformative of this tendency, at the very least run against its grain. It is important to identify these, for they are spaces of possibility that, depending on evolving circumstances and political interlocutors, are capable of expansion, retraction, and influence upon pentecostalism as a movement.

In this process of identification, the role of black women is especially important. Women make up more than two-thirds of the pentecostal movement in Rio de Janeiro.[19] In the churches surveyed by ISER, black women comprised about 15 percent of total church membership. Thus, if we are to understand to the complex relationships between evangelical and black identity, a focus on black evangelical women's experience is a good place to start.

This is especially true since so much of how pentecostalism interacts with the race/color system in Brazil passes through the question of its construction of an alternative vision of physical beauty. I will examine, in particular, the impact of pentecostal belief and practice on black women's lives in connection to their self-identification by color; relations to dominant stereotypes; beauty, love, and marriage; and antiracism. I will conclude by discussing how women of different colors feel about some of the burgeoning efforts, organized and led by evangelical men, to articulate the matter of color publicly. My argument is that for each of these arenas, pentecostal belief and action form a field of contradictory forces, that can both stimulate and hold in check the development of racial identities. How an individual woman responds to these forces and which ones work most effectively on her depend on a variety of circumstances. Still, an overall conclusion may be drawn: pentecostalism is far from being the monolithic brake upon ethnic consciousness that Brazilian black activists depict. It is, rather, a field of meaning in which, just as often as not, religious language and practice contribute to the forging, enrichment, and extension of black ethnic identity and commitment.

THE MAJOR THEOLOGICAL TENSIONS WITH BLACK IDENTITY

Exploring the potential for dialogue between pentecostalism and the black movement requires recognizing the potent tensions that exist between these perspectives. All of our informants—even those who were closest to embracing explicit ethnic discourse—articulated one or more of the following tensions.

First, a tension exists between pentecostalism and the development of strong social identities intermediate between the universal and the individual. As Sanchis and Csordas have pointed out, pentecostalism encourages believers to see themselves as belonging to a transcendent worldwide brotherhood of the saved. Such a view is at odds with the ethnic project, for the universalizing insistence that before Christ every human being is the same is in tension with a focus on group-centered discourse. Indeed, raising the issue of ethnicity in conversations with pentecostals often produces awkward silences, since the issue implies that there are identities in the world that are as worthy of attention as that of Christian. "Look," said one informant, in a typical statement, "do you think Christ's message needs these groups? Needs to be dressed up for these groups, in one way or another? No! Christ's message is very simple, it doesn't need to be connected to any group. It is something universal."

Group identity is also in tension with pentecostalism's vision of the transformation of the individual. Jesus encounters each soul, not as a representative of a group, but as an irreducibly individual moral being. One informant said, "Jesus did not come to save any particular group. He came to meet *you*, as a particular, distinct human being." As a distinct being, the new creature in Christ sheds all prior baggage, including social and cultural anxieties and concerns. "I do not accept any effort," declared one informant, "to isolate some part of the human being, of his soul. Christ saves the soul totally, not piecemeal. Everything starts anew."

Ethnic discourse is also at odds with the strong otherworldly perspective of pentecostalism. If the only truly important thing in the universe is salvation, then ethnic identity is an expression of spiritual immaturity. "Yes, there are people who are concerned about that," said an informant. "They think a lot: I want to valorize this or that in my material life. But that is all it is: the material life. When someone is truly mature in Christ, when he is truly converted, he comes to see that none of that is important. Race and ethnicity: none of that saves. Only Jesus saves."

Pentecostal belief is also in tension with the discourse of the black consciousness movement in particular. Pentecostals reject all belief connected to African spirits. Many pentecostal churches maintain an image of Africa as a continent immersed in idolatry, being slowly retrieved from the mire by heroic evangelical missionaries. Some churches endorse the doctrine of hereditary sin, that all converts must ask forgiveness for the sins of their ancestors, including the idolatry of one's African forebears.

The tensions between pentecostalism and black identity are thus quite pronounced. Still, I will argue that pentecostalism includes a host of beliefs and practices that encourage believers to focus their attention on their color, to reflect on the spiritual and social meaning of racial identity and on the immorality of racism. These beliefs and practices, while not dominant, exist in tense interaction with the discourses that are antagonistic to black identity. They carve out spaces of possibility, full of inner tension and contradiction, but full of possibility nonetheless.

OVERCOMING SHAME

I am walking in the winding streets of a *favela* with Edite, an evangelist of the Assembly of God Church. She is in her thirties, and calls herself *negra*. A young black man, no older than seventeen, shirtless, with hip-hop pants, razor-cut, and wraparound sunglasses, is standing guard outside a *boca de fumo*, a "smoke-house" where hemp and cocaine are consumed. Under his arm is an AK-47, pointed down. Edite smiles and approaches the boy. "Hello, brother," she says sweetly. He doesn't respond, eyes her suspiciously, then shows a few teeth. "I want to talk to you."

"Friend," he replies, "I don't want to talk to you."

"That's all right. You don't have to talk. Just listen."

He's listening.

"Brother, you and I know that if you keep carrying that gun, you'll be dead by this time next year."

He snorts. "What's that to you? One less hoodlum!"

"No, brother," Edite replies, without skipping a beat, her voice brimming with warmth. "One less chance for you to feel what true love is."

This response, I think, startles him.

"Brother, you're here to make your hundred *reais*. To survive. I know that. These guys, you know, they don't care if you live or die. You'll get killed, or something will happen and they'll kill you, and they'll replace you with someone else."

He was standing stock-still, his fingers stroking the AK-47.

"And you don't really care because you don't care about yourself. You figure you could die tomorrow, and that'll be that. No one ever cared about you, and you don't care about yourself. You think you aren't worth anything."

Then she laughed a laugh of joy, which startled both of us, this laughter in the face of death, atop the angry hills of Rio de Janeiro.

"Brother, you couldn't be more wrong. You couldn't. Because you don't know a simple little fact, the most important truth there is: for Jesus Christ, you are the most important thing in the world. You don't care if you die tomorrow; no one else here cares either. But there is a person who cares. For Him you have infinite value. You are the most valuable thing there is."

That was all Edite had to say. She gave the young man a little slip of paper with the address of her church. "Brother, the name of this place isn't worth a thing, because the love of Jesus is everywhere, if you open your eyes. You can open your eyes there, or here, or somewhere else: I don't care, and He doesn't care where you do it. What He cares about is that you open your eyes. Because that's all that's left to do. He has always loved you. You have always been in His heart. Now you have to put Him in yours."

And with that, she turned away and we continued our walk. I glanced back. The boy with the AK-47 was still standing there, holding the piece of paper, looking at it.

I have no idea whether the boy went to the place named on that slip of paper. What I do know is that in her comments to him, Edite had articulated the core message of her faith: You think you have no value, you think you are worthless; but you are wrong. For Jesus, your value is infinite.

Edite's message was contained in more than just her words. The way she held her chin slightly upraised; the way she had walked toward the boy, as if his AK-47 were no different than a boom box; the way she had looked directly, happily, unashamedly into his eyes; the way she had engaged him, every cell in her body expressing love, both for herself and for him; the way she had laughed. Edite was a woman—a dark, black, nappy-haired woman—who valued herself.

This message of self-valorization inhabits every moment of the evangelical's daily round: in sermons, hymns, Sunday school, and informal conversation and action. A hymn sung in every pentecostal church we visited declares:

> You have value!
> The Holy Spirit lives within you!
> End your inferiority complex!
> You are a child of God!
> You have value!

Crente calls to self-valorize do not, it is true, employ the language of color. The songs, the sermons, and street-corner evangelizing are all couched in universalizing language that can be applied to any group, ethnicity, or gender. It is, however, precisely the lability of this universal language that, I will argue, renders it susceptible to being understood in specific group-based ways. Pentecostal self-valorization is not the subjective equivalent of whitening. When I told Caroline, a middle-aged *preta* in the Assembly of God, that there were people who said that *pretos* became *crentes* in order to feel whiter, she burst out laughing. "Want to be white? I don't want to be anything other than a child of God. Let whites be whites. *Preto* is *preto*. We should be happy with who we are, as God made us."

Being a creature of God and child of Christ, the black becomes as valuable as a person of any other color, no more, no less. "I always used to avoid situations," explained Edite, the *favela* evangelist, "where I thought I would be among people who did not respect me because of my color. I wouldn't go to places where I felt out of place. . . . In *crença*, happiness comes when you realize, when you really understand, that *negros* are just as good as whites. In the sight of men there may be difference, but in the sight of God there is none. Because of the freedom Jesus gave me, His liberation of me, I can speak to you about this. Before being *crente*, I was afraid of mixing in, of going to places where I didn't belong. After converting, this changed. Because, before, if I were invited to a wedding, I would say: 'No, I'm not going there, no way. There will only by whites.' And today, no: today, if the wedding is of whites, I'll go; if the wedding is of blacks, I'll go."

The most sustained theological reflection I encountered on this matter came from Dona Marta, a sixtiesh *preta* who periodically stands in front of her Jesus is the Truth Church and holds forth on the Bible. Although, she said, she rarely touches on the issue of color, she had incisive things to say about the subject. "Knowing the Bible more deeply was fundamental," she told me. "First of all, because the Bible teaches us that God made us in His image. No matter what my color, I am a masterpiece of God, in his image. And Jesus: His blood was spilled not only for whites; He came for me too. So you see, I have value. . . . We only find our true identity when we find God: because we are the image and likeness of God. You cannot see yourself without a mirror; and to know yourself in your fullness, your truth, you must look into the mirror of God. As long as I haven't looked into that mirror, the mirror I use are the eyes of other people: I am looking at myself through their eyes."

Theology is supported by everyday practice. In Brazilian society there are few places where a dark-skinned black can feel treated more equally than in a pentecostal church. This equality is embodied in a variety of gestures. First, there is the moment of evangelizing contact. Several black informants insisted that being approached was itself a powerfully affecting experience. "When the evangelist comes to you," said Dona Carmina, a middle-aged *crente* of the Renovated Baptist Church, "it is something entirely new, entirely different from anything you have seen or felt before. Because here, I am this *pretinha*, and they come and treat you with such love and respect. No one else does that."

Once inside the church, other gestures drive home the point. Services include a call to all congregants to greet each other with a hug. The significance of this embrace may be overlooked by an outsider, but not by the black women who spoke to us. "Inside church, we are all equal," said Dona Ruth, an elderly woman from the Assembly of God. "You can see when we embrace each other. That for me is a very important thing. It doesn't matter your color, whether you are rich or poor. The love of Jesus brings us all together." The feeling is reinforced by the sight of dark-black women standing before the congregation and singing, testifying, prophesying, even preaching. In one Universal Church the majority of the *obreiras* (spiritual assistants) were dark-black women. I asked a dark-skinned member what she thought of this. "Yes, it is wonderful, isn't it," she replied, "that God chooses anyone He wills to fulfill His plan. Here there is no separation, no discrimination. In God and Jesus we are all equal." Or listen again to Dona Ruth: "Before being in church, no one cared about my opinion. Who cares about the opinion of a *preta*? But there, people come to me, they want to know what I think." A *negra* in her forties named Danubia pointed meaningfully to the cover of her Bible lesson booklet, adorned by a photograph of a black female hand guiding a white male hand in its first attempts to write. "See how we are valued? Here the *negra* has the same value as anyone else."

Black female evangelicals carry this self-worth into their interactions outside the church. In Brazil, one of the most hierarchical societies in the world, the poor have built into their bodily habitus expressions of deference and self-effacement, especially in the presence of doctors. I once scheduled an interview with a white doctor, the director of a small public hospital. As I was ushered into her office, she was at the end of a meeting with two nurses. One nurse remained silent while the other, a dark-black woman, spoke in a clear, self-assured tone. Her voice solid as a rock, she said: "Yes, and another thing, Senhora. We need to have fifteen minutes set aside for prayer each day. You see . . ." "But Maira!" the director interjected. "We are so busy!" With quiet civility, Maira replied, "Please, Senhora. I will explain. Please do me the kindness of allowing me to finish." She then went on to detail the various arguments for the fifteen-minute break.

I spoke with her later. She was a member of the Assembly of God. When I told her I was trying to understand what it was like to be *negra* in church, she smiled and beckoned me to sit with her on the clinic's lawn.

"Until I was a young woman," she began, "I didn't accept myself as a *negra*. This affected my whole life: relationships, everything. Until I was able to accept myself as a *negra*, as a Christian, through Christianity itself, and started to live this, only then was I cured! Until then, believe it or not, I was angry at my parents for being *negros*. That was a problem, of which I had to be cured. But once I was able to abandon my old self, with that inferiority, once I was able to realize that God loves me as I am, that I am a child of God, in his image: that is a cure! For you must love yourself, like who you are, how you are."

She stretched her arms and looked down at her belly, where a child was growing.

"Before coming to know the Gospel, I did not love myself for who I was. I was embarrassed by being *escura*. I wanted to disappear. But when I read that line in the Bible, 'Love your neighbor as you love yourself,' I thought, 'I can't do that until I love myself. And Jesus is telling me to love myself.' So that feeling of shame left me."

Then she added: "I used to wonder: Is what they say true about us? Are we really so evil? When I accepted Jesus, and began to feel the Spirit move within me, then I knew that was a lie."

As I began to talk with more black evangelical women, it became clear that Maira's feelings were not uncommon. Although the public language of pentecostalism does not highlight color, in informal, one-on-one conversations the connection is often present. This was apparent in the story told to my assistant Ruth by Edineire, a nineteen-year-old *negra* who is a member of the Renovated Baptist Church. Recently Edineire was subjected to an experience familiar to young black men and women in Rio de Janeiro. Entering a clothing store, she was immediately shadowed by a security guard. She told Ruth that she turned to him and spoke, gently but firmly. "I asked him why he was following me. He didn't say anything. So I asked him, was it because I was *negra*? He denied it, but I could see it in his face."

"Why did you ask him that?" asked Ruth.

"Because they try so hard to shame you. But for us, who know the Word of God, we know that it is impossible for one person to shame another. When you have Jesus with you, when you know that Jesus is your savior, that He loves you, what man can shame you? None."

FROM LIES TO TRUTH

The discovery of spiritual equality, while central to black evangelical women's self-valorization, in no way exhausts the connection between pentecostal and black experience. There are other, more direct connections. One of the most important is that evangelical conversion is very often framed as a move from a life of "falsehood" to one of "truth." "God entreats us to truth," preached pastor Sergio, in the Jesus is the Truth Church on a hot summer morning, as the single ceiling fan battled the sticky air. "When we are Christians, we do not vacillate. Listen, friends, to Ephesians: 'With regard to your former way of life, put off your old self, which is being corrupted by its deceitful desires. Be made new in the attitude of your minds. And put on the new self, created to be like God in true righteousness and holiness.' Amen, friends? Hallelulah."

The church filled with hallelujahs.

"What is God telling us?" he asked. "I'll tell you: to leave aside all lies. The worst lies are not to others, they are to ourselves. 'Then we will no longer be infants, tossed back and forth by the waves, and blown here and there by every wind of teaching and by the cunning and craftiness of men in their deceitful scheming.' Hallelujah! That is what the Apostle said."

The image of being "tossed back and forth by the waves" spoke directly to the experience of several of the black women we interviewed. Several of our informants recounted having felt, before conversion, not just shame about their blackness, but deep ambivalence about how to think of themselves. In retrospect, these women now speak of that phase of their lives as their flirtation with falsehood, a flirtation resolved through coming to know the Gospel. For them, being reborn in Christ moved them from a life of self-deception to one of truth.

Tereza carries her certitudes quietly. For the past thirteen years a baptized member of the God is Love Church, this large, jovial, supremely self-confident woman in her forties, who works as a domestic servant, speaks of religion only when asked. We sat in the kitchen of the house where she worked one afternoon, after her work was done and the employer, a friend of mine, had left for the day. A cool breeze wafted through the window that looked out on the white and pink apartment buildings of Copacabana.

One of the things about which Tereza is certain is her color identity. "*Morena* I am not," she assured me. "I consider myself *preta, escura.*"

But she had not always been so certain: "Before, I vacillated, like on a seesaw. Like a child, learning to walk: falling down, getting up. It used to be that I would try to fool people, say that I was something I was not."

"What did you say you were that you were not?"

She laughed. "I would say . . ." She laughed again. "I would say I was *mulata, marrom bom-bom.* I didn't just say it. I tried to be it."

She placed her right hand on her hair and stroked it gently. It was nappy and untreated, pulled back in a bun.

"I straightened my hair! Because when it was very curly, I would get angry. I even wore a wig for awhile. I watched TV, right? And there were stars on TV, like the *mulata* Sargenteli, who had a program, *Obá! Obá!*, and I wanted to look like her, with hair like that; and so the wig. I would look in the mirror, and want my hair to be different, I imitated the *mulata*s."

Now, she says, "I am firm. I *assume* who I am."

The word "assume" shot through the air like lightning. I had heard the word often among black activists. But Tereza denied knowing anything about the black movement; in fact, she said, she had never heard of it. I asked where she had picked up the phrase "assuming who I am."

"Ah, that is all the church, all in the church. Because it is right there, in the Word of God."

She invoked the Apostle Paul: "In one of the books of the Bible, it says something about how when we are in Christ, we will no longer be infants, tossed back and forth by the waves, blown here and there. Now, when I passed to *crença*, I could finally stop using that straightener, which gave me headaches, that hurt me every day. I had been using that stuff for years; and finally when I stopped I felt so relieved! When you don't understand things, you feel obliged to put that straightener on; you are enslaved by it."

This was not the only time I heard of *negra* identity emerging from an understanding of the Bible. Listen to Adalva, a young, very dark woman in the Assembly of God:

> I don't have courage any longer to lie, to myself, to others. I used to think, when I was in the world, that I could choose my color. I used to say: "I am not *negra*, I am *marrom-bom-bom*." Today I have totally changed. Because now I know I cannot live a lie; I must love myself as God made me. If you ask me today what my color is, I will tell you: "I am *negra*." I like my color. For I am truly converted. You can't run away from what you are: I am *negra*. I think the worst thing in the world is trying to live something that you are not. It is like being tossed on the sea.

The tendency of black evangelical women to assume their identity as black is corroborated by ISER'S survey of 277 evangelical women, in which 15 percent identified themselves as belonging to the dark end of the color continuum, compared to a national figure of 6 percent. Three-quarters of these used the term *negra*.[20] That the use of the latter term was of long standing is suggested by the fact that, in the survey, black evangelical women older than forty-five used the term twice as often as their younger counterparts.

Such black evangelical women seem to be engaged in a synthesis of biblical precept with subjective experience. "Whoever knows the Truth," said Adriana, a black woman in her forties, a mother of five, and member of the Renovated Baptist Church, "knows the differences between right and wrong, good and evil. As a *crente*, you can't fool yourself: just as you can't lie to anyone else, you can't lie to yourself. We can't try to fool ourselves that we are something that we are not. You must convert, really."

She too was talking about her color.

"Once I didn't know right from wrong. But now I know the wrong side is to want to be one thing, but you really are another. I am that, I am this color, and so amen! Now, people say my color is *morena*, but it isn't! You are what God created, I think."

I asked her to tell me what she meant by wanting to be one thing and really being another.

"Before becoming a *crente*," she explained, "I was divided within myself. A part of me wanted to be white, another wanted to be *negra*. It was like I was divided in two. But Hallelulah, Jesus! Accepting Jesus ended this, it brought the two parts together. Now I know I'm *negra*, I don't wish to be anything else. That is how God created me."

BEAUTY, COURTSHIP, AND MARRIAGE

While it is true that the aesthetic norms of Brazilian society continue to influence attitudes inside pentecostal churches, dark-skinned, nappy-haired women encounter in those churches two powerful ideas about female beauty that run counter to the dominant trend in Brazilian society. These are, first, that however God made you should be appreciated for the virtue inherent in all of God's creation; and second, that physical beauty should not be allowed to distract from the beauty of the soul.

Although the notion that a woman should not seek to alter her God-given appearance beyond the requirements of hygiene and decency is partly rooted in the Apostolic tradition of trying to minimize male distraction from the faith, it has come to be interpreted in evangelical churches as expressing a respect for "natural beauty." While Peter's entreaty to Christian wives that "Your beauty should not come from outward adornment" (Peter 3:3) aims mainly at getting them to cultivate their inner spiritual beauty, I have heard a preacher say Peter meant that "what God gave them was already beautiful enough!" Paul's reference to women's hair as their "glory" (1 Corinthians) is also frequently alluded to. One minister said: "In our church we say that women must come as they are, as God has made them. Does God make anything ugly? Of course not. Why then all the need to beautify? This is like saying that God does not already make nature sufficiently beautiful."

If this is not convincing enough as a break with the social standard of beauty, pentecostalism delivers a *coup de grâce*: it insists vociferously that external beauty is but a passing shadow. "All is vanity," declares Ecclesiastes (Ecc. 1:14) in a refrain that comes easily and often to the lips of good *crentes*. Peter's advice to Christian wives, that "your beauty must be in your hearts, for that is a beauty that is never lost" (Peter 3:4) can be heard in Sunday school teachers' explanation to girls of why they must not use makeup or fancy hairstyles. Congregants learn by heart the thirty-first Proverb, that declares: "Fairness is an illusion, and beauty will one day come to an end: but the woman who fears God shall be praised." (Prov. 31:30).

The attractiveness of this doctrine for black women comes through in Edith's account of how she slowly gave up the practices of the "world." Edith, who calls herself *escura*, is now in her forties. She converted to the Renovated Baptist Church twenty years ago. She said:

> I stopped wearing fingernail polish and earrings right away but it took
> me longer to give up wearing Henné. I asked myself: "How can I wear
> my hair frizzy and hard, my God?" I prayed a lot over that. Because if

I stop using Henné, my hair is going to be very hard. Wow, how will that be? But I thought, my hair, that God gave me, is my glory. It says so in Corinthians. And God makes nothing that is ugly. Everything made by the hand of God is beautiful. Who am I to fiddle with it?

Edith recounted this like a major spiritual revelation.

So God helped me, He released me from the terrible pressure to straighten my hair. Because I thought that is what society wants. But what God wants is more than anything you see in the magazines. God released me step by step. First, He allowed me to stop using Henné, but to continue for awhile using the hotcomb. Then I stopped using that.

For young *preta*s, this new aesthetic creates a more even playing field for courtship than any they have known in the "world." Although *branca* and *morena* evangelical women still enjoy advantages in attracting the most desirable mates, *preta*s get to taste the pleasure of being considered seriously by men who, in the "world," would pass them by. This pleasure is far from unqualified; it carries with it the price of heightened tension with *morena* and *mulata* women, a tension softened but not eliminated by the language of Christian fellowship. *Preta* evangelicals thus experience the space of courtship in their churches as a web of agonistic feelings: of liberation and constraint, sincerity and hypocrisy. Still, overall, the young black women we spoke with far preferred this web to the rigidities and humiliations of love in "the world."

In the pentecostal universe, the young man who seeks the hand of a fair-haired, fair-skinned woman, or the woman who runs after a handsome man, find themselves confronted by stern-faced counselors. "Before I will give my blessing to a marriage," said a pastor of the Assembly of God, "I talk it over with them. I ask the boy, Have you prayed over this? Has God spoken to you? Has He shown you that this is the one? I tell him not to be led astray by superficial things, by the hair, the face, the body. These things will not last. Only that which is within will last." A Sunday school teacher, also of the Assembly of God, said:

All this must be handled delicately. Young people can be very stubborn. When I see a boy who is trying to marry a girl just for her looks, I talk to him, I do! I question him, to find out if all he wants is beauty. And I know there are also a lot of young girls who want to marry an attractive boy because that way they will gain a certain status in church. So it is up to me to say something about this! [I say] if you are marrying that boy for his looks, that marriage, I can assure you, will not be blessed by God.

Theological precept and social pressure seem to have little influence on the courting behavior of black men. About 23 percent of the Brazilian black men surveyed nationwide in 1995 reported being married to white women, almost the same as the 22 percent of the black evangelical men surveyed in 1994.[21] About 60 percent of both groups were married to *preta*s. Apparently, for black evangelical men, as for black men in general, the rewards of finding a white girl and "marrying up" are not outweighed by the ideology of the church. Although the black men I spoke with denied this, black, *morena*, and white women all agreed: when he can, the black evangelical man, like all black men, marries a girl who is lighter than he is. "Of course this is not pleasing to God," said Marluce, a black evangelical. "The black boy wants the pretty white girl. And she wants him too."

This "she wants him too" is an important element in the color politics of evangelical marriage. For while the ideology of pentecostalism may not alter the desire of black men for white wives, it does seem to make white women more willing to accept black men as husbands. Claudete, a young woman who identifies herself as white, is eighteen years old. She lives at home with her parents and several siblings, is finishing high school at night, and is working as a tutor during the day. She has no time to waste, she says, on any but serious boyfriends. "Look," she said, "I have been going steady with a boy I've been with now for two years: so far, the longest I've ever been with a boy. He's black, but on the inside . . . well, you won't find anyone who says they don't like him. A very serious, responsible boy."

Such attitudes have statistical consequences. The 1995 Datafolha survey found that white women in general were about three times more likely to date a black man than marry one, but that only 5 percent of them had taken the final plunge.[22] In contrast, in the 1994 ISER survey of evangelicals, fully 13 percent of evangelical white women were married to black men. Put differently, white evangelical women were about two to three times more likely to marry a black man than were white Brazilian women more generally.

This being said, I did notice that black evangelical men who had opted to marry black women tended to conceive of this choice in more positive terms than do their non-evangelical counterparts. Whereas the non-evangelical black man might regard his marriage to a black woman as "settling" for second best when a white woman would not have him, I found black evangelical men speaking in glowing terms of their black wives, as especially spiritual, or prayerful, or knowledgeable of the Word of God. It is as if being a pentecostal made available a new set of ways to praise the black woman. I will return to this point.

Still, in general, the precepts of the church seem to have made a deeper impression on light-skinned than on black men. Perhaps light-skinned men have less to lose by courting and marrying black women. Whatever the reason, church precepts appear to have led light-skinned evangelical boys to be more willing than their non-evangelical counter-parts to be serious about *preta*s.

Non-evangelical white men are, of course, notorious for liking to go out with black women, while being uninterested in marrying them: in 1995, 20 percent of a sample of 1,242 white men said they had gone out with a *preta*, but only 2 percent had married one.[23] In contrast, 21.5 percent of the white evangelical men surveyed in 1994 reported being married to women darker than they were.[24] The alteration in atti-tude is tangible in individual accounts. "Before I converted," said Wag-ner, a twenty-year-old white man in the Assembly of God, "I used to be attracted to another type of beauty. Let me tell you: I would not have been attracted to my fiancée. She has very natty hair. I would not have gone for that. But for me, now, she is very beautiful. Because I now look at something else: that which is inside, not the outside." Or listen to Gilcemar, a *moreno* in his early twenties:

> Before I was a *crente*, I was very concerned about the looks of the girls I went out with. I wanted a girl who had long flowing hair, who was *morena*, so I could show her off to my friends. All I wanted was to be with the prettiest girl to show off. . . . Before converting, I only looked at the exterior, at beauty. But once I accepted Jesus, it was much less important to me.

But all is not bright. Some of the white men who court black women report having encountered flack in church. As Wagner said, "There are many girls who have commented: 'Man, he is so good-looking, he could have any girl he wants, but he chooses this black one.'" Wagner's convictions have allowed him to stand firm against such gossip. But he has learned a tough lesson. He now knows that "in church, there are really two types of young people. Those who are truly converted, and those who are not. The ones who aren't are still bound to the standards of the world. They just look at the surface. They look to color and hair, to decide whom they will go out with." At a deeper level, some light-skinned men report continued struggle with demons on this issue. "From time to time," said Gilcemar, "I will see a pretty girl and feel attracted. But then I tell myself: what counts is what is within. I tell myself: what good is it to pay attention to that physical appearance, which one day will deteriorate, will become corrupt? Only character will remain forever."

Evangelical *morenas*, meanwhile, find themselves entering for the first time into serious competition with *pretas*. In "the world," this competition is usually not very intense, since *morenas* know that, in the end, they have the greater likelihood of victory. This is less obviously the case in the evangelical courting arena. *Morena* evangelicals do not experience this change simply in negative terms. After all, they too are engaged in serious religious reflection, and their religion teaches them that *pretas* have just as much a right as they do to fairness. They know that the *preta*, as well as the white woman and the *morena*, should be judged by what is "within." That is why young *morenas* could, like Sandra, tell us that "when it comes to dating, there is no color. That is not what should be looked at. It is the character and spirit of the person. And these have nothing to do with color."

But these young women are also heirs to their prior lives, and are not cut off from the values of the larger society. It is difficult simply to abandon the privileges they have always been told were their birthright. Many *morena* evangelical women thus find themselves in an intrapsychic bind. While yearning to embrace their religion's decrees, they continue to have feelings of superiority to black women, and resentment that black women are starting to take what never used to belong to them.

This, at least, is how I interpret an important pattern in our interviews with young *morenas*: a certain edginess, even irritation, when they spoke of their *preta* co-religionists. Their main complaint was that *pretas* were "so proud of themselves for catching white boys." Touting themselves as knowing that color is irrelevant to love, they criticized *pretas* for choosing their partners not for love but for looks and status. Marcia, a nineteen-year-old *morena* who has been a convert to the God is Love Church for three years, articulated this view. "I have seen racism among *pretinhas*," she said. "If they weren't racist, they would like a black husband as much as a white one. But look how they go out trying to steal away a white man from some girl."

"But why would they want to do this?" I asked.

"They want him so they can lighten their child's color. That is prejudice. And when they get him, you should see the way they take on airs! They will walk down the street and into church with their white boy on their arm, like he is their prized possession, no one better touch him. Nose in the air. So I ask you, who is really racist?"

In the context of black evangelical men's continued desire for white women, white men's greater receptivity to black women, *morenas*' hostility, and their own self-valorization, our most significant finding was that many *preta* evangelicals pursued relationships with men lighter than they. They experienced this as a personal triumph. Before conversion they were no more than bodies to white men; now, they felt, they finally had the chance of being recognized body and soul.

Some young women told stories of having felt rejected or used by lighter men before their conversion. Alessandra, a sixteen-year-old *preta* now in the Assembly of God, converted a year ago. Before her conversion, she says, she was a constant frequenter of *funk* dances. "There the white girls go for the black boys, and the black boys go for the lighter girls," she said. "Someone who looks like me ends up dancing with other girls. There was this white guy who wanted to go out with me." She looked pained. "He was so good-looking, I couldn't believe he wanted to be with me. I was afraid he was making fun of me."

"Did you go out with him?"

Her eyes moistened. "Yes," she said slowly. "But I couldn't stay with him for long. It wasn't meant to be. I felt ashamed to be with him."

"But why ashamed?"

She looked away. "Because I always thought he was just with me for sex; and I knew that's what everyone else thought. I would look in the mirror and say: 'What else can he want you for? You, who are so black?'"

"My life changed a lot when I accepted Jesus," she went on. "I used to want to be with a white boy because I didn't value myself. But now I do value myself."

Now Alessandra has a hankering for lighter men, but this feeling is not about filling an emptiness, nor even about lightening the skin of the next generation. It is about wanting to know what it is like to have a white boy love and respect her. She is theologically ready. "Since God made me this way," she said, "they have to accept it, right? Because God does not make ugly things. For God I am never ugly, I am always beautiful. If I am a creature of God, then I am beautiful."

Her desire for a white boy is still abstract. "I am not saying that if I meet a *preto* that God has prepared for me, I will not go with him. Not at all! For God teaches us to look at the inside of the person, not at his shell."

"Then why do you still think about being with a lighter boy?"

She paused. "I don't know. Maybe because being a *crente*, I'll know he chose me from sincerity, not just for sex."

"But that would be true for a black boy, too."

She smiled. "Yes, but there's the difference: if the black boy comes to you, it may be because he couldn't find a lighter girl. With the white boy I know he could be with anyone he wants, but is choosing me."

One result of this structure of feeling is that a black woman who is evangelical is more likely then a black woman in the population at large to marry a lighter or white man. Our analysis of the 1994 ISER sample of seventy-four married black evangelical women revealed that 47 percent were married to men lighter than they, and 27 percent of these were married to white men. If the black woman was raised in church, this increased her likelihood of marrying a white man almost three times: 17 percent of the black women not raised in church were married to white men, compared to half of all black women raised in church. By way of comparison, a separate survey of 294 *preta* women found that 26 percent were married to lighter men and 20 percent were married to white men.[25] In other words, if a black woman was evangelical, she was about twice as likely to be married to a lighter man than if she was not evangelical.

But this is not the end of the story. The valorization of inner beauty has put on trial for at least some of these women their desire to seek a lighter partner and has persuaded them to pursue black men instead. Luciana, a very dark woman in her early twenties who calls herself *preta*, had before her conversion five years ago, clear notions about the color of her ideal spouse. She spoke to Ruth:

> While I was growing up, I always said I would marry a very handsome man, *moreno*, with much hair, thick. I always said this to my mother. . . . I didn't want my children to be as dark as me. I didn't want to marry a man who was pure white: I thought he would not respect me. So my idea was to marry a man in between, a *moreno*, who was just right. Someone who was not as black as me, but who was not white.

Conversion had, Luciana recounted, an irrevocable impact upon these ideas. "When I became a Christian," she said, "I stopped looking at the outside of the boy. What good is it to see someone for their outside, when it is what is inside that counts?" Currently she is seeing Luiz, a dark-black evangelical man in his mid-twenties.

I never would have been interested in him before. He is not that pretty *moreno* I had hoped for: but it is the power of the Holy Spirit that I see in him! When I first converted, and I saw him, I was not attracted to him, because I didn't want my children to be so dark. But God worked His will in me, and changed my opinion, and I went to him; and then He showed me how *escuros* can be good husbands.

But matters are not always so easy. For some *pretas* the process of becoming detached from the aesthetic of lightness remains a daily spiritual challenge. Consider Edilene, a thoughtful, well-spoken seventeen-year-old who identifies herself as *negra* and works as a domestic servant in Rio de Janeiro. She has been a convert to the Renovated Baptist Church for three years.

At first Edilene insisted, in her interview with Marcia, that conversion had brought about a radical break in her thinking about color. Yet the desire to lighten her offspring ran deep for her, so deep that even a powerful dose of the Holy Spirit has not been able to exorcise it. Edilene admitted that even now, long after conversion, she still thinks a good deal about the color of prospective boyfriends. "I must admit," she said, "that I understand why young people want lighter boyfriends. Because I myself still have a little of that feeling in me."

She lives in a state of inner tension about this. "Sometimes I think about wanting to marry only a white boy. But then I say 'no, stop this!' and I remember that to be happy, it isn't important for the boy to be white or black." Yet she cannot quash her longing. "You know, that ideal of the prince, the white boy, that I had before converting? Well, I cannot lie: I still have it."

What difference then has conversion made for Edilene's feelings about the color of love? By introducing the constant eye of God and making such feelings "un-Christian," it has forced her to become her own observing eye. Whereas before conversion she accepted her own values uncritically, she now possesses a divine discourse that obliges her to think about them critically, even to feel guilty about them. "It is a weakness, " she says, "this desire of mine. It is my flesh, it is that part of me that cannot conform to the will of God."

RESHAPING THE IMAGE OF THE MATURE BLACK WOMAN

Mature black evangelical women find themselves in a complex relationship with the dominant images of themselves in Brazilian society. The new roles they adopt in church, such as prayer healer, hymn singer, and prophesier, are partly influenced by, and reinforce, these images. At the same time, their religion also includes strong ideas that run counter to these images. The give and take between these two processes creates something altogether new: the social identity of the mature black pentecostal woman. This is, I submit, a genuinely new identity in Brazilian culture, not reducible either to a simple perpetuation of received stereotypes, or the creation, *ex nihilo*, of entirely new ones.

Mature black women in Brazil are supposed to be humble creatures. The self-effacing black maid on television, the affectionate, self-deprecating black mother in the Afro-Brazilian religion of *umbanda*, or the old ex-slave eager to please are standard figures in the Brazilian imagination. Given that humility is a necessary precondition for receiving the gifts of the Holy Spirit, it is not surprising that many evangelicals of all colors assume that mature black women are more likely than not to be endowed with spiritual gifts. "It's because we are more humble," said Dona Edite. "We do nor exalt ourselves. So the Spirit has more space to work in with us."

Yet the humility Edite is referring to has a rather different feeling-tone from that of the self-effacing maid or slave. It is, after all, humility before God, not before man. In contrast to the slave or maid who must know when to hold her tongue, the black woman filled with the Spirit knows she must speak truth to power. The *mãe preta* speaks softly, curves her back, and keeps her gaze rooted to the ground; the black evangelical woman in the Spirit holds her back straight as a rod, looks up and into the eyes of everyone she meets, and fears no man. There is very little that is obviously humble about Irmã Silvia, a great prayer leader and prophet, when she stands up amid a full congregation and denounces the sinfulness of the presbyters of her church.

The figure of the black female prayer healer also partly reproduces the stereotype of black woman as nurse. "We are good at laying on hands," said Sandra, "because we are more sensitive. I think the black woman thinks more about others, about taking care of others." The spiritual meaning of sickness in the pentecostal context, however, complicates this role. For sickness here is sometimes seen as a trial applied directly by God. If a woman lays on hands and invokes Jesus' name to no effect, she knows that what is needed are not her ministrations but rather the patient's getting right with God. From merciful healer, the black woman thus slips into the role of prophet. At one prayer session I heard the following testimony: "He had come again to be prayed over," said the testifier, "But it was to no avail. I prayed there, I spoke the name of Jesus. Hallelujah. But brothers, I tell you this: the judgment of the Lord was upon him. Hallelujah. For there comes a time when nothing is to be done but for you to look into your soul and see how little you love the Lord, that you have forgotten Him." Not exactly the voice of the merciful healer. Where else in Brazilian society is such a "voice" possible for any woman, let alone a black one?

The other side of the coin of healing is, of course, sorcery. The image of the black woman as practitioner of black magic is rooted in the history of slavery, and is now disseminated in popular culture and media. Black women are assumed to possess arcane magical knowledge; children are routinely warned not to go inside the houses of those old black women suspected of being *macumbeiras*. But black women's conversions to evangelicalism have a direct impact on the stereotype. Now that they have received Jesus into their lives, they prove their rejection of black magic through their prayer, prophecy, healing, tongues, and faith. Their visible evangelical identity is usually enough to dispel suspicion that they may be secret practitioners of the black arts. "Before I was a *crente*," said Dona Julia, a *preta* and member of the Assembly of God, "my neighbors were always accusing me of being a *macumbeira*. Since I passed into the church, I never hear that any more. They know that a child of God cannot mess with that stuff."

Yet even in their new roles as enemies of witchcraft, black women live with the legacy of the stereotype. Both *crente*s and non*crente*s commonly assume that a black woman who is an evangelical was once a *macumbeira*. Even without knowing her personal story, co-religionists will assume that her conversion involved fleeing from *macumba*. Said Rodrigo, a white presbyter in the Assembly of God, "if you look closely, you will find that 90 percent of the *pretas* in church were once *macumbeiras.*" This presumption has contradictory consequences. On the one hand, it reinforces the image of black women as especially committed to things of the Spirit. After all, having known firsthand the worst evils of *macumba,* black women will be that much more resolute in sustaining their faith and enveloping themselves in the safety of the Holy Spirit. On the other hand, the image makes possible the danger that a black woman may fail to distinguish between possession by the devil and by the Holy Spirit, making her prone to backsliding. I have heard examples of this kind of stereotyping, as when Carmen, herself a black woman, explained that black women needed to be especially vigilant lest they become subject once again to the wiles of the devil, and slip back into the world of *macumba*.

On yet another stereotypical front, pentecostalism makes room for the old cultural fiction of the black woman as innately robust, made of a fiber that bends but will not break. While knowing that God chooses whomever He wishes as His vessels, *crentes* also believe that the fasting, self-purification, and all-night vigils required to prepare for the Spirit, as well as actual possession by the Spirit itself, are not for the faint-hearted or weak of body. The prophesier or speaker in tongues who falls or loses control is sometimes characterized by his fellow *crentes* as "too weak" or "too frail" for the Spirit. Such ideas of "strong blood" come into play when *crentes* turn their attention to men and women touched by the Spirit. "It is that the *negro's* blood is stronger," said Ruth. "Put a white or even a *mulato* on his knees all night long at a prayer vigil and see what happens. They won't make it to morning." A black female evangelical may thus turn "black blood" to her spiritual advantage, concluding that her access to the Spirit is due in part to the very thing that "in the world" justifies placing upon her shoulders a heavier burden of manual labor.

The one who carries that burden in the world is the "black mother." The *mãe preta* role presumes that the black woman's identity is defined by the life of the heavy labor of the household, whether as mother, housewife, or domestic servant. Pentecostalism, in contrast, although entreating women to fulfill their duties in the home, also challenges them to try their hand at an entirely new assortment of unmistakeably nondomestic occupations: street-corner evangelizing, missionary work, preaching to the congregation, prophecy, and organizing interchurch exchanges. Although Christian mothers are assigned the responsibility of socializing children, exposing them to the faith, and instilling in them a love for Christian values, they are also taught that no human affection may upstage the love of God. Since maternal feeling is the closest competitor to divine love, it must be handled with caution. Ideally a woman will encounter God through her love for her children, but *crentes* are well aware that such love may lead a woman to forget God. A story was circulating in the Jesus is the Truth Church, about a *crente* whose son had been killed in a terrible accident. She had, in consequence, stopped attending church. The churchgoers I spoke with felt she was committing a sin, because her motherly love had crowded out her trust in God.

One of the most pervasive of ideas in Brazilian society is the belief that *swingue*—a natural bodily response to syncopated, percussive music—is carried genetically "in *negro* blood." When a *crente* observes that "the strongest voices in the choir are those of the *negros*" or that "people with black blood have more musicality" she is simply expressing a view shared by most Brazilians. In church, said Roberto, a deacon of the Assembly of God, "it is true God gives the gift of music more to blacks than whites. The blacks are the ones to play the tambourine loudest. This too comes from our blood, from what we have inherited from our ancestors."

This belief is accompanied by an important division of labor: black men are regarded as naturally talented at instrumental music, particularly percussion, while black women are reckoned to be gifted singers. This pattern has become a significant basis for black women's prominence in evangelical churches. In a small, crowded Assembly of God in the *favela* of Cantagalo, I saw young men drench their suits in sweat as they pounded tambourines, accompanied by the high-pitched voices of an almost entirely black female choir. In the Renovated Baptist Church in Nova Iguaçu, almost all the lead singers identify themselves as *pretas*. In the Assembly of God Church in São Jorge, on the periphery of Rio, all the women's choirs were directed by dark-black women.

While black women's musicality in pentecostalism is thus rooted in stereotype, it also accretes new meanings. First, the image of "black rhythms" in Brazil, especially samba, is that they are ineluctably tied to sensuality, eroticism, and danger. But pentecostals regard evangelical blacks' natural propensity to music and the music they like to play as means to realize the goal of salvation. Although in traditional churches almost all the music belongs to a repertoire that originated in the United States and Europe, in some smaller, "hotter" churches one can hear tambourines beaten to the same metronome of certain variants of samba. The men and women who play this music recognize it as "*a musica do negro*" (black music), which they have retrieved from the devil and put to divine use. "Isn't it wonderful? Isn't it mysterious?" asked Stella, a black member of the Assembly of God. Just as churches are founded on the sites of ex-*umbanda* centers, or outdoor evangelization takes place in front of brothels, so too "it is a victory for God when this rhythm is taken from the world and put to the service of salvation."

Overall, then, the mature black woman finds constructed in pentecostalism an identity, fashioned from the materials at hand in Brazilian culture, but invested with a variety of new meanings that make it unique in the culture. It is an identity that is certainly a relief from the burdensome, negative stereotypes she faces in secular society.

PENTECOSTAL ANTIRACISM

Virtually every *crente* I spoke with embraced, at least at the level of discourse, the radical equality of all people in the sight of God, irrespective of color, gender, age, or class; and the biblical injunction that Christians must feel and practice universal love for all humankind. In sermons, Sunday school, and hymns, *crentes* are constantly reminded to "love others as you love yourself," and that God "discriminates against no one" (James 2:1–10). This latter biblical passage was without doubt the most frequently cited whenever our conversations with informants turned to the matter of color prejudice. "In the Bible," said Maria, a white woman, "it says that we cannot discriminate. So it is a sin to feel prejudice."[26]

Evangelical belief seems to have had little relevance to woman's views about whether color prejudice was common in Brazil. Opinions on these matters were shaped less by religious belief than by personal experiences and ideological forces outside the church. Thus, the women in our sample said that they had known that racism was a problem, in Brazil or in their own life, before converting, and that, in the words of Alessandra, "becoming a *crente* had nothing to do with knowing this."

When it came to the moral evaluation of color prejudice, however, all the women we interviewed agreed that conversion had brought about an intensification of the opprobrium they felt toward racism. Almost all the black female evangelicals we interviewed said that involvement in the church moved them from the simple commonsense feeling that prejudice was wrong, to a much stronger moral stance bolstered by their new evangelical understanding. Black women referred to their certainty that prejudice was against the will of God. "Before I was a *crente*," Ruth told Marcia, "I saw all this, and I didn't like it. But knowing the word of God leads you to new insight. The Bible says 'Do not discriminate,' in James. Jesus taught us to love our brother. So I realized that racism is not the will of God, that He doesn't want this thing of prejudice."

While the radical egalitarianism of the Bible provides the theological foundation for such invigorated antiracist views, we found that these views also provide black evangelical women a way to experience in an unprecedentedly clear fashion the hypocrisy of their co-religionists. The high standards of behavior evangelicals learn to expect from each other led some of our informants to become attuned to gaps between word and deed among other evangelicals who profess to be good Christians. Many of the examples of this hypocrisy revolved around the courting market. "They say that they are good Christians," Alessandra told us. "And what hit me was, how can they be good Christians and feel the way they do? Because I heard the commentaries, I saw how those other girls would say: 'How can he go out with that black girl?' And there are families that say they are Christian, and they don't allow their sons to go out with a black girl. Is that Christian? The Bible says we cannot discriminate."[27]

Several of the women we interviewed bore witness to their beliefs in everyday interactions. Cristina, whenever she hears or sees a racist comment, speaks up right away. "I don't let that pass. If I think someone is discriminating, I will recall to that person what is written in the Bible." Rosângela reported that whenever she had the opportunity to speak of prejudice in private conversations or in class at her seminary, she did. "I assume this in a very clear way, because it is biblical! I assume this as a woman, and as a black woman."

It should by now be clear that far from being a simple corrosive of black identity or antiracist sentiment, pentecostalism can and does in various ways articulate elements of both of these agendas. These elements do not, of course, constitute a coherent, sustained, self-conscious ethnic identity or agenda. If anything, the black identity articulated in pentecostalism remains largely at the level of practice, of diffuse sentiment, of relatively unreflective consciousness.[28] Such practices and sentiments are the very stuff of everyday life, and with all their contradictions are at the heart of the most intimate mixed feelings of self-esteem and self-doubt. It would be arrogant to expect these practices and sentiments to form themselves into neat packages of political consciousness.

Still, an entirely legitimate question remains: To what extent has this sporadic, fragmentary sense of blackness contributed to joint action in the service of that ethnicity? Has pentecostal "everyday" black ethnicity ever become translated into "non-everyday" politicized ethnicity?

The short answer to this question is "yes." We identified a surprising number of efforts on the part of black pentecostals to make the defense of black ethnic identity and the fight against racism ongoing projects of their churches. Furthermore, we found that black evangelical women's particular mix of sentiments about color inspired some of them to participate in these efforts.

In 1985, a certain Pastor Rubens returned from a visit to the United States and founded, in a São Paulo suburb, a congregation of the Church of God in Christ, a southern black pentecostal church. At the same time, Pastor Rubens also started the Comunidade Martin Luther King, Jr., which included a weekly seminar on black issues. From the publications of the group, it is clear that women played a key role in it. The seminar, a place in which to read the Bible through the lens of black concerns, became a virtual school for black pentecostal leaders who went on to influence other congregations.

One young man influenced by these leaders was Hernani da Silva, who in 1991 founded the Cultural Association of the Quilombo Mission in his pentecostal Brazil for Christ Church. The association's main objective, according to its founding document, was "through seminars, talks, and conferences, to push the Brazilian church to reflect on the evils of racism in society and even within the churches in a direct and indirect way." The association now promotes monthly discussions and debates on the theme of racism, produces a series of pamphlets on "the black in the Bible," maintains contacts with São Paulo's black movement, and strives to form black leaders in pentecostal congregations. The membership of the group is currently about twenty, of which the majority are women.

The Quilombo Mission has not only influenced the attitudes of members of the Brasil Para Cristo congregation where it originated, but has also produced several charismatic leaders who are establishing an Afro-Brazilian pentecostal discourse in their respective congregations.

We even found a few voices calling for a more radical proposal—that of founding an exclusively black evangelical church. There was an effort to do this in São Paulo in 1992, but it was short-lived.[29] In Londrinha, Paraná, Pastor Paulo has founded a congregation of the Wesleyan Methodist Church with the hope of creating a strictly black congregation. He has formed the Community of Studies of the Life of the Black, which nurtures the desire to "found a church which is black, Biblical, pentecostal, and with Afro-Brazilian consciousness." In his group of about thirty people, three-quarters are women. Although still not exclusively black, this congregation may one day become so. It is relevant that Pastor Paulo works in the far south of Brazil, where residential segregation of blacks is tangible. It may be that if a black-only church is ever formed in Brazil, it will happen in the south.

These groups are developing, with the help of women, readings of the Bible from, as Pastor Paulo puts it, "a black pentecostal point of view." In a series of pamphlets on "The Black in the Bible," Hernani has argued that the myth that associates Cain with blackness must be rejected, while the African origin of many of the great figures of the Bible, such as Simeon (Acts 13:1) or Simon (Matthew 27:32) must be emphasized. The image of Jesus himself as white and blue-eyed must be replaced either with a dark-skinned Christ, or at least an open question about Jesus' color.

Small, tentative spaces are just starting to open up in several pentecostal churches in which black women have begun to articulate in public their own readings of the Bible. For example, Elinete, a participant in the Quilombo Mission, has prepared her own written analysis of Numbers 12, in which Moses returns to his family after marrying

Zipora the Ethiopian. In her text, Elinete shows Aaron and Miriam rejecting Moses because of this marriage. God is enraged and visits upon Miriam a disease that turns her "white as snow." Here, Elinete argues, God is demonstrating that "one cannot associate blackness with evil and whiteness with good; here, the colors symbolize exactly the opposite." What potentialities lie ahead for such theological reflections?

CONCLUSION

There is at present in Brazil a deep antagonism, and virtually no lines of communication, between the organized black movement and the pentecostal movement. On the side of the black movement, pentecostalism is regarded as the enemy because it is steeped in the European religious tradition and because it has declared war on Afro-religiosity. Pentecostals who are sympathetic to the struggle against racism, meanwhile, feel alienated from the black movement because, among other things, of its commitment to Afro-religions. These are undoubtedly formidable ideological barriers to collaboration between the two movements.

At the same time, it is possible that some of the ideas emerging from everyday and noneveryday pentecostal thought and practice in relation to blackness and antiracism may be of considerable interest to secular black activists. Many of those activists, for example, have not questioned their own presupposition that black women's self-valorization must occur through a focus on adorning her surface and making her spectacular. To what extent might pentecostal ideas about inner beauty contribute to a broader conception of self-valorization? To what extent do black evangelical women's views about courting white men problematize the position that authentic black consciousness manifests itself primarily through racial endogamy? How might a dialogue with black pentecostals committed to the antiracist struggle challenge activists to assess more closely the taken-for-granted centrality of Afro-religiosity to black identity? And to the extent that the black movements are eager to work with black youth and salvage them from the drug culture, what insights might pentecostalism have to offer about what moves them?

Suggesting that such questions might actually some day be explored may not be pure fantasy. Later in this book, I will return to a concrete effort to explore them.

FIVE

The Eyes of Anastácia

Political Readings of a Popular Catholic Devotion

A DEVOTION AND A SUBMERGED CONSCIOUSNESS

In this chapter, I will discuss how a religious devotion to the image of a tortured black woman is understood by different social actors, and the impact those understandings have upon the actors' everyday lives. In what follows I move between the voices of black movement activists, white, *morena*, and *negra* devotees, and my own roving, restless, ever-glossing voice. My objective is to gather these voices together onto the same pages, to place them into contact and confrontation with one other. Activists may hear some voices that confirm their presuppositions about the color politics at work among Anastácia's devotees, and some that complicate them. White, *morena*, and *negra* devotees may encounter here surprising differences among themselves. My own voice, rooted in North American history, brings to this meeting place its own distinctive set of ideas about race, and I feel alternately vindicated and frustrated at every turn.

This meeting of voices will suggest that there are good reasons for the black movement's skepticism about Anastácia. In many ways, especially with regard to how white and *morena* devotees relate to her, the devotion does indeed fail to challenge norms and attitudes that are prejudicial to black women's dignity and agency. Yet the crux of my argument is that other dimensions of the devotion often go undetected by the distanced eye. I will suggest that the devotion helps *negras* in small, everyday ways to value themselves physically, challenge dominant aesthetic values, cope with spousal abuse, and imagine possibilities of racial healing based upon a fusion of real experiences with utopian hope. At no point does the devotion effect these things with earth-shaking clarity and self-consciousness. Quite the contrary: at every step, the consciousnesses of Anastácia's devotees are full of ideological tensions. Keepers of ideological purity will find much amiss here. Yet there is also much that is surprising. Paying attention to these surprises, I suggest, will make for a richer depiction of the variety of black consciousness in Brazil, and for a more nuanced assessment of that consciousness's political potential.

The forms of consciousness linked to Anastácia do not remain limited to the realm of images and attitudes. The love and gratitude devotees feel for Anastácia have inspired some of them to different kinds of social action. Most strikingly, the devotion has led to the formation of a variety of informal and formalizing networks and groups, some with quite explicit social agendas. These submerged networks, I will conclude, could conceivably be a source of challenging ideas for black activists.

THE *MOVIMENTO NEGRO'S* AMBIVALENCE TOWARD ANASTÁCIA

While it may be understandable why Rio de Janeiro's black consciousness movements adopt an adversarial stance toward pentecostal churches, their attitude toward the devotion to Anastácia is more difficult to fathom. It is a stance of avoidance. Activists will, it is true, sometimes refer to Anastácia as a model of the strong black woman. Black women's groups like Criola in Rio de Janeiro and Gelêdes in São Paulo sometimes place her name in lists alongside other black heroines like Dandara, Acotirene, Carolina de Jesus, and Benedita da Silva.[1]

Yet in the everyday cultural work of the movements, Anastácia is conspicuously absent. The posters and visual art of the movements rarely include her. Upon the walls of movement organizations one encounters the faces of the great Zumbi, of the generic "African woman," of the gods of *candomblé*, and of black street children, but not of Anastácia. When organizations such as *Odo-Ya* strategize about where to go at the base to bring educational materials on AIDS to black women, they identify *candomblé* centers, but never the Anastácia temples located in the Zona Norte.[2] When one attends panels, discussion groups, or lectures sponsored by IPCN, CEAA, or any other black movement organization in Rio, one is regaled with analyses of the counter-hegemonic values at work in *candomblé*; but no mention is made of Anastácia. Only once in its five-year history has Criola, the leading black women's organization in Rio, mobilized any action in relation to the slave saint: when the musical troupe Banda Didá, which wears Anastácia's face-iron as an emblem, was ridiculed in the *Jornal do Brasil*, Criola sent a letter to the paper calling the critic's attitude "racist." Otherwise, the movement in general and the black women's movement in particular have remained deafeningly silent about this most massive of Brazil's mythic images.[3]

The black movement's reticence about Anastácia has numerous sources. First, the devotion originated in the Catholic Church, and continues to be worshiped primarily by Catholic women. Activists feel that the Church was the ideological apparatus of the white colonizer and oppressor, and Catholicism was the religion shoved down the throats of slaves to turn them into docile subjects. "How can we forget what the Church did to our ancestors?" asked Joscelina, an activist in Criola. "Anything that originates in the Catholic Church," said Ivanir dos Santos, the director of CEAP, "is the responsibility of Catholics, not us. The ones who need to assume Anastácia are those who profess the Catholic faith. Not us."[4]

The Catholic black pastoral has, however, been only slightly less ambivalent than the secular movement in its relationship to the slave saint. The pastoral's steps in Anastácia's direction have been tentative. Two groups of laypeople, one in São Paulo and one in Rio, have christened themselves with names that include "Anastácia." Medallions, T-shirts, and buttons with her image are sporadically worn by participants in the pastoral. Her bust was used by the black pastoral as part of its insignia in the 1988 march against racism. And during the inculturated Mass, her name appears alongside those of other black heroes. Yet there are limits. The pastoral has composed no hymn or song to celebrate the slave saint. While Zumbi is a constant presence in the pastoral's iconography and discourse, Anastácia is rarely mentioned in published material of the pastoral, and she was studiously avoided in the black pastoral's recent compilation of the lives of the great black saints.[5] Moreover, the clergy of the pastoral do not permit her image to enter the church.

What, then, are the deeper ideological anxieties produced by Anastácia among people committed to raising consciousness about black identity? The reservations fall into four main categories: 1) the devotion focuses on individual health and miraculous healing, and is therefore a weak source of critical reflection about society; 2) her image is a concession to the ideology of whitening; 3) her story reinforces fatalism toward racism; and 4) her story endorses facile racial conciliation. In discussing these concerns, I do not mean to imply that all activists share them. What I am suggesting is that the concerns are strong and widespread, and, to my knowledge, have yet to meet any sustained countervailing argument. There is no explicit discussion about Anastácia within the movements. There are, rather, taken-for-granted views, less than fully conscious understandings built into the habitus of neglect. Such understandings surface only by getting activists to reflect upon why they have expended so little energy to work with the image of Anastácia, while making a gargantuan investment in the figure of Zumbi.

DISTRACTIONS FROM BLACK ETHNIC IDENTITY AND ANTIRACISM

Black activists' first reservation is that the devotion to Anastácia is so concentrated on nonethnic longings that these effectively crowd out any thought of black ethnic identity. Cleonilda, an activist in her forties who works with an African dance troupe, summed up the concern: "The people who go to Anastácia are not going there to think about racism. It's a spiritual, religious thing, not a political one. . . . What people want from Anastácia are cures and miracles. They don't want to develop black consciousness."

It is true that much of what transpires in relation to Anastácia seems to have little to do with black ethnic identity. Many of the problems brought and resolutions attained through Anastácia have meanings that overflow the categories of race or color. Even for devotees for whom Anastácia carries important color-bound meanings, the slave saint is not exhausted by such meanings.

Elenira, a *preta* in her fifties who is a public-sector nurse, had never put any chemical products on her hair, because she had no interest in changing the way she looked. She was a lifelong *preta* who felt comfortable in her skin. "I have seen prejudice, every day," she said. "Brazilians are terrible racists. They say they are not, but they are." She told me of the many times she had been treated with disdain because of her blackness.

But none of that was involved in her devotion to Anastácia. She told me that story as we sat in a small room in the medical clinic where she worked. It was her nephew's condition that brought her to the slave saint—his affliction, she said, had made life miserable for her and her sister. "I did not know what would set him off. Everything would be fine, then he would go on a rampage through the house." Although that was a long time ago, emotion still rose in her voice. An acquaintance, she said, urged her to seek a miracle through the infinite power of Anastácia. Although she had no idea who Anastácia was, she went to her shrine in search of help. As she remembered her first sight of the slave saint, her eyes moistened. "When I saw the muzzle," she said, "that torture, I saw that she had suffered. So I said to her 'The way you have suffered, I don't want my nephew to suffer.'"

"What did you think Anastácia had suffered?" I asked.

"That face-mask. She had suffered so much. And that's what I thought: that she could understand my nephew's suffering."

"Did you think of her suffering as a slave?"

Elenira looked at me quizzically. "As a slave? No. No, not at all. I just saw that she was suffering, that she felt pain."

Insistent anthropologist: "Did you identify with anything about that pain?"

Patient Elenira: "No, of course not. I was not the one who was suffering. It was my nephew."

"Did you feel anything in common with her suffering because she, like you, is a *negra*?"

Another quizzical look. "No. I didn't even think of that. I just saw someone who was suffering, someone who could sympathize with my nephew's suffering."

"What is your nephew's color?"

"He is white, he is your color."

Here what was meaningful about Anastácia transcended color. Similarly, for Nete, a *negra* in her late thirties who runs a rural school, the primary emotional meaning of Anastácia had little to do with her ethnic identity. Like Elenira, Nete had a very strong sense of herself as a *negra*. "I've always called myself that," she said. "I grew up knowing I was a *negra*. Why should I ever deny that? I am proud of my color."

We sat together in the bare-brick annex to her house that she had built in honor of Anastácia, and where every day she taught twenty children, aged seven to twelve, how to read and write. The children had to wear cotton T-shirts printed with Anastácia's image. Some parents had withdrawn their children when they learned of this detail, but that was of no concern to Nete.

"When I was ten," she told Ruth and me, "my father died in a horrible accident. With a lot of blood. And it was not long before my mother went insane and was put in a hospital." The years lay like a soft blanket between that pain and now. "I went through a long time," she said, "when I thought God couldn't exist. How could there be God if I had lost my father, and my mother was spending her life in a mental hospital?"

Although Nete knew that the *Escrava's* separation from her own parents had been caused by enslavement, it was not slavery, but losing parents that remained foremost in her sense of commonality with the *Escrava*. What had bound her for life to Anastácia was her feeling that the slave saint had known, like her, the pain of this loss. "When I learned more about Anastácia's life," she told us, "I began to feel better about my own. I felt, if she could endure that, so could I."

Ruth, whom I had asked to seek out a racial meaning wherever it might lurk, pursued the theme. "When you felt that, did you also think about Anastácia's color? That she had been a slave?"

Nete looked at Ruth, who is the same color as she is. Because of Ruth's youth and university education, Nete suspected that the right answer should be "yes." Ruth told me this later, but Nete said so right away. "Well, maybe I should have thought about those things. But to tell you the truth, I didn't. I just saw her as someone who had lost her parents young, like me, and who had been forced to live uprooted from family, and dependent on strangers. Maybe her color should have come into it. But it didn't."

Color also sometimes fails to show its relevance to the phenomenon of miraculous cure. Such cures are flooding experiences that can rearrange all emotional priorities in their path. We found that black women who had been recipients of miraculous blessings at the hands of the slave saint often thought about her in nonracial terms.

Listen to Dalila, a dark-black devotee in her forties with a headful of long, tightly woven braids. Like Elenira and Nete, Dalila had virtually no contact with any black movement group; but, also like them, this had not prevented her from developing a clear sense of herself as a black woman. She spoke at length to Ruth, Marcia, and me about what it was like to be black. "You know how it is," she said, speaking to Ruth. "You know how people look at us."

Yet although she recognized that Anastácia was a dark-black woman like herself, she said this did not carry much emotional weight for her. "Anastácia is a *negra*," she said, "but when I look at her, it is not her color that I see. I do not see her as a *negra*, I do not identify with her that way at all. When I look at her image, she is not a *negra* for me, she is not a slave."

These statements become understandable when we learn that Dalila came to know Anastácia when her only child became ill. "I was entering despair," Dalila said quietly. "That day that I went to her church, I made a promise: I said that if my son improved, from that moment on I would be her devotee." She received the blessing. Now, whenever she interacts with Anastácia, it is with the spirit that saved her son's life. The intensity of this feeling overwhelms any other sentiment in connection with the slave saint. "I am so thankful for the miracle she performed for me," Dalila explained, "that now I hardly see her face-mask or anything about her like that. I am entirely focused on what she did for me."

The idea of "flooding" also helps us understand the account of Gegê. Gegê participated for years in the black movement and has a strong identity as a black woman. I got to know her first through her participation in the inculturated Mass, when I noticed that she was wearing an Anastácia button.

"Ah," she had said, eyeing me closely. "You want to talk about Anastácia? OK. But be careful. Anastácia is different from this other stuff. She is very special, very sacred."

Gegê had never married and had devoted her life to activism in the Church. We talked at her kitchen table over cups of *cafezinho*, with busts of Anastácia and Aparecida do Norte watching us from her bookshelf, and a poster of Zumbi peering at us from the wall.

She had known Anastácia for many years. At first, as I will recount momentarily, the slave saint had a powerful ethnic meaning for her in her symbolization of black beauty and pride. But the *Escrava* took on a new dimension for her in the 1990s, when she blessed Gegê with a cure of what may have been cancer. "I was at the edge of death," she said, "and Anastácia brought me back to life." The cure added a whole new layer to Anastácia's meaning. "When I first knew Anastácia, she helped me accept myself as a *negra*," Gegê said. "But now she is no longer just about that. Now when I pray to her, I am not praying to a symbol of black struggle. I pray to her as a saint who is an intermediary between me and God. So she means far more now to me than just my identity as a *negra*."

In addition to such emotional forces, the theology of universalism has a strong relativizing effect on how devotees perceive Anastácia's blackness and her condition as slave. Regina, a *negra* housewife in her late twenties, spoke to Ruth and me of her own slave ancestry, her pride in her color, and her hatred of racism. None of this, she insisted, had anything to do with Anastácia. I remember how, sitting in the *sala* of her house in the Zona Norte, against the background noise of the afternoon soap opera, she held up her hand to stop our insistent queries. "Look," she said, "I do not identify with Anastácia as a *negra*. For me she is a saint, like other saints. I do not choose my saints because they are *negra*s! My faith in her is a faith that goes beyond identifying. If I only had faith in her because I see she is like me, is that really faith?" She paused to let her words sink in.

"Imagine this," she continued, "God says to you, 'believe in me, have faith in me, because I am white like you!' Isn't that an offense to your faith? You cannot have faith in God because of His color. Color has nothing to do with it. So this thing of 'identification' is a problem."

"So," I asked, once again, science sticking in my throat, "looking at Anastácia, you don't see her as being like you?"

She went over the point patiently once again for my benefit.

John, must I have faith in someone just because she is black? If I don't identify with her, I can't have faith in her? That is not what faith is, John. My faith is larger than that. In my case, I could say, to satisfy you, 'because we are *negra*s. My race! She suffered!' I could say to you, John: that I feel what she suffered, and so on. But I can't say that, because it just isn't true. I am very sorry she went through so much suffering. Maybe she went through that suffering for us *negra*s, but I do not know, and I do not identify with it.[6]

By now it should be clear that the image of Anastácia, despite its seemingly overpowering ethnic referents, does not always contribute to black devotees' black ethnic identity, nor to reflection on the issues of prejudice and racism.

As true as this is, it is far from the whole story. For the slave saint's image and legend also have frequent occasion to enter into relation with popular ideas about Brazilian history and slavery, and present-day ethnic identity and racism. I will suggest that these relations are more extensive at the popular level than activists believe. We found that in a large number of cases, the devotion to Anastácia actually played a significant role for its devotees in articulating the issue of color and developing modalities of action about it.

ANASTÁCIA, COLOR IDENTITY, AND THE WHITENING AESTHETIC

"What I want to know," said Efigênia, an activist in the black movement and a Workers' Party operative, "is this thing about the eyes. Why do Anastácia's eyes have to be so blue?" She was not alone in asking this question. I heard other activists express a similar concern, that the image of Anastácia reinforced the dominant aesthetic of *embranquecimento* (whitening), the aesthetic that makes Brazilian doll manufacturers add blue tint to the eyes of their dark-skinned dolls. "There we have it again," said Cirleia, an activist at Criola, "for a black woman to be attractive, she must be a *mulata*." To the extent that Anastácia's beauty figures centrally in her mystique, and to the extent that her beauty is understood as derived from mixture with European blood, she presents a problem to anyone striving to challenge Eurocentric aesthetics. "My concern," said Jurema, an activist in the Movimento Negro Unificado, "is that the only way a black woman can be considered beautiful is if she possesses traits of the white woman. I much prefer images of Dandara [the wife of Zumbi], the African queen, or Benedita, who are pure black women."

But how do Anastácia's devotees actually understand the meaning of her physical appearance? What is the meaning of her "beauty" to them? How do they interpret her blue eyes? What are their beliefs about her racial ancestry? What relevance do these beliefs have to their everyday lives?

Activists' concern that Anastácia's beauty may be viewed as a sign of European blood appears most warranted in the case of devotees who identify themselves along the middle of the color continuum. Yet even among them, this connection is neither absolute nor unanimous, for the devotion has the power of highlighting the value of rethinking the link between beauty and white genetic inheritance. With few exceptions, female devotees with middle-continuum identities identified Anastácia as being, like themselves, *mulata*, *morena*, or *mestiça*. The "proof" of this, cited by all of them, was the color of Anastácia's eyes. Those who acknowledged that Anastácia was usually depicted with dark skin were still sure she had been the offspring of a mixed union. Said Sandra, a middle-aged *morena*, "She had dark skin, but one could tell by the fineness of her features and her eyes that she had a white father." This is also what Isabel Fillardis, the famous *mulata*, told me when I interviewed her about why she had wanted to play Anastácia in the stage production of her life.

This insistence on Anastácia's *mulatismo* or *morenidade* reveals a strong whitening standard of female beauty. For most of our *morena* and *mulata* informants it was inconceivable that Anastácia could have been anything other than a *mulata*: for, they asked, how else could she have been so attractive to a white man? "The master fell in love with her," said Janainha, a *mulata* in her thirties, "because she was a fine *mulatinha*. He had never seen a woman like that before, with those incredible eyes." This view could lead to selective memory. The 1990 television miniseries represented Anastácia as the child of two "pure" Africans. Yet Lurdes, a middle-aged woman who regards herself as of mixed parentage, remembered (incorrectly) the TV Anastácia as a *mulata* born in Brazil. "On TV her ancestors were mixed," she reported. "Because in the series, her parents were not those creatures, you know, those kind of ugly blacks. She was a beautiful creature."

We also heard two of these women articulating countervailing views. For them, having become devotees of Anastácia helped them to reinforce and articulate their own skepticism about prevailing racial aesthetics. Carla, a middle-aged *morena*, accepted the image of Anastácia as a dark black, and decried all efforts to deny her heritage based on her beauty. "Beautiful she was," Carla said. "She was a beautiful *negra*. I used to think that *negra*s could not be beautiful. But all you have to do is look at Anastácia and you see that is a lie."

"Wasn't Anastácia a *mulata*?"

"No, no, no. She was a pure *negra*, brought from Africa."

The dominant view in middle-continuum women's understanding of Anastácia's ancestry is embedded in Brazilian moral history. Middle-continuum informants who acknowledge having a slave ancestor have a special stake in embracing the Freyrean vision of affectionate, paternalistic slavery. Several of our *mestiça* informants transferred this stake to their version of Anastácia's myth, in which they depicted the slave saint's master as caring deeply about her, because he was her *father* and loved her true mother. In their accounts, this fact infuriated the master's wife, who, powerless before her husband, vented her vindictive rage upon an innocent Anastácia.[7]

Listen, for example, to Solange, an elderly working-class *mestiça,* who recounted her version of the slave saint's story on a cool afternoon on the porch of her house in the Zona Norte. "The way I understand Anastácia's story is this," she said. "You see, the baron [master] had two daughters, one a *mulatinha* named Anastácia, with a slave woman, and the other a white girl. The baron was really in love with the mother of Anastácia. But the *baronesa* suspected that her husband planned to elope with her. So she had Anastácia's mother sent away and killed by other slaves." Solange paused to let the horrific detail sink in. Then she continued: "With this heartache, the baron doted on Anastácia, the daughter of the woman he loved. But the white daughter wanted to take vengeance." Again she paused, so that I might fully appreciate the magnitude of Anastácia's adversity. She breathed deeply. "In spite of this, Anastácia loved her sister as a sister. She even took care of her when she was ill. But despite all this, the sister and her mother had that awful face-iron placed on Anastácia."

Solange's version, variations of which we heard from other *mulata* and *morena* devotees, refigures the history of miscegenation as tragic romance, in which true love does battle against the sinister jealousy of white women. The appeal of this version to women who regard themselves as the heirs of miscegenation is, I believe, its reassuring message that whatever evil accompanied miscegenation was external to the miscgenating act itself, that indeed the mixed-color person's ancestors were moral, loving, even heroic people. In a culture that embraces so strongly the notion of character as genetically transmitted, the appeal of such narratives to the mixed-color descendants of slave-master unions is not difficult to fathom.

Our white female informants tended to prefer to think of Anastácia as a quintessentially dark-black slave. Most referred to her as *preta*, *pretinha*, or *negra*, often preceded by the pronoun "my." Only two said she was *mulata* or *mestiça*. Maria Luiza, an elderly *preta* who has worked for ten years as caretaker of one of Anastácia's temples, told me that "the ones who prefer the blackest image of Anastácia are the whitest." Some called her blue eyes the result of divine intervention. Others ventured that there must be people in Africa with blue eyes. Overall, white informants were simply more ready and willing than were *mestiças* to regard Anastácia as a dark-black woman, and a beautiful one at that. Why should this be the case?

A key variable in our sample of white women was class: we spoke to four middle- and upper-class white women, and seven poor or working-class white women. Among the middle-class women, a strong motivation seemed to be that the darker Anastácia was, the less ambiguous was their own authority in relation to her. By keeping Anastácia at the polar opposite of themselves on the color continuum, they seemed to be able to mark a clear boundary between themselves and the slave saint. We noted, for example, that these white devotees frequently mentioned Anastácia's color spontaneously, in prayer to her or in speaking of her. "The *negro* is not preoccupied with his color," observed the black caretaker Maria Luiza, "but the white is. Whites are afraid someone will think they are like Anastácia."

Keeping their distance from her socially, middle-class white women can approximate a patron-client relation with her. "I think," said Lucia, a middle-class white journalist in her fifties, "that it is a certain homage that we whites give to Anastácia by becoming her devotee: we show that even though she is a poor *negra*, we love her too." Yet the only devotees I met who seemed to feel the right to challenge or talk back to Anastácia were middle-class whites. "I have often fought with Anastácia," explained Lucia. "I'll say, 'Hey, you're not going to help me with this? Hey, what are you up to? If you don't do this for me, I'll never speak your name again!' I threaten, I cajole, I flatter. My mother says, 'You should be able to get whatever you want from that *neguinha*!'"

All white devotees, including those in the working class, tended to have pity but little empathy for Anastácia. They spoke of the slave saint's pain, hunger, and thirst behind the mask, but not of her feelings of humiliation or isolation. "I felt so sorry for her!" said Rosilda, a working-class white devotee in her sixties. "Pity for the pain she must have gone through! I have horror of feeling pain; so anyone in pain I feel terrible for them. I thought: 'She suffered so much she must have gone straight to heaven.'"

For all white devotees, as well, placing Anastácia's birth in Africa neatly avoided the tricky moral questions surrounding miscegenation on the plantation, in which both the white man and woman have less than honorable mythic associations. None of the white women we spoke to seemed keen on rehearsing tales of plantation wives standing by as their husbands raped black women.

Not only were these women eager to locate Anastácia's origin in Africa, they were also more willing than middle-continuum women to accept the idea that a "pure" African might actually possess beauty. Although part of this beauty reproduced European standards of blue eyes, fine nose, and high cheekbones, it also meant accepting as part of her beauty her nappy hair. "Who says that this hair is 'bad'?" asked Luzia. "No, it is beautiful, beautiful in her. She was a very beautiful woman." To the extent that some white devotees could imagine a dark black with "bad" hair to be exquisitely beautiful, a rather dramatic step was being taken away from dominant aesthetic norms. It is as if white women, personally unthreatened by black beauty, could afford to acknowledge it, at least in this context. Could it be that a psychic exchange was taking place: recognition of beauty in return for relief from the moral ambiguity of white-black concubinage under slavery?

What of the largest segment of our sample, dark-black, *preta* devotees? What do they make of Anastácia's color, eyes, and ancestry? Our data are quite clear: most of our *preta* informants felt that in life Anastácia had been a dark-black woman, not a *mulata*. They were quite sure of this, because they believed that no master would have allowed a light-skinned slave to be so cruelly treated. The suggestion made by *mestiça* devotees that Anastácia may have been the master's own daughter they found ludicrous. "If she had been his daughter," said Gegê, scarcely suppressing a laugh, "she wouldn't have been treated like this: because *fazendeiros* [planters] gave protection to their own daughters. And you can see she didn't have this protection!"

What made Anastácia's color a matter of emotional interest for many dark-black devotees was that, as everyone knew, she was that rare occurence, a dark-black and beautiful woman. By this they all meant one thing: that she possessed facial beauty. From their point of view, if Anastácia could be considered beautiful—black skin, nappy hair, and all—then the notion that black equals ugly could not be so ineluctable after all.

We encountered several stories of dark-skinned, nappy-haired women whose shame in their own appearance began to dissipate once they became convinced that Anastácia's looks were not so very differ-ent from their own. Listen to Jania, a *negra* in her forties who now runs a small black beauty salon named after the slave saint. Many years ago, she said, she had been unhappy with just about everything about her appearance. "I didn't like having hard hair," she said, "I didn't like being called '*negra*.' Because for me that meant 'ugly.'" Back in the 1960s and early 1970s, her visits to the hairdresser were to "ask him to do everything he could to make my hair long and flowing. I even put lightening cream on my skin. I avoided the sun, put on a lot of makeup, and tried to hide my rear."

When she became a devotee of Anastácia in the mid-1970s, her views about her appearance began to change. "It is hard to explain," she says. "But there I was, always struggling to stay out of the rain so my hair would not lose its straightness, using a hot iron, doing all that. And then you look at Anastácia, and she puts things in perspective. This woman who struggled, was tortured, who was ready to die—and here I am worrying about keeping my hair straight? To be a black woman, with hair like hers, all natural, and skin like hers, all dark, was some-thing to be proud of. I mean, she helped me to like my race." Soon thereafter Jania finished training as a hairdresser for black women. "That is how I am today, partly thanks to her: because I used to be afraid of who I was." What, then, to make of Anastácia's blue eyes? Jania believed they were a genetic inheritance from Africa too. But did she think they were more beautiful because they were blue? "No, it is not just their color," she said. "It is the contrast, that you have these blue eyes in a black face. That is what makes them so striking."

In this connection it is significant that statuettes and prints of Anastá-cia commonly adorn the walls of Rio de Janeiro's hair salons specializ-ing in black hair; we tracked down no fewer than four salons in the Rio area that use "Anastácia" in their names. One of them was founded by Janir, a devotee who feels that Anastácia inspires and guides her work of bringing aesthetic self-esteem to black women. "Anastácia was so beautiful," she said. "She is saying, 'Black woman, be proud of yourself. Dare to take your beauty seriously.' That is what we do here in the salon, with Anastácia blessing us!" Among other things, Janir passes out small pamphlets to her customers describing how they can care for their hair without the use of chemicals.

We discovered three loosely organized networks of devotees that had been meeting as a informal mutual aid and conversation groups. One of the groups emerged in Vaz Lobo among black women who are devotees at the same Anastácia temple. "Anastácia helped me to think better, but she also helped me to talk," said Silvia. With other dark-skinned devotees who felt similarly, "we have talked about this issue of color. Anastácia has to help us, she being *escura* like us. We get a lot off our chests among ourselves. And it is as though an *escrava* is present in these conversations, helping us along." These women meet in each other's homes to drink coffee, share news, keep track of each other's health, organize visits to the shrine, fulfill promises for blessings received, and, among other things, talk about color prejudice. "Before being a devotee," said Silvia, "I never talked about this subject with anyone. After being a devotee, this became important, and I was able to have these conversations. To talk about this matter of color prejudice. I had never done this before. It was all bottled up; but I didn't talk about it."

THE POLITICS OF SERENITY

There are some in the black movement who feel uncomfortable with the devotion to Anastácia because, in their opinion, she reinforces the image of the victimized slave. Olivia, a black intellectual with a long history of involvement in various black movements, said that looking at the face of Anastácia made her feel "a certain weariness, sort of depressed. The face-mask emphasizes victimization. Anastácia is the image of the disempowered woman, women who are silenced, tortured. I think it weakens you politically just to focus on the chains, on that. What is the positive project? Where do you get if you call upon people to identify with a suffering slave? We must go beyond slavery." A co-director of CEAP wrinkled his nose at the mention of Anastácia: "The problem with Anastácia," he said, "is that she is that slave who stayed on the plantation, who refused to run away and join a *quilombo*. She is that slave who just was resigned, who endured suffering, who did not revolt against it. That is not the model we feel want to project. We need positive models of action." The figure if Zumbi, in contrast, accomplishes what Anastácia does not: he was agent of his destiny, the slave willing to risk death, first by running away and establishing the *quilombo*, then by fighting back.

Anastácia's face-iron is particularly problematic. How is a political movement committed to inspiring people to *speak* supposed to relate to this symbol of silencing? The sporadic efforts by the movement to appropriate Anastácia's face has had to contend with this problem, leading to compromises that have satisfied no one. In 1988, when movement leaders agreed to allow her image to be carried aloft at the march against racism, it was widely argued that the face-iron should come off. As Januário Garcia, then president of IPCN said at the time, "If I had my way, I would take that mask off right away, so that she could proclaim to all the world: I am silenced no more."

Some images of Anastácia tried to work against this appearance of passivity. In 1985, Marizete Kuhn's multipart radio drama depicted Anastácia as a prophet of rebellion, intervening to stop whippings, smuggling food to imprisoned slaves, and acting as lookout to run-aways. The face-iron in this version became an effort to silence her; her penetrating blue gaze became her ability, even from behind the mask, to transmit telepathically her love of freedom. The 1990 television drama retained this image, and went even further, portraying Anastácia as the inspiration for a full-scale slave rebellion and flight. When activists conceded any place at all to Anastácia in the pantheon of heroes, it was this media-constructed Anastácia they chose to think of.

Anastácia the great rebel leader, however, was not the Anastácia embraced by the majority of her poor and working-class black devotees. None of the women we spoke with believed that Anastácia had desired to foment flight from or rebellion against the plantation, and several explicitly rejected that part of the television series. For them the hallmark of the slave saint was not her desire to plan rebellions; it was the imperious fact of her torture, the visibility of her face-iron, and her serenity before it all. "Her face, that face in the middle of torture, the face iron," said Dona Maria, an elderly black woman. "It was her serenity, her calm as she suffered, without bitterness, without renouncing her faith: that is what I would want to pass along to my grandchildren." How should we understand this? How might we grasp black devotees' sentiments about Anastácia's face-iron and her serene willingness to endure horrible torture and suffering?

There is, to begin with, the power of Anastácia to convey in graphic terms that any notion that slavery was a warm, easygoing system is a lie. No other devotees were as emphatic about this aspect of the image as were our black informants. "There are still people," said Sandra, a black devotee in her forties, "who say that slavery was not hard. That the slaves ate well and that they had a roof over their heads. That things got worse after slavery was abolished. But I would prefer to have rain on my head than a neck-iron around my neck."

In the context of an ideological world in which such attitudes exist, it is understandable that black devotees might feel that any effort to remove the face-iron from Anastácia's image is tantamount to a denial of her suffering. Several of them spoke of how important it was to them to see the instruments of torture in Anastácia's shrine at the Museum of the Negro. Looking at her image and telling her story were occasions for keeping alive the memory of the horrors of slavery, in towering negation of romanticized visions of gentle, kind slave-master relations. "In those days," said Dona Maria, a *preta* devotee in her seventies, "no one saw how wrong this was if you were *negro*: they just said, to the dungeon! They didn't have any rights. Sold like dogs."

Even more important than Anastácia's negation of the myth of affectionate slavery, however, is the fact that for her black devotees, Anastácia's serenity in the face of torture was the direct outcome of her refusal to be raped by the master. In response to our question, "What is the most important part of Anastácia's story?" black devotees' most frequent answer was that Anastácia successfully resisted being raped. Listen to Izolina, a black devotee in her forties: "When I think of Anastácia's story, the most important thing is how she wouldn't allow her body to be taken by the master. She would not allow it. He came to her and tried to force himself on her, but she said 'no,' and would not permit it. So she suffered for that."

This response originated in the hearts of these women themselves, for it runs counter to all written texts, which depict Anastácia as protesting in vain against her ultimate violation. *Preta* and *negra* informants, moreover, repeatedly underlined the point that Anastácia refused to sleep with the master in order to protect not her virginity but her dignity. "She was not a virgin," said Izolina. "But she had a commitment not to give her body to anyone. Her owner wanted to use her, and she did not accept." "She had already had lovers in the slave quarters," said Francisca, a devotee in her thirties. "She was not a virgin. She was not trying to save her virginity. She just did not want to be raped." "In the TV show," Carolina, a devotee in her sixties, reminded me, "Anastácia got married in Africa. I thought that was very pretty, with the ceremony and dancing. And there she slept with her husband for the first time. So she was no virgin."

And when we asked how they knew that she had successfully

resisted, the answer was unanimous: hadn't she been tortured, with that horrible face-iron? Margarida, a devotee in her thirties, said, "Of course she wouldn't give in."

"How do you know?"

"Hah! Look at her mask. Why do you think they put that on her?"

For these women, then, Anastácia's face-iron did not symbolize passivity before torture; it was, rather, emblematic of her willingness to suffer to protect her dignity as a woman, as a *negra*, as a person. In 1988, the IPCN proposed taking Anastácia's face-mask off in the antiracism march, in order to symbolize the will of black women to no longer be silenced; the black devotees I mentioned this to were horrified. This was before I fully understood the deeper motivations at stake in the reaction. I was inclined at that time to agree with the comment of the activist who wrote this reaction off to religious conservatism. Little did we understand that without this visible sign of her torture, Anastácia's heroism, her towering "no" to the master, would remain in doubt.[8]

Far from perpetuating the image of the passive slave, then, black women's version of Anastácia's willingness to submit to torture, even unto death, helps retrieve for them an honor robbed by the stereotype of the slave woman as ready to give her body in exchange for a little better treatment. To this extent, the figure of Anastácia extends Hegel's claim that the truly free person prefers death to unfreedom: Anastácia prefers death to rape. "She would not give in," said Aparecida, her eyes shining with admiration. "She would rather die. She would have been so well treated if she had gone along. She didn't care about being better treated; she cared about her honor." Anastácia's serenity is actually a preference for death, a preference that allows her black devotees today triumphantly to refute the idea that they are the descendants of natural slaves.[9]

The specificity for black devotees of Anastácia's resistance to rape comes clearly into view when we find out that this resistance is constructed in entirely different ways by white and *morena* female devotees. We found that white devotees accepted without much concern the notion that Anastácia, like other slave women, had been fair game for white men. None of our white informants, in response to the question, "What is the most important part of Anastácia's story for you?" spoke of her defense of her honor. Instead they said that Anastácia had submitted, not only to her master but to all the *feitores* (foremen), and had given birth to many children from these encounters as well. "That part of the story," said Maria, an elderly white working-class woman, in a comment that went to the heart of the political matter, "that she was abused and raped, I don't think is real. I think she just slept with the master because she was a slave and the other was the master." As an indication of the strength of such views, white female devotees did not hesitate to turn to Anastácia for help in matters of romantic love: I met no fewer than three working-class white women who attributed their love matches and marriages to Anastácia's intervention.

There were some white devotees who were willing to believe that Anastácia had refused sex with the master, but were quite cynical about the refusal. "At the time," said Josefina, a white working-class devotee in her forties, "it was the commonest thing in the world for masters to sleep with slaves. So I was never impressed by her refusal here. I thought that was sort of silly, to be honest."

The views of *morena*s and *mulata*s on the role of sexual encounters in Anastácia's story are strong indicators of their subjective historico-existential predicament. We found two chief patterns here. First, like *preta* devotees, some *morena*s and *mulata*s said that what moved them about the slave saint's story was that she had refused the slaveowner's sexual importunities. For them, however, this detail reinforced rather than problematized stereotyped images of licentious black women. While for *preta*s Anastácia's refusal was about preserving her human dignity, irrespective of considerations of virginity, for some devotees who identified themselves as of mixed ancestry, the main drama in the slave saint's life was that of a virgin keeping her virtue intact. For them Anastácia was that rare thing, a virgin slave in the midst of the generally licentious lot of slave women.

Listen to Zefa, a working-class housewife, a light-skinned *morena* in her sixties. What impressed Zefa about Anastácia was not her color; it was not that she had suffered as a slave; it was not that she had rejected slavery. What impressed Zefa was, quite simply, that despite her abject condition, she had refused to sacrifice her virtue. Slavery served only as a backdrop for the real drama, a woman's struggle against "temptation." "She was a virgin," she told me. "A pure person. Because, look: she was a slave, but she didn't let herself be dominated by temptation. She refused temptation, she refused money, refused becoming a prostitute." Zefa could be certain Anastácia was a virgin because, once a slave woman had "fallen," she would have no further reason to resist sexual advances. "All the other slave women were jumping into the masters' beds," she said.

But not all *morena* informants embraced this version. A second, more complex variant among these devotees portrayed the master as having genuinely *fallen in love* with Anastácia, and Anastácia as having reciprocated. Dona Penha, a working-class *morena* in her fifties, told me: "The master fell in love with her. He had real feelings for her, and had a romance with her. Later she even bore some of his children. The mistress discovered this, and ordered a face-iron to be placed on her as punishment, so she wouldn't kiss any more, so she could no longer speak to the master." We only heard this rendering of Anastácia's tale from *morena* informants. The underlying motive for this rendition is probably similar to the stakes involved in *morenas'* representation of Anastácia as the fruit of love, not rape: to rehabilitate the white contribution to their own ancestry, to humanize both sides of the encounter to which they are genetically, socially, and characterologically heir.[10]

Black devotees' views about how Anastácia nurtured self-respect and dignity were far from abstract; they had repercussions on how race and gender relations figured in devotees' everyday lives. Some of these repercussions remain limited to the intrapsychic level. It was, for example, Anastácia's serene dignity, transmitted to Silvia, that allowed her to cope with racial assaults on her daughter's right to become a doctor. Silvia, a gentle, soft-spoken *escura* in her sixties, ran away from a bad marriage thirty years ago, coming to Rio to work as a domestic servant. The problem was the employer's son, who

> didn't like my daughter because he felt that his father liked her more than he did his own granddaughters. Silvania could not play with them or touch their toys. This created a very big pain inside of me. I knew it had to do with color. Later the son said Silvania should not be a doctor because she is black, that she should be a maid, like me. Because of her color. That gave me so much pain to hear that.

Silvia spoke to Anastácia about the employer's son. She said,

> I spoke a lot about this with her. She had gone through this, I knew she would understand, because she was *negra*. I knew Anastácia would understand this problem. I would say to her: "Oh, my *Escrava* Anastácia, you can understand this, because you too are *escura*, you have suffered for this." So I asked strength from Anastácia to help me deal with this prejudice at home. . . . I don't know what I would have done without her. When he would say things like "*negras* don't belong in doctors' offices," I would close my eyes and think of Anastácia, serene, knowing she was as good as any white. And that saved me.

In other cases, the self-respect inspired by Anastácia has helped black women to pry open new discursive spaces, ranging from the one-on-one dyad to wider, more polyadic flows of speech. As an example of the former, some informants said that Anastácia's protection of her dignity had helped them confront employers. Nete said,

> When I thought of Anastácia having the courage to refuse the master, I began to say to myself, Don't bow your head anymore, say what's on your mind, say what you believe. I said, From now on, I'll be like her. And so when I went back to the house where I was raised, I said: "Senhora, from today forward no one is going to step on me any more. I am going to say what I think and what I don't think. Because I have many years of having stayed quiet."[11]

But Anastácia's symbolization of dignity did not only strengthen these women's own self-esteem; it also led them to try and improve the self-esteem of other women, starting with those of their own families. For black women, such issues are often highly charged with racialized gender meanings. Aparecida explained:

> My daughters go to dances. I tell them about Anastácia, how she did not let herself be taken advantage of. Because the black woman is told again and again that all she is worth is her sexual part. And at those dances, there are boys ready to take advantage of that, that she doesn't value herself. So I tell the story of Anastácia, saying look, she valued herself so much she resisted the master; are you gonna let some kid take what's not his?

It is awkward that the adversary in such situations is not always a white man. Aparecida is a dark-black woman in her thirties who, among other things, started a children's literacy program named after the slave saint. "Sometimes," Aparecida said, "I turn to Anastácia because when that man tried to take her, to have sex with her, Anastácia said no. I saw this on the television show. That was really something." She then proceeded to recount the story of a rocky relationship with a partner, who had happened to be black. "The man," she said, "told me he would do this and that to me. And I told him that he could try, but that one of us, either me or him, would die if he did. He left me alone. For this I thank Anastácia. That was the spirit of Anastácia, guiding me and giving me strength. Only her."

Telling the story of how Anastácia had made it possible for her to resist this man also provided the opportunity to say a few choice things about black men more generally. "They treat us like shit. The black man, let me tell you, he does not respect a black woman. He would come home and expect me to wait on him hand and foot, and if I didn't he would say how he would get himself a white woman who knew how to treat a man. Well, with Anastácia helping me, I wouldn't take that shit."

Aparecida's complaint against "black men" cries out for further comment, for it is, I think, another clue to the lack of enthusiasm for Anastácia among black activists. Both male and female black activists (but especially male ones) have placed most of their hero-symbol eggs in the basket of Zumbi. They are reluctant to invest too much energy into developing any icon that might distract from the chief—and male—hero of the movement.

The fact of Zumbi's maleness is, it turns out, of considerable importance. When we look closely at the issues focused on by the black women's movement in Rio, we find primarily work on self-esteem, aesthetics, and women's health. In their everyday practice, black women's groups avoid articulating and debating issues that might be regarded as a threat to male power and self-esteem, such as sexism, spousal abuse, domestic violence, the division of labor in the household, child support, adultery, or alcoholism. As a member of Criola explained "The priority is to focus on women, not on women's relationships with men. We don't feel that in a racist society it is a good thing to raise issues that can hurt or weaken men. We must struggle alongside of them." "The black woman can take care of herself," explained a prominent activist and writer on black women in Brazil.

> She has not suffered as much as the black man. Under slavery and after, the black woman never lost her social role as mother, as sustainer of the group, of the community, of the family. It was the black man who lost his identity as a leader, as head of the household. It is the men who need to build their self-esteem. We want black men to be happy with themselves, so they will leave white women alone, come home again and help raise strong black families with us. We don't need heroines. We are all naturally heroines already. What we need are heroes.

To the extent that the ideological focus in the black women's groups is on a a fantasy future black family rather than on the gender tensions and problems of the families that exist, the figure of Anastácia has little symbolic utility. It is revealing that the other black women in the pantheon were in one way or another wives and mothers of the black race; Anastácia, in contrast, never joined with a black man, and she never had black children. To the extent that the image of Anastácia provides a vehicle for criticizing black men, for articulating the problem of domestic violence, or articulating current problems in the family, it is a distraction from the priority of forming a common front for valorizing masculine black power and reconstituting the black family around the figure of a strong, self-confident, breadwinning male.

FORGIVENESS AND HEALING

The myth of Anastácia, and above all its denoument in the slave saint's choice to heal her torturers' children embodies the Christian ethos of conciliation, forgiveness, and healing. It is therefore at odds with the political desire on the part of much of Brazil's black movement to instill the values and passions of righteous anger, resentment, self-defense, and the willingness to be confrontational. In a resounding counter to Anastácia, one activist embraced the vision of Fanon: "The man maimed so many slaves," he said. "Then he wants her help and she just gives it to him? Is that the only way the slave can be complete, by giving the white man what he wants? Blacks must take pride in healing themselves, not healing their oppressors. As long as we are more concerned about healing the master's children than ourselves, we will never be truly liberated."

This Fanonesque perspective is for many black activists all the more imperative in Brazil, which does not have a history of killing rage carving out a space of moral legitimacy for the struggle for racial justice. One activist explained:

> Especially here in Brazil, we cannot afford the loving, forgiving route. That has been the problem all along: we are supposed to be so cordial, and loving, and forgiving. Brazil is a Christian country. It is the country of the beer at the corner bar which is supposed to mend all fences, heal all wounds. But those things just leave the real causes of the wounds untouched. It is time for us to stop all the smiling.

A brief detour into the idea of black forgiveness toward whites in the United States draws a helpful comparison. In recent discussions of the possibility of forging "meaningful bonds of intimacy between blacks and whites,"[12] North American black writers have emphasized that the sentiment of forgiveness cannot be initiated on the black side unilaterally, cannot simply happen in order to satisfy white longing to be forgiven. If it happens at all (which many blacks do not regard as necessarily desirable or feasible), its precondition is for whites genuinely to recognize their own deep-seated racism and the privileges they derive from racist society and to join hands in the antiracist struggle. "It is imperative," writes Dalton, "that White folk accept joint ownership of America's race problem."[13] Certainly forgiveness, if it is to come at all, cannot come as a gratuitous act, carried out in the naive hope that it will have the redemptive effect of finally getting whites to change their racist ways.

If North American blacks are this deeply skeptical about forgiveness, one can imagine how problematic it seems to the Brazilian black activist, who faces a society in which the very legitimacy of his resentment has yet to be fully acknowledged. It is no wonder that activists in Brazil share what the political philosopher Peter Strawson has identified as the concern that moving too easily toward forgiveness conveys "that we do not take our rights very seriously."[14] Recall that Anastácia's master has in fact not repented of anything when he comes to her to heal his child: hers is a totally free, unconditional gift. Why then should Brazilian black activists turn to an icon whose life, at the moment of her death, realizes its meaning through such unconditionality?[15]

Once again, let us pause to listen more carefully to the moral and political significance of Anastácia's forgiveness for her devotees. Does the legend evoke in black devotees the self-debasement and morbid dependency that activists fear? Does it produce among white devotees feelings of unjustified transcendence of their own evil?

Black activists' concerns seem to be vindicated, partly, in the way white devotees think about Anastácia's forgivingness. In order to understand white devotees' feelings about Anastácia's grand gesture, we must realize that present in Brazilian popular political culture is a deeply rooted strain of white fear of black vengeance for having been chained and tortured under slavery. The common experience of being outnumbered by slaves, the legacy of the *quilombos*, the proximity to the Caribbean, the large size of plantations, the constant running away, the Bahian uprisings of the 1830s, the turmoil leading to the final ending of slavery—all of these historical forces produced a constant, powerful suspicion and anxiety on the part of whites that, given the chance, slaves would not hesitate to cut their throats, and that, once freed, they would use their powers, occult and otherwise, to wreak joyful vengeance upon the class that had so long made them suffer. In Brazil, the image of the docile slave, far less than in the United States, was an expression not so much of the everyday modes of social interaction as a fantasy designed to allay the ruling class's worst fears.[16]

The angry, resentful, vindictive slave is a presence in Brazilian literature, especially before the Freyrean myth of the affectionate Big House swept the image under the rug. Joaquim Macedo's 1873 novel *As vitimas-algozes* (The victim-executioners) explicitly invoked the memory of that quintessence of revenge, Haiti, and depicted slaves betraying and massacring the master's family.[17] Fagundes Varela's poem "Mauro, o escravo" (1864) portrays the slave who takes vengeance on his master, who has raped and killed his sister; and Castro Alves' poem "Bandido Negro" warns: "Grow, grow fierce vengeance."[18] The black maid, too, is seen as potentially dangerous, even at the very moment she is supposedly most engaged in taking care of the master. The character of the old slave woman in Cornelio Penna's *Dois romances de Nico Horta* (1939) is tyrannized by her masters but is able to balance the scales "during those violent illnesses that every so often toppled them from their altars. And then her vengenace knew no bounds, in a complicated web of cures."[19]

The echoes of nineteenth-century white fears of black resentment continue to reverberate today, just below the surface of cordiality. In 1988 on the occasion of the centennial of abolition, I had numerous conversations with poor and working-class whites in the urban periphery of Rio, in which they expressed serious fears that blacks should not be allowed to have access to jobs in authority over whites, "because they are still angry about slavery and will take it out on us."[20]

In this context, then, we can begin to understand the fuller import of Anastácia's loving, healing gesture: it stands in towering contrast to a tradition of fear. Anastácia's forgiveness is especially reassuring for middle-class white devotees because it reminds them of, and idealizes, their most comforting relationships with blacks. The sense of this came through to me as I was talking with Camila, a middle-aged white actress and devotee, about Anastácia's cure of the master's children. All of a sudden she remembered the elderly black woman who had lived with her family while she was growing up. She explained:

> In Minas Gerais, that was very common. To have a kind of "pet black" [*preto de estimação*] at home. She was not a servant; she was treated like a member of the family. And what I remember best about Dindinha was that she was the only one who would keep her cool, who would not get angry. She always kept control, would make biscuits for the rest of us, while everyone was yelling. This aspect of her, I believe this may

have influenced my interest in Anastácia. Today, with you, I am seeing for the first time that the figure of Dindinha—always happy, always calm, always helpful—that this figure may indeed have nourished my interest in Anastácia.

In language that mixed desire, fantasy, and precept, Camila said, "Thinking about Dindinha, the black has a certain humility. You know, our blacks here in Brazil are not like yours in the United States. There it seems all they can think of is anger and resentment and getting back for the centuries of slavery. But our blacks are not like that. Our blacks are not vindictive."

Here the image of Anastácia clearly permitted the division of the social world into the good, forgiving subjects ("our blacks" like Anastácia and Dindinha) who can ally themselves with whites in order to impose discipline on "bad," unforgiving black subjects. This relation of appropriating the power of good subjects to help control the bad is made explicit in many white requests for Anastácia's miracles. "The fact that she is not full of hatred toward whites is very important," says Luzia, "because I think by asking her she won't let her people, other *negros*, hurt or rob me. When I find myself in a public place, close to a *negro*, and I am feeling afraid, I say to her, in my mind: 'Oh, Anastácia, this is your brother, it is our brother, please hold on to him!' Because she can be a kind of intermediary to him, work on his mind, do something to make him not want to rob me." From the white point of view Anastácia's forgivingness can indeed serve the project of continued white domination.

All of this confirms black activists' worst fears, at least where whites are concerned. At the same time, we discovered that the image of Anastácia's forgivingness for some white devotees also makes possible new ways of thinking about race, racism, and their own prejudices. For some whites, asking Anastácia to intervene to protect them from other blacks brings their own attitudes to the surface, allowing them to be subjected to self-scrutiny. "When I ask Anastácia to protect me from her brothers," Luzia explained, "this is not subconscious; this is conscious on my part. It makes me stop and think: wow! That's really what I feel." In her case, at least, turning to Anastácia "made me more aware of my prejudice. After that episode with the white and black, I was filled with remorse. So I asked forgiveness from Anastácia, as my black friend. Because I saw that this was prejudice inside of me, latent." The outcome of this process has been a generally greater awareness, not only of others' racism, but of her own. "Being a devotee of Anastácia has made me more aware of the prejudice that I do have, because she sees it and I feel the need to see her forgiveness for this. I already knew about prejudice outside of me; what Anastácia did was to sensitize me to the prejudice that I have inside."

One of our most remarkable findings was that the episode at Anastácia's deathbed, when she cured the master's children, was regarded by a majority of our black female informants as the single most important detail of her life. "When she saved the master's children," said Aparecida, without hesitating. "That was the most important, because she put anger away. I wonder if I would ever be able to do that. That is what moved me most."

The importance conferred upon this narrative detail is, I believe, in part an expression of the power of the ideology of racial democracy to move psyches away from their immediate experience and get them to focus on distant or unreal fantasies and utopias. Anastácia is the model here of the ideal self-denying black woman, who pours her healing powers into the bodies of white men, assuring their health even as she dies. This ideal is, in part, what whites want black women to want of themselves.

At the same time, black women's willingness to take on this burdensome role model for themselves does not simply float; it must be sustained by already existing ideas, experiences, or longings. These are connected in agonistic, dialectical relation with the fabric of everyday life, partly reflecting it, partly transmuting and changing it through selective memory, even sometimes transcending it. Anastácia's act of love provides a space in which black women can articulate their experience of Brazilian social reality to themselves and others on all these planes simultanoeusly. Therein lies one of the keys to her symbolic power.

To begin with, for at least some black women, the episode of healing brought back memories of genuine, strongly felt emotions for the white children they had cared for when they had worked as maids. Chica, a tall black woman her sixties, is deeply aware of racism in Brazil, is committed to "valorizing the race," and observes the national day of black consciousness. And yet the part of Anastácia's story that was most important to her was when the slave saint cured the children. "I felt," she said, "my soul echoing with Anastácia's desire to do that." She went on: "We black women carry this knowledge inside of us. I breast-fed two white children. And I did that with great pleasure and satisfaction." She tried to describe the experience. "Because nursing really puts you close. Women know how this is: the closeness of the skin, skin contact, the smell, the warmth, you can't help but feel love for the child, pass your love to the child." This love, for Chica, was all the more poignant because of the racism of the surrounding society. "The white child," said Chica, "is seen by society as superior to you: but there, in your arms, that disappears. He is totally innocent, totally dependent. The parents may be terrible racists, but the children don't understand any of that. Being with them fills you with hope."

Chica then extrapolated this to the experience of slave wet nurses.

Some say that the slave who nursed the white child must have felt anger, for having been forced to do this and not feed her own children. Maybe. But there was something else, too. The wet nurse had love for those children. Their feelings for them were genuine. How can the woman feel hatred for the other race when she has passed her own milk, her own blood to the child?

"The sins of the parents are not the child's fault," she concluded, synthesizing personal experience with redemptive theology. "I really identified with Anastácia's love and hope for the children. They are the next generation. The adults may be too late. When you nurse a child, you are giving a transfusion of blood, it is like a Communion. Perhaps we can teach the next generation not to be racists like their parents." The woman who is reminded of intimacy with children is simultaneously reproducing the most limiting stereotype of the Freyrean racial democracy canon and remembering a genuine experience of intimacy, connection, and moral transcendence, in which she had insights into the possibilities of a future without racism.

This view of the political potentialities symbolized in the nursing relation, became manifest in at least one oral version of Anastácia I collected several years ago. In the Museum of the Negro, the image of Anastácia used to be affixed in close proximity to the sarcophagus of Princess Isabel, the so-called liberator of the slaves. In the version of Anastácia's story I heard from an elderly black devotee at the museum, the slave saint had been the nursemaid of Princess Isabel. "She fed her when she was a baby, right at the breast," this woman told me. "And that is why she freed the slaves." Through Anastácia's breasts flows the redemptive substance, the love of freedom, transmitted to the Great Liberator herself.

But there are obvious psychological limits to such forward-looking views. A far more immediate gratification from Anastácia's final act is its turning of the moral tables. "Anastácia refused," explained Car-

olina, a devotee in her fifties, "to become like her torturers. She wanted
to show them what true love is. She was better than they were. Much
better. So she became a saint and is now a model for us." In this sense
it embodies all the deepest impulses that gave Martin Luther King his
appeal among many sectors of the black Christian community. For
these black women, the power of the episode resided in Anastácia's
moral triumph over her enslavers and its undeniable proof that images
of black moral inferiority are falsehoods. Here the black woman can
simultaneously imagine a larger moral community while savoring
sweet moral victory. Gegê said:

> The most beautiful point in Anastácia's story is that she took care of the
> daughter. When I heard that, I recalled: they say my people, the *negros*,
> that we are bad. But look: if we were so bad, there would not be a sin-
> gle white person in Brazil! Who were, and who are, the midwives, the
> wet nurses, the babysitters? We, who are black women. And if we had
> been evil, we would have gotten rid of white children a long time ago.
> But we have never wanted to kill a white child, because we love life,
> and we loved that white child. Look at how good we are: knowing that
> that very life, of the white child, might end up killing her own children,
> might even kill her, sell her, torture her. But she would never destroy
> life. We were not made to be evil! Anyone who says this need only lis-
> ten to the story of Anastácia.

FROM PSYCHIC HEALING TO INSTITUTIONAL SOCIAL ACTION

I have already mentioned several types of social action more complex
than the individual and intrapsychic: dyadic relations with family members, the creation of informal conversation groups and friendship networks, and the establishment of black beauty salons. Here I want to
focus on yet another level of organization: the creation of future-ori-
ented institutions designed to influence the consciousness of the next
generation.

We met four of Anastácia's black devotees who were inspired—not
only by Anastácia's dignity and self-respect but also by what she represented about building a nonracist world through working with children—to create small, fledgling groups and semiformal institutions
designed to realize this goal.

Three of these were small literacy schools for local children, in which
Anastácia became present both in the school's name, her image, and in
some of the philosophy of the founders. When the local school would
not take the children of the squatter settlement in which she lived

"because we lived on the street," Aparecida resolved to found a literacy program and day-care center that would serve the needs of her neighbors' children. "I asked for a lot of strength from Anastácia when I wanted to start the school," she reported. The slave saint was very obliging, so much so that Aparecida, after a long year of struggle, could proudly inaugurate the "Informal School of Escrava Anastácia." Although it was no more than two cramped spaces underneath the elevated train track enclosed by wood and cardboard, the school succeeded during its five years of existence to provide several dozen children of the squatter settlement with basic literacy. "My goal," said Aparecida, "is to live out the ideal I learned from Anastácia: to love yourself, to love others, and to help them to love themselves."

Most of the children at Aparecida's school were black, and Aparecida thought of her initiative as, in practice, helping black kids. But she did not want the school to be color-exclusive. "I have kids here of all colors. Most are black, because this is where we live. But you can see that there are *moreninhos* and white kids too. I mean, it would be entirely against what Anastácia wants me to do to have this school be only for one group ar another."

The most elaborate organization to emerge from a devotion to the slave saint was shaped by the ideal of bringing children of all colors together to appreciate black history and culture. This was a group founded by Rivanilda, a dark-black devotee in her fifties who had some exposure to the black movement in the 1960s, but who now swears off any involvement with black activists. In 1988 Rivanilda established the "Associação Feminina Escrava Anastácia" (the Anastácia Feminine Association, recently renamed the Assocation for the Descendants of Africans in Brazil), in a poor, semirural district on the outskirts of Rio.

Rivanilda explained to me how her devotion to Anastácia inspired her to take up this work.

> I wanted to start something in her name, because she was a strong, resistant woman. Resistant to that barbaric slavery, to rape and everything. She refused to deliver herself into rape until the very end, she suffered for that until the very end. That is the suffering of the black woman, that suffering. She gave me that power to resist, to struggle, she passed a lot of that to me. To resist, to never stop, not give up: she has taught me that it's not because I am discriminated against that I should fall into depression. No, she was powerful, she endured serenely all that for the sake of her honor, her person. If it had not been for the example she gives me in this work, I would have given up a long time ago.

The group is structured around a series of free weekly traditional African dance and music classes for local children, designed to nurture love and respect for African and Afro-Brazilian culture. Rivanilda also organizes periodic "black beauty contests" for kids in the neighborhood, and teaches local children the rudiments of the Yoruba language.

On the basis of her work with local children, Rivanilda has drawn mothers into a series of bimonthly meetings dedicated to educate local women about health, reproductive, cultural, and political issues. I attended various all-day seminars at Rivanilda's home in Sepetiba, a small fishing town on the ocean, at which she led discussions on everything from plants and herbs to personal hygiene, abortion, and clothing. A key innovation in her thinking is that she urges women to bring their husbands along to these meetings. "How will women be able to solve their problems if men aren't part of the process too?" Rivanilda says.

The association, which currently has about twenty adult members and their children, is entirely independent of any larger Rio-based organization. As director of a local public school, Rivanilda has access to the school's xerox machine and typewriter, which she uses to produce a monthly newsletter, but beyond this she is hesitant to become too dependent on larger institutions. Although she constantly bemoans the reluctance of members to donate the money she needs to run the group, she is very reluctant to seek outside help or funding. "The instant any other group starts giving you money," she said, "they will want to take over and control you."

She also has little use for the black movement or black activists. "They talk and talk but do nothing," she said. "They are all speeches and 'We must do this to transform Brazil this way, and we must do that to transform Brazil that way.' I've heard it all before. And they say blacks first, right or wrong. I say no: I say blacks along with whites and all the rest, we need to build things from the bottom up together, not separately."

CONCLUSION

I hope to have persuaded the reader that while some of the opinions black activists hold about the incompatibility of the devotion to Anastácia with the development of a strong, self-affirming, antiracist black identity are entirely accurate, many of them are less so, and correspond mainly to the views and behavior of white and *morena* devotees, rather than those of *preta*s and *negra*s. If anything, the portrait that emerges here is of a system of symbol, myth, and practice that contributes in various ways to the development of a stronger, more self-valorizing, and in some ways more critical black consciousness.

But if this portrait has any claim to accuracy, what to do with it? Are there any implications here for practice?

No and yes. First, it is still crucial to reflect critically about the nature of a religious system that, while bringing people of all color self-identifications together, has rather different impacts on each groups' racial attitudes and identities (and, of course, on their individual attitudes and identities as well). The black devotees who come to feel more self-confident as black women through their devotion to Anastácia continue to share her and to interact with other devotees for whom she has had no impact; indeed, as I have documented, for some, she has actually deepened and reinforced racist stereotypes. Does this imply that those concerned with black consciousness should therefore wash their hands of her?

Perhaps; but then again, if the kinds of everyday impact on black women's lives are any indication, the fact of coexisting alongside whites and *morena*s with strongly contrasting views from theirs is in no way an insurmountable barrier to putting into practice new levels of consciousness. These forms of practice, in their physical separation from the actual shrines of the slave saint, suggest that it is likely that Anastácia's self-identified religious centers are not the most suitable organizational level for the articulation of race/gender issues.

But what would be the purpose of anyone other than an Anastácia devotee trying to articulate race/gender issues in conversation with a devotee? Isn't this perilously close to political instrumentalism, the simple effort of political groups to seize upon and co-opt for their purposes already existing networks of people?

That is not my idea at all. The point is not to seek out devotees and try to recruit them, and far less to visit networks and groups and try to co-opt them. The point is, above all, to become aware of what the devotees of Anastácia say, believe, and do. The question is: Has relating intensely to the spirit of a tortured black slave generated ideas and experiences capable of stimulating people concerned about racism in Brazil to deeper and more critical reflection? How might hearing more from devotees, whether individually or in groups, deepen and enrich a common fund of critical consciousness about race and racism in Brazil?

To what extent, for instance, might black devotees' feelings of indifference about claims that Anastácia was of royal blood push activists to think more deeply about their general notion that royalism is a crucial ideological element in building popular black consciousness in Brazil? (This can be seen, for example, in the movement's insistence on Zumbi's royalty, on the fascination with African royalty, and so on). To what extent might the devotion's response to black devotees' concerns about rape and the defense against sexual violence encourage reflection on the need to articulate these issues more openly within the black movement? To what extent might the lessons that Rivanilda draws from her devotion—that men need to be included with women in consciousness-raising efforts—be submitted to discussion and scrutiny by black women activists?

And to what extent might Anastácia's admittedly hard-to-swallow example of racial conciliation challenge activists at least to reflect on the tense dialectic between moral exclusion and moral triumph, and invigorate a more plural, less dogmatic engagement with popular culture? Might such an engagement, for example, deepen a critique of the ideological rejection of Christianity and privileging of *candomblé* as the proper vehicle for black identity? Most generally, to what extent might increased awareness of the ideological doubleness present in this sphere of popular black consciousness—its simultaneous expression of a longing for the universal, while also making possible the affirmation of the ethnically specific—provoke a deeper engagement with this doubleness as a widespread ideological reality of Brazilian blacks?

At the same time, to what extent might activists be of greater benefit to devotees than they are now? To what extent might, for example, Rivanilda's preoccupations about control feed into a more supportive but also more self-critical and more democratic relationship between groups like Criola and Rivanilda's? If Rivanilda were invited to share her insights and practices at various meetings, what new ideas might she herself receive and take home? To what extent, for example, might she become more aware of similar initiatives elsewhere, whose experiences could be of direct benefit to her? To what extent would her own local practice become richer and fuller of energy if she became more cognizant of black women's struggles elsewhere?

These are just questions, of course. The point here is not to prescribe answers. In the conclusion, I will explore some of my own small tentative attempts at intervention in this regard. The first step, as Anastácia has taught us, is to use our eyes.

SIX

The Politics of Ethnography

Translating Knowledge Claims into Practice

ETHNOGRAPHIC PRAXIS AND SOCIAL MOVEMENT GROUPS

This book has been an effort to convey what I learned about patterns of spiritual and social belief and action among nonwhite women in Rio de Janeiro. Is there anything to do with claims about patterns other than write a book about them?

The anxieties of anthropologists around the utility of their work remains a constant feature of their identity. Each generation of anthropologists since World War II has criticized the one that came before for not being political enough, and produces new calls for the discipline to put its ethical house in order and commit itself anew to a "reinvented anthropology,"[1] an "advocacy" anthropology,[2] an anthropology of "collaboration,"[3] an "anthropology of liberation,"[4] a "re-imagined anthropology,"[5] an anthropology of "transformation,"[6] and, most recently, a "committed and barefoot" anthropology.[7]

Yet for all its urgency, the practical, everyday mechanisms by which anthropological knowledge might be made to contribute to liberation remains unanalyzed. What is needed is reflection on the various ways "utility" can be defined: by whom and for whom it is defined; how "useful" anthropological knowledge claims come to be generated; and the range of contexts and channels through which any such claims come to be presented, scrutinized, and acted upon by the people for whom they are supposed to be useful.

I suggest that a social movement group can benefit from ethnographic work that strives to represent the movement to itself. Ethnographic knowledge claims become one voice in helping to refine debates and self-critiques within a social movement. Ethnography, I believe, can help activists develop a broader awareness that the people in targeted constituencies who continue to remain indifferent to the movement cannot be dismissed as simply "alienated," but rather must be regarded as having complex forms of consciousness that include some of the very ideological elements activists are hoping to bring about.[8]

Anthropologists seeking to make their knowledge claims useful have adopted a variety of approaches,[9] of which one of the more democratic is that of participatory action research. The approach is supposed to include "an ongoing conversation between activist community members ... and anthropologists with a long-term commitment to local community collaboration."[10] The problem with this approach however, is that it calls upon the researcher to assume that "activist community members" are usually the carriers of the best or fullest understanding of the problems the group faces. Barger and Reza, for example, make it a point of honor to assume that local activists "are in the best position to determine what is good for their own group," and that the community action group "knows best what rights and conditions are needed" by its constituency.[11]

While this assumption may be fair in many cases, to accept it uncritically requires downplaying the fact that a social movement group exists in practice alongside other groups, networks, and individuals who, while they are part of the population served or benefited by the organization, often have ideas and life experiences that differ from those the organization is seeking to articulate and emphasize. My point is simple: we must take methodological care to include these groups, networks, and individuals in our description and analysis, lest we perpetuate the idea that they have nothing of value to add to the views articulated by the social movement organization.

It is precisely this idea, I believe, that makes much recent writing about praxis and anthropology problematic. While this writing has much to say about the necessity of taking sides in conflicts between the social movements of the disempowered and the powerful institutions that are their adversaries,[12] it has less to say about what, if any, side to take when members of a social movement group remain uninterested in listening to people in their targeted constituency who say things they don't want to hear. What is one to do, for example, with testimony from someone who is supposed to feel aggrieved but does not, at least not very intensely? Does one put such testimony quietly in the drawer? Is it testimony that one duly acknowledges but hastens to call "exceptional"? Or is it testimony that maybe, just maybe, challenges us to reconsider some of our own presuppositions?

The dilemmas posed by these questions are exemplified in Anglin's work (1997). In the 1980s, Anglin carried out a project in connection with NORCAL, a New England group striving to redress, against an insensitive biomedical establishment, the grievances of women with breast cancer. The initial statement of the research agenda came from the chair of NORCAL's research committee. "Based on her activities as recording secretary for NORCAL and as a breast cancer activist in northern California," Anglin reports, "she presented the work of the committee as documenting the fact that women were receiving negligent care from their physicians."

Anglin, however, had engaged in preliminary conversations with prospective informants and was already starting to hear from some of them stories about entirely satisfactory encounters with the medical profession. Other informants had been initially frustrated and then had figured out how to extract from the profession what they needed. Still others had had disastrous experiences. This kind of variation began to convince Anglin that perhaps the most useful thing her research could accomplish was not to offer direct evidence to the antiphysician battle, but rather to help educate women and doctors about what worked in the system and what did not. In order to achieve this goal, Anglin had to insist that the sample of women surveyed be expanded beyond the membership of NORCAL, to include women with no involvement or even knowledge of the organization. This shift transformed the goal of the project "from documenting examples of physician negligence to assessing the range of women's experiences and the type/frequency of problems they encountered with both diagnosis and treatment." No longer just a way to attack the medical establishment, the project became a way to "to educate women as potential patients on how to negotiate the medical system so as to receive better and more timely care."[13] However, the project did not get very far, because the director of NORCAL was less interested in hearing a range of experiences than in registering those that could specifically strengthen the antiphysician struggle.

The failure of Anglin's study to get off the ground points to a key challenge in making ethnographic knowledge useful to activists. Activists, understandably, regard such utility as long-term at best, or, at worst, a distraction from the immediate need to act against the enemies of justice. In the context of such sentiments, Anglin might have engaged the director of NORCAL in conversations about the specific ways, both short- and long-term, that research such as hers might have contributed to the organization's larger goals of protecting women's health.

What kinds of things can I as an anthropologist say about anything like this?

What follows is a report on several of the paths I traveled in my effort to make ethnographic knowledge claims of practical interest to activists in the black movement. I do not claim that these approaches are the best I could have adopted, and certainly not that they are exhaustive. They were, rather, opportunities seized upon. My aim in discussing them is not to suggest a recipe for intervention, but to stimulate others to become more self-conscious about the concrete contexts in which they strive to turn knowledge into practice.

I came to believe that the knowledge claims generated by my project had two main potential uses in relation to the antiracist struggle in Brazil. First, some of my findings, I thought, might help erode activists' stereotypes about people and groups in their targeted constituency who remained aloof from the movement. And second, some of my conclusions might help bring to activists' attention important gaps between their rhetoric and the feelings and attitudes of at least some of the people in their targeted constituency.

I tried to introduce these views into the political process in three different ways. First, I brought my observations to the attention of key social movement actors and leaders, both individually in long conversations and collectively in group presentations. Second, I sought at several points to place activists into contact with non-movement individuals and groups whom they had traditionally avoided, but with whom, I believed, they shared surprisingly extensive ideological ground. And third, my research process positioned me to facilitate the building of small networks among non-movement individuals who shared similar political views.

At every step of the way, I was aware that the willingness of a leader to listen to my findings had much to do with her prior dispositions. When what I had to say strengthened a view already held, it was given a warmer reception. When the ideological barriers were too high, what I had to say was given little credence. These were not, however, hermetically sealed processes. They were accidented and fractured, in the sense that opening up space on one front sometimes had repercussions on others as well.

Eroding Stereotypes about Nonparticipants

Isabel is the cultural director at Criola, the largest black women's consciousness organization in Rio de Janeiro. She is in her forties, a veteran of twenty years of activism, and wears her hair in an impressive mane of braids. As cultural director, her job is to strengthen connections with autonomous cultural groups throughout the city. When I met her at an event in downtown Rio, I asked her what cultural groups she had contacted. "You know," she replied, "reggae-samba bands, grassroots groups, *terreiros* of *candomblé*." I asked her if she had considered outreach to any of the Anastácia temples. She smiled wryly. "Why? That is not my bailiwick." Nor had she taken any initiative to speak to black women in Protestant churches, least of all the pentecostal ones. When I mentioned that my research team and I had been unearthing patterns of ideas among these groups that might be of interest to her, she showed interest, and invited me to come by the headquarters of Criola for a more in-depth discussion.

When I visited Criola's offices the following week, we sat in the anteroom, while a cool afternoon breeze entered through the southern window. We were on the fourteenth floor of a building in downtown Rio and through the window I could see the cobalt blue of Guanabara Bay. We sat amid the appurtenances of the black movement: the chest-high wooden masks and shields from Nigeria, the small images of *orixás* perched on bookshelves, the walls plastered with recent and upcoming cultural events: a black beauty pageant, a march to Brasilia commemorating the 300th anniversary since Zumbi's death, a meeting on affirmative action, a panel on prostitution.

I decided to start with what I suspected would be the easier topic of conversation—Anastácia, rather than the pentecostals. "Let me begin with a question," I said. "When I saw you last, you said that the temples of Anastácia were not your bailiwick. What did you mean by that?" She replied:

"Well, neither we nor the movement as a whole spend much energy on Anastácia. I think it was only once that we did something about her: when Zózimo wrote a nasty article about that Banda Didá, saying they should be handcuffed as well as face-masked. Criola sent an e-mail to Zózimo directly, complaining that this was an immoral and racist attitude to adopt. So when the image of Anastácia is attacked, we will come to her defense. Otherwise, we don't do much in relation to her."

"Why not?"

"Well, we have other heroines."

"Like who?"

"Well, like Dandara, for example."

"OK, right. Dandara. But let me push you on that, Isabel: if you asked a poor, working-class woman to recall the name of a historical slave, whom do you think she would say?"

Isabel thought for a moment. "Well, for me, the name that would come to her lips would be Dandara's."

"But Isabel, don't you think that is the name you would *like* to come to her lips?"

"Yes, I suppose so. Not many people really have heard of Dandara."

"What would be the name of the slave woman that most of them would recognize?"

"Hmmm," she said. "It's true that not many would recognize who Dandara was. We ourselves hardly know anything about her. But that is all the more reason to emphasize her, rather than Anastácia. We need to spread Dandara's name, not Anastácia's."

I felt her point.

"You know, John, the point of cultural work is not simply to say what people want to hear. We need to educate them about what they do not know. And they do not know about Dandara. Because Zumbi and Dandara are much better for inspiring political action than is Anastácia. They struggled for a whole people. Their struggle was political; Anastácia's was purely individual."

Isabel's point was sinking in. After all, what in the world was I suggesting? That just because Anastácia was more popular she should therefore be brought into the cultural work of the movement? No, that was not my intent. I was quiet for a moment and then tried again.

"Isabel, certainly it makes sense to teach people about Dandara, to the extent that you know about her. But doesn't it also make sense to learn from Anastácia's devotees what she means to them? You say that what is important is learning new things, and I believe there are things about the political meaning of Anastácia to her devotees about which you may be unaware."

Isabel smiled and said: "OK, I'm listening."

"First, at the individual level, it seems Anastácia helps some black women valorize their own natural beauty more. We have heard a number of women say this. And, I don't know if you realize this, but there are many black beauty salons around Rio that were inspired by her and are named after her."

Isabel was listening intently.

"We have also heard cases of black women who feel that the example Anastácia set is important for them. Her example is to stand up and fight back against domestic abuse and rape. In one story, a woman told us that the example of Anastácia had given her the courage to say 'no' to her abusive husband."

"Really? That is interesting." Her tone was flat.

"We also found that lots of black women take pride in Anastácia's power to say 'no' to the master's sexual assault. And that they take pride in her having forgiven him in the end, as a kind of moral triumph over him. We have learned other things too. We found instances of women who, inspired by Anastácia, have done things like starting a consciousness-raising group for black women, and literacy programs and schools for kids in the *favela*."

"You found that? Well, that is important to know about."

But Isabel was resistant. She was seeking some other reason for objecting to Anastácia. "Everything you say may be true," she said, "but basically I cannot accept Anastácia as a vehicle for black consciousness. It must be the fact that she is so close to the Catholic Church. We just cannot accept that."

"But the Catholic Church has rejected her," I reminded her. "Shouldn't Criola take greater interest in a popular practice that people are carrying on against the official policy of the Church?"

"Perhaps," she replied. "Perhaps. Well, I have to say: I have never had a chance to discuss Anastácia like this before." I offered to show her a copy of a paper I had on Anastácia, and she took it.

Up to this point, Isabel had been quite tolerant of the ideas I was presenting to her. She became rather more skeptical when the topic shifted to the pentecostals.

"I also wanted to talk a bit about the *crentes* with you," I began. Isabel tensed visibly. I pressed on. "Because it seems to me that it is hard to ignore them nowadays. In terms of the numbers of black women, certainly the *crente* churches are among the most popular."

She agreed with this, but wrinkled her nose. "Yes, it is a shame. It is a terrible loss to us."

"But that is exactly what I want to raise a question about with you. Because . . ."

"Well, I know there are some efforts in the Methodist Church, which we support. But overall, we feel that the person who has become a *crente* is falling away from their true identity. They are running away from African culture, which the Protestants say is the devil. How can we accept that?"

"Of course you can't. But that is not the only thing that is happening among them about the black question."

She was hardly listening. The reasons for her antipathy started to tumble out.

"First of all," Isabel insisted, "these women put everything into the hands of Jesus, and then they wash their hands of everything. They are passive before the problems of the world, they just say 'Let us pray.' They are so dogmatic, so puritanical about sexual matters, that they will refuse to sit through a discussion about them. How can you work with that? And what is more, they say you don't need to fight racism because all you have to do is become a *crente* and the problem is solved. So I have to say, I haven't had much to do with them."

"OK, OK," I said, "I don't deny any of it, it all captures something very real about the *crentes*. But let me ask you something: What do you make of the fact that Benedita da Silva is a *crente*?"

Isabel rolled her eyes.

"Her case, yes, it is a puzzle. But I believe it is entirely unique. She is the exception. And I must say, I always avoid talking about religion with her. Out of respect for her. Because if I started in on the *crentes*, there'd be no end of it. I don't understand how she can reconcile her involvement in the movement with her Protestantism."

"Well, in our interviews with black women who are pentecostals, we have found that perhaps Benedita's identity as a *crente* may not be so strange after all. We found several interesting patterns. First, lots of women say that becoming a *crente* allowed them to question the European aesthetic values which they grew up with. That they were finally able to valorize the beauty that God gave them. Others said that being a *crente* no longer permitted them to lie to themselves about their identity, that they had to take pride in the person God had made them, as black. Enough of pretending to be *morena* or *marrom bom-bom*."

She had started to listen.

"In fact, because many of the boys of the church learn to look beyond color, black girls in church are able to marry lighter boys far more frequently inside the church than out. So you see . . ."

I had, from Isabel's point of view, said the wrong thing.

"There, you see? All they want to do is become white, to marry whites and lighten the line."

I tried to protest. "No, no, from their point of view, as I understand it, there is more at stake than that. They don't want to be white, they want to have the same choices and freedom as white girls."

Isabel was sitting quietly. She mulled this over.

"Well, this may be true, too. But I'm not sure what we are supposed to do about it. If these women are thinking these things, let them think them. That's good for them. Do you think we have a role in going in there? There's no way! They would never open their doors to us, and they have trouble adapting to our environment."

"Of course, that certainly is a problem. I'd be the last to suggest that you try to go to a pentecostal church with your message. The important thing for now may just be for you to know that such things are possible and are occurring. That maybe if you or others were more aware of these things—you know, that maybe even in one-on-one contacts there might be more possibility for discussion and . . ."

Isabel looked skeptical, but nodded diplomatically.

"OK, John, I have to say I'm not sure about this part. The points about Anastácia are more convincing to me. Maybe I'm just too biased against the *crentes*. But please do give me what you have about them too, and I will read it."

I encountered rather more openness to the idea of conscious black pentecostalism among Christians. I had numerous contacts, for example, with Olimpio Sant'Anna and Gerson Martins, the principal leaders of the Methodist Ministry to Combat Racism. They listened carefully, read the work I gave them, and even took steps to make my work available to a larger Methodist audience. "We have long believed," said Olimpio, "that the future of this question inevitably will pass through the pentecostals. And now you have given us something we can show to prove it." As I left the field, Olimpio told me he planned to place the issue of pentecostalism high on the agenda of the Ministry to Combat Racism in the year ahead.

I also received a receptive individual hearing about the pentecostals from Frei David. Although he was critical of the Protestants for their rejection of Afro-religiosity, his own identity was not fundamentally threatened by the Protestant stance. Certainly for someone concerned about reaching the masses, the idea that the *crentes* were not quite so irredeemable as he had believed was of interest. He photocopied my paper on the pentecostals and made it available to pastoral agents.

If someone of Isabel's convictions had been so resistant in private to the idea of linking pentecostalism to black identity, it should come as no surprise that this resistance became more dogmatic whenever I spoke of this linkage to groups with black activists present. I remember talking about the issue to a group of young black activists and sympathizers in Rocinha, a large *favela*, at a meeting of the vestibular preparation course. My comments about the *crentes* were met with icy stares and much fidgeting. Only one young man saw fit to ask a question.

"Are you saying that you think there is potential among the *crentes* to work in solidarity with the movement against racism?"

"Yes, I suppose I am saying that."

"Then you don't understand Brazilian reality," he said. Many in the group nodded approvingly. "You have been here only for a short time. The truth is that the *crentes* will always be dead set against us, against our movement, against our religion and culture. Because they want one thing only: to be white."

I spent several minutes describing counterexamples, but it soon became clear that any such evidence would do little to dissuade my collective interlocutors. When I had finished, the same person who had addressed me before said, "You have understood incorrectly. There is no way you could have understood what you saw. Or if you heard anything at all like that, it was the exception." Someone else finally chimed in, "What are you doing here anyway, doing this kind of research? What is your interest? Do you work for the *crentes*?"

I assured them that I did not, but the damage had been done. In a one-on-one conversation, Isabel had been willing, at least, to entertain what I had to say as a possibility; in the public group, this kind of flexibility was all but gone.

In another situation, however, I intervened more directly and put people into contact across the divide between the black movement and the pentecostal church. The contacts I had found in São Paulo between the *Quilombo* Mission and São Paulo's black movements had suggested to me that the agenda of combating racism could indeed create an incentive for dialogue. Of even greater potential, I thought, was the ideological convergence between interested pentecostals and those in the few groups on the fringes of the orthodox black movement who, in the past few years, have come to emphasize Afro-religiosity less and Brazilianness more, such as the Afro-Reggae Cultural Group (GCAR). This group is dedicated to helping the youth of Rio's *favelas* find in popular black and Brazilian music and culture an alternative to narcotraffic.[14] Officially, the director of GCAR declares that his organization is not the black movement. Yet there can be no doubt about the group's various connections to IPCN, CEAP, and Criola. Precisely because it has no strong stake in Afro-religion, I reasoned, GCAR could serve as a bridge between Rio's black movements and at least some of the city's black pentecostals.

A promising point of contact here seemed to be music itself. Since the mid-1980s, many pentecostal churches have opened their doors to various nontraditional musics, including many that are typically considered "black," such as reggae, samba, pagode, rap, and hip-hop. While the objective is obviously to gain more souls for Christ, some of the young evangelical blacks who have started to play these rhythms are discovering through them new sources of pride. In an Assembly of God church in the suburb of Abolição, blacks sing American soul music with great gusto, and say they are drawn to it "because it is in our blood, our black blood." In Niteroi, a pentecostal church has generated the group called the Chosen Race (*A Raça Eleita*), which plays reggae, samba, and pagode. "Of course," one of the musicians told me, "this music comes from our blood. We have that from birth."

The GCAR has until recently kept its distance from evangelical reggae, rap, and soul because of the assumption that these efforts were little more than a strategy to gain converts. The GCAR has therefore remained uninformed about groups such as Chosen Race or Grato Soul, in which young evangelical blacks are making incipient connections between music and black identity.

I got to know the current director of GCAR quite well, and told him what I was learning about the various Protestant musical groups in the area. He expressed an interest in learning more about such new groups and in opening up space in the GCAR's monthly publication (a newspaper with a circulation of twelve thousand nationwide) to articles dealing with black evangelical music. So I wrote an article, along with photographs, for publication in the newsletter. Since leaving Brazil, I have received news that GCAR has pursued various new groups like this and is opening up a periodic column on evangelical black music.

It is still too soon to tell where such a step might lead. There are numerous practical and ideological obstacles in the path of collaboration between black pentecostals and the black movement. Still, it may be possible at least to pose the question: Could points of connection such as the one between Grato Soul and GCAR embody sufficient ideological convergence—black identity, Brazilianness, hostility to narcotraffic, commitment to youth, love of music—to write a new chapter in the still-evolving history of Brazil's black consciousness movement?

Gaps Between Rhetorics and Constituencies

The second principal way I hoped my findings might be relevant to activists was in reporting the patterned testimony of people in the movement's targeted constituency who on the one hand held views and engaged in actions very much in line with movement goals, but who on the other hand felt strongly put off, alienated, or marginalized by one or another aspect of movement rhetoric or practice. It seemed to me that becoming aware of such people and their reservations about the movement could be useful to activists. Could activists learn from such people? Might their criticisms create opportunities for reflection and self-critique?

I will focus here on two movement ideas that produced particularly negative reactions among people who otherwise felt positively about movement goals. The "conscious" black must first feel a deep-down preference for things "African," especially drums and percussive instruments, and second, must feel that his African ancestry is intrinsically more self-defining than ancestry from any other source. I have already discussed these issues in this book; I now want to share how I tried to bring them to the attention of movement leaders, and how the leaders responded.

When I told Frei David that several self-identified blacks, including a *candomblecista*, had expressed the longing for more quiet during the Mass, he began by reiterating, once again, the official position: "In Africa," he said, "in authentic African rituals, what is the strongest moment, equivalent to the bread and wine? The moment of receiving the energies of the ancestors. Or the spirits. What is the posture that the religious men require of the people in that moment? Maximum beating of the drum. Profuse and profound dancing. Incorporation by the spirits and falling to the ground."

"So," I replied, "what would you say to the black person who assumed her negritude, but who said that she still liked a moment of silence? I spoke to several people who strongly identified themselves as blacks, recognized that Brazil is a racist society, and were committed to battling racism. But they still said they felt uncomfortable with the constant thrum of drums throughout the Mass. Do you think such people are denying their heritage? Their race?"

Frei David stopped and looked at me. He looked down and shut his eyes, and thought for a moment. Then his eyes met mine again.

"If such people say that they only like silence, and do not like drumming at all, then I would be concerned about their negritude, yes."

"But that is not what they are saying. At least not to me. They are saying that they wonder whether there might be something universal in the desire to have at least some moments of quiet during the Mass, to connect spiritually to God. And they wonder whether in Africa there are no cultures which also value at least some quiet."

"Well," David replied, "I don't know of any, but it is a very interesting, very sincere issue. That is one to think about. And as you spoke, I began to think of something. Because, you know, I personally need, every day, to have moments of silence. And I make sure that, every day, I get these moments, when I meditate, and lie down in my bed, close my eyes, and indescribable images play before me. Of light, energy, points of light. Have you ever had this experience? It is an amazing, amazing, amazing mystical experience. And when this ends, I open my eyes and I am in a very wonderful spiritual state."

He looked at me again, and smiled. "So, yes. What am I saying? I mean to say the following: there are many, many different methods for a person to make contact with the spiritual force that God has in him and that he has in God. I am not privileging one. All the meditative methods, when they are authentically human, they bring us to God. All the methods of meditation. Extroverted or introverted, when they are authentically human, and when assumed with authenticity, they carry us closer to God."

There had been a tangible shift in Frei David's language. Until this exchange, whenever he had used the word "authenticity," it was in reference to ethnic authenticity, to the expression of a group-bound value. Yet here we had entered a new terrain of "human authenticity." Frei David proceeded to the next logical step.

"I confess that this issue needs closer examination. I need more information to really come to a conclusion about this. I don't have a neat response for you on this. I confess I'm a bit afraid of this one. But I'll say this: I really don't want to say that the only place the *negro* can find himself mystically with God is in the inculturated Mass. I am sure that there will be *negros* who find a deep connection with God through the traditional European Mass. As for whether African culture also has moments of silence and concentration: I confess, this is a great plate to be researched."

We ended the conversation with Frei David in an animated mood. He asked that I transcribe the interview for him right away, because, he said, "there are issues here that I have never really thought about before and would like to think about some more."

My interviews with the few people who identified themselves as *mestiço* had suggested to me the possibility that the activist's insistence that nonwhites take on a monolithic, undivided black identity might be failing to mobilize people who otherwise might be mobilized into the antiracist struggle.

I knew Daniela, a thirtiesh leader at CEAP, quite well. We had spent a good deal of time together over the years, and had a warm, easygoing friendship. I had met her in 1988; at that time, she was very active in the MNU in Duque de Caxias, where I was working on my dissertation. Because of this friendship, I felt I could dare to tread on one of the most tender of all issues in the black movement: defining who is black.

So I raised with Daniela my finding that there existed people proud of their black ancestry, and ready to lend energy, ideas, and time to the antiracist struggle, but who felt that the undivided identity of *"negro"* did not correspond to their own social experience. I also reported my finding that there were other, similar, people who—while identifying themselves as *"negros"*— still felt uncomfortable with the label, and not from lack of pride in their *negro* ancestors but because they felt the term denied and glossed over the other facets of their identity.

I turned this report of findings into a direct question: "What would be wrong," I asked, "to say that those people who felt moved to do so should call themselves '*negro*', but that others who wished to enter the antiracist struggle but who felt that their life experience and identity did not correspond to the label *negro* could simply state that they valued their blackness and slave ancestry, but that their more diverse inheritance led them to regard themselves as, say, *mestiços*?" I pointed to several important examples of this trend, including the leader of the Grupo Cultural Afro-Reggae, and the singer Carlinhos Brown, both of whom are people who enjoy high standing with the movement.

Daniela at first resisted the idea. She immediately launched into a historical diatribe about how miscegenation had been a strategy of the white ruling class to divide blacks from each other, how nowadays light-skinned blacks might like to think they were better off than dark-skinned ones, but that they were not.

At the same time, she noted some events that complicated her own response. First, she had been present, she said, at a discussion about affirmative action at which a white professor had raised the question about who was *"negro,"* and said she knew there was growing sentiment among *mestiços* that they resented being grouped in a way that denied their specific experience. The woman, Daniela told me, was denounced wildly and silenced.

"It may be possible some time in the future," she said, "to talk about such things in public, but we are not there yet."

With me, she said, she was willing to broach the subject thoughtfully, but she made it clear that in public she might avoid or even speak against the very things she was allowing—between us—might be legitimate. For now, she said, such talk in public would simply play into the hands of those who would divide the movement. She gave as an example a debate she had witnessed between a light- and dark-skinned person, a debate that broke down when the latter had finally hurled at the former the epithet: *"filha de estupro"* (daughter of rape).

I responded to Daniela in two ways. First, I suggested tentatively, the question of timing—whether now or in the future—might be neither absolute nor objective. For the question about when it might be raised: Who had the authority to make such judgments about timing and impose them on others? For whom was it "not the right time"? Perhaps it was the right time for some and not others? The second question was: If not now, when? For twenty years or more the black movements had, I suggested, been avoiding open discussion of alternatives to the homogeneous *"negro"* identity.

"Look," I said, "I know it's not my place to comment on this. I am just giving my opinion. But it seems to me that open discussion of this issue might build the tools necessary to help avoid precisely the kind of rupture you described in that meeting. Have you considered that without open discussion of this issue, the black movements might in fact be playing into the hands of the white ruling elites? Because if someone who *could* participate feels alienated, is this not weakening the movement? Who knows: if the movement could accommodate a range of legitimate self-identities, of people who could work together to combat racism, this would represent a break with the divide-and-conquer strategy of the whites."

"Well, let me respond," said Daniela. "What you are saying is not entirely new to me. I see this happening in various places. In my own work, I make sure to emphasize that what I support is an Afro-Brazilian identity, not an exclusively *negro* one. The point is to value your African and slave heritage, not necessarily to be totally this."

"Yes," I replied, "I recognize that. But let me stick my neck out here: Why is it necessary even to require this much? Why not make *negro* and *afro-brasileiro* available alongside *mestiço* as well? Because *afro-brasileiro* already assumes that the person would have to identify the "Afro" part as the most important part of their identity. Right? And what if what was important to the person were not that the "Afro" predominate, but that it simply be valorized? Certainly a key struggle, as you have long pointed out to me, is to get people who deny any slave ancestry to acknowledge and take pride in it. But that is different from requiring that they turn such recognition into the claim that this predominate in their lives. What about people like Junior, the director of GCAR, or like Carlinhos Brown, who personally value their blackness but continue to identify themselves as *mestiço*? Sometimes, as with

Junior, these are people with more commitment to the valorization of blackness and the antiracist struggle than many people who call themselves '*negros.*'"

"But John, after all, this is a movement about identity. And who ever heard of a mixed identity? If that's what they want, then they should start their own movement."

"But Daniela, do you mean they don't have enough in common with you to fight alongside you? Are you saying you would be unwilling to fight alongside the likes of Junior? Aren't you slipping into the trap that whites want you to slip into?"

"Maybe, maybe. OK, you've made your point. Let me think about this one."

Connections and Networks

Up to this point, I have been describing interventions in which my main objective was to plant a bee in the bonnet of activist leaders. These interventions depended on my privileged access to these leaders, and they depended for any value they might have on the ongoing involvement of these leaders in articulating issues within their own circles and networks. But I also tried to intervene not in relation to activist leaders, but in relation to the pentecostal men and women we had gotten to know, who expressed strong views about their black identities and antiracism, but who neither knew each other nor had had much exposure to the black movement. These people held in common a feeling of frustration about not having any space within their churches to articulate their views. They were quite unaware that other *crentes* had similar views that they too had difficulty articulating publicly.

To the extent that these people had something important in common, and to the extent that it was still impossible for them to become engaged in the black movement, it struck me as desirable to invite them to meet each other and talk. It seemed to me that if indeed these *crentes'* views were as strong as they appeared, they ought to be able to develop and maintain a network around the identity of black pentecostalism. Although there had been no public articulation of a black pentecostal identity in Rio, I knew that small groups had formed in São Paulo that were in fact striving to articulate just such an identity. In particular, I had come to know the *Missões Quilombo* of São Paulo, and I invited the leader of this group, Hernani, to come to Rio and chair a meeting of the various black pentecostals we had come to know.

I had developed rather strong relations with Hernani. I had visited him in São Paulo several times and knew his work well, and had come to São Paulo, at his invitation, to speak to the Organization of Brazilian Lawyers about affirmative action in the United States. Hernani was using an article I had written about black pentecostals as a discussion pamphlet and he asked me to serve on the board of directors of the Missões. When I asked him to come to Rio, he regarded the trip as part of his normal political work.

We ended up organizing two meetings of the group, one in September and one in November of 1996. Half a dozen people attended each meeting, which took place at a research institute in downtown Rio de Janeiro. Each meeting lasted about five hours. The point of the meetings was to help local black pentecostals interested in racial politics to become aware of each other's existence, to create a context in which they could network and exchange ideas, and to initiate the process of forming a group that might serve in the longer run as a source of ideas, comparative experiences, and support for pentecostals who wanted to work on the issue of color/race in their own churches.

These meetings and the group that emerged from them revealed, I think, one of the potentialities of ethnographic research in relation to social movements. As ethnographers, Marcia, Ruth, and I had entered into a wide range of intense, qualitatively rich, dyadic encounters through which it became clear that a particular constellation of beliefs that were not supposed to occur together not only did so but did so quite vibrantly. This was the ethnographic knowledge claim that became the justification for the meetings. The ethnographic process had served as a catalyst, bringing together people who otherwise might not have known about, much less believed in, each other's existence.

The shock of this coming together was clear at the first meeting, when one of the invitees, a *crente* of the Assembly of God who had been reluctant to come, was rendered speechless when he heard a presbyter of the Assembly of God speak of the need for pentecostal blacks to fight racism in their churches and in the larger society. "I was almost ready to leave the meeting," Sergio told me later, "but when I heard that, I thought, there really is something going on here." He ended up coming to the second meeting, despite a long commute, and has continued to participate in the group.

The meetings themselves led in a direction about which I had some reservations, but that ended up overwhelming the meetings and my articulated concerns. My feeling was that some kind of support group or submerged network was needed that would help sustain group members efforts within their respective congregations. These could include getting the pastor to acknowledge the theme of color as important and worthy of being treated in sermons; carving out some space on the subject in Sunday School meetings; obtaining the right to establish a discussion group on race and the Bible; or starting semi-autonomous discussion groups on this topic.

As the discussion in our group proceeded, however, it became clear that the issue of color/race was so taboo in church, and the battle to establish its legitimacy so uphill, that it was likely to lead to intense frustration before the battle was over. None of the participants was a full-fledged pastor and none of the participants felt they could manage these fights unless the way was blazed by a pastor. By the end of the second meeting, therefore, the group took the decision to start meeting not as a support group for initiatives taken elsewhere but as a fully autonomous group, perhaps even a new black pentecostal church, that would systematically deal with the issue of black identity and its connection to pentecostalism. When I left Brazil in December 1996, the group was planning a series of meetings to incorporate itself legally as a church.

CONCLUSION

The idea that guided me throughout these fairly haphazard interventions was that rather than any single standard legislating how researchers ought to go about translating knowledge claims into practice, it was preferable to participate in a wide range of efforts. The model of advocacy anthropology, in which the research agenda is set entirely by the activists, is important but should not be taken as exhaustive. To the extent that there are important issues that can only be addressed by gathering the widest possible range of political views, activists may be less than sufficiently detached, or perhaps unwilling to undertake this research themselves.

And yet it is of great importance to listen carefully to what activists have to say, and to seek their influence over the form and content of research. It should be possible to avoid the easy romanticization of "the people" while at the same time making the goals, ambitions, hopes, and fears of activists the main engine of a project. What are the types of issues that are best addressed in this way? Could it be, for example, that the kind of research that aims to produce information of clear short-term utility is best defined and even conducted by activists, but that research aiming to explore the understandings of nonmobilized people is best conducted by an outsider? I have no clear answers to these questions. I only suggest that they must continue to be asked.

CONCLUSION

An Agenda for the Ethnography of Social Movements

IMPLICATIONS FOR THE STUDY OF SOCIAL MOVEMENTS

The perspective I have adopted in this book has implications for several areas of reflection and criticism. First, the method of examining a social movement as a set of practices on a par with other practices within a cultural field has the advantage of approximating the point of view of people on the ground. Although a particular group activity may be understood from an academic perspective as a social movement, it is, more often than not, perceived by local people as but one of a number of concurrent, and by their lights, more or less coequal, activities occurring in the neighborhood. Grasping this phenomenological reality has positive consequences for the analysis of social movements. One of the chief aims of such analyses has been to trace the processes through which ways of thinking and living that contest socially dominant ones come into being, evolve, become influential, and move people to various kinds of social action. A problem has always been how to identify what counts as a social movement. While there have been a wide range of efforts to define the term,[1] in the absence of a fully satisfactory definition, the rule of thumb has been to focus on groups and organizations that have an explicit agenda for social change. This focus, in my view, leads to overemphasizing organizational behavior as an object of study rather than processes of change in consciousness and their concomitant forms of action. By choosing to focus on the self-identified social movement organization, the analyst in effect presumes or accepts the claim of the movement to be a privileged site in the contestation and change in social values.

The focus on the perspective from the street problematizes this claim, making it a hypothesis to be tested rather than assumed. From the point of view of the locale, people of various ages, ethnicities, classes, and genders encounter and move through a field of social activities—avoiding some, participating fervently in others, passing half-heartedly through yet others—any of which may have more or less impact on consciousness and the predisposition to act in concert with others to change society. By conceiving of the study of social movements as a study of such cultural fields, the observer avoids the trap of a priori assumptions about which cultural locus is actually the most promising harbinger of change.[2] To study a social movement, we need to place it alongside other social groups and activities that are not themselves organically linked to the social movement. We need to be able to see the possibility of people who choose to stay away from the social movement, in part because they find for themselves the same, or more of the same, rewards of evolving consciousness, resonance, and even social action, in *other* local groups and activities.

When we broaden our perspective this way, we are better able to avoid, for starters, the pitfall of interpreting a lack of participation as either freeloading, or false consciousness. It may very well be that the person who appears to be freeloading on all the good work of a social movement organization is actually busily engaged in various forms of informal culture-change work herself. Failure to recognize this makes much of the sociological writing on the "freeloader" problem ring a bit hollow and even a bit arrogant in its presumption, once again, that social movement organizational action is the only, or best, social change game in town.[3]

The perspective I am suggesting also helps us to avoid the teleological view that social phenomena such as informal networks are only relevant to social change to the extent that they provide the recruiting ground, or "micromobilizational context" for self-conscious social movement organizations.[4] This is, in my view, a limited way of conceptualizing the potential social influence of such phenomena as networks, religious groups, and so on. While such phenomena may indeed create a pool of people predisposed to participate in social movement organizations, their social effectiveness should not be reduced to the creation of such pools. Religious groups and informal networks also create pools of people predisposed to act upon the world, but *away* from social movement organizations.

Again, if we insist on privileging social movement organizations, we miss this field of social action. It remains an open question and one that calls for careful analysis and debate, whether, for example, women's participation in pentecostal churches in Latin America represent on its own a more effective challenge to patriarchy than the effort of Latin American women to organize themselves into groups expressly with this as a goal.[5] It is also an open question whether, say, interracial friendships generated by common church attendance represents more or less social change than efforts to build a particular coalition of social movement groups across the racial divide. I am in no way suggesting that non-movement groups can or should substitute for and replace social movement organizations and mobilization. What I am suggesting is that until we recognize that the question of actual social impact and effectiveness are empirical rather than ideological or theoretical, we will continue to blind ourselves to the multiple sites and tracks through which cultures can and do change.

IMPLICATIONS FOR INTERPRETING THE POLITICS OF CULTURAL PRACTICES

In analyzing the cultural field of religion in Rio de Janeiro, I have been moved to reflect on the limitations of the Gramscian position that hegemonic and counterhegemonic beliefs coexist simultaneously within the subaltern's contradictory consciousness. The problem here is the assumption that we can always distinguish which is which. Gramsci is probably right that the socially disempowered almost always have a mixture of ideas, some deriving from horizontal social relations and some coming from on high. But the question still needs to be posed: Whatever the social origin of an idea, to what extent does it contribute to a social group's long-run liberation or subordination? Answers to this question remain far from simple.

Here is an example. Among other patterns, I found that young evangelical women who call themselves *pretas* or *negras* ended up marrying white men at a much higher rate than did non-evangelical black women. How to interpret this pattern politically? The women themselves spoke consistently about the pleasure they felt participating in a marriage market where their skin color had less salience than in the outside world, how being an evangelical increased their ability to choose a mate by love rather than by color alone. From one point of view these women's choices—when given the freedom through pentecostalism—to marry white men is interpretable as the internalization of the ideology of whitening; this was, for example, how this result was interpreted by

Isabel at Criola. From another point of view, however, this pattern may be viewed as the radical transcendence of color through the power of the Holy Spirit. Gramsci's concept of contradictory consciousness provides, on its own, no independent criteria by which to decide which element in these women's consciousness is the "really liberatory" one. The simple quotation of the women's voices themselves, while relevant, cannot decide this issue. It is, ultimately, an issue decided more by the observer's politics than by the realities on the ground. Reading this cultural practice, then, is not the simple undertaking of finding the truth out about it; it is rather a summoning of it, or mapping upon it, of one's own political stance.[6]

Or, to take an example through which we can see Brazil and the United States converge culturally, consider black women's use of hair straighteners. To what extent is a woman's intentionality relevant to how one reads this practice politically? To many true believers—whether inspired by Fanon or Elijah Muhammed—intent is rather beside the point: the practice is slavish subjection to Europe. To champions of "total freedom," on the other hand, a black woman's decision to straighten her hair can be the expression either of her desire to conquer for herself the same freedom for creative self-adornment that white women enjoy, or even the expression of the robust ludic space of the black woman's hair salon. The problem is that quoting women's voices on one side or the other of this issue cannot itself decide it. Interpreting the practice will be largely shaped by the ideological views of the interpreter.

Given this kind of ideological indeterminacy, I believe that the right thing to do is to avoid two methodological temptations. First, we need to avoid relegating to the drawer those passages of our fieldnotes or interview transcripts that give voice to a point of view we would prefer not to hear. We must also avoid another temptation: that of moving too quickly to judge which view is the predominant one. This calls for careful methodological self-criticism. Have we ended up talking with the folks who give us the answers we want to hear? How hard have we tried to seek out alternative points of view? The point is not to declare coequality among all points of view. The point is to do our best to assess the relative social force of each. But to do that, we need to hear more of the range to begin with.

In the end, of course, simply pushing ourselves to include wider ranges of variation cannot solve the problem of how to represent the complexity of consciousness. It still always matters how we, as researchers, hear voices through our own ideological filters. For exam-

ple, I insist that the views of the actual practitioners of a cultural practice of that practice's meaning can never be regarded as irrelevant to the
political meaning of the practice. It matters, in my view, whether a
woman who straightens her hair feels this is a way to experience a fuller
range of creativity; and it matters if a black evangelical woman who
marries a white man feels that the evangelical church has increased
rather than narrowed her marriage choices. I recognize the relevance of
my own political values here. Whereas I, feeling uncomfortable with the
attribution of false consciousness, am likely to accept the cultural practitioner's reading of her own practice, I also recognize that this, too,
involves a political choice. The ultimate political meaning of the action
therefore will always remain elusive.

IMPLICATIONS FOR THE POLITICS OF ETHNOGRAPHY

But when all is said and done, representation of such political meanings
for what reason? In the last chapter I explored one possible set of
responses to this question. It is important to emphasize that the intention of linking ethnography to politics is not reducible to the cultural-
ist fantasy in which popular culture rises to save the day. It is also not
my intention to call on social movements to move in and appropriate
cultural practices. The point is not to move from analysis and understanding to the propagandistic, imperial impulse to appropriate cultural
sites. The point is to learn about and from them, respecting their
integrity, specificity, and autonomy. This is why a careful, measured
ethnographic voice is a valuable *added* presence in a movement's political analyses of culture. To the extent that a greater awareness of these
sites leads to exchange and dialogue, so much the better. To the extent
that such exchanges may lead to actual moments of networking, cooperation, alliance, coalition, and even solidarity around joint projects,
that is all to the good. The point is that stages cannot be rushed or
skipped and that the process is slow and must be based upon respect
and a genuine willingness to accept that all ideas and practices, one's
own included, involve complex simultaneities that both perpetuate and
challenge the ideas and practices against which the movement sets itself.
If we have learned anything at all from this postrevolutionary period it
is that the greatest revolution of all is patience.

I have already suggested some of the ways an ethnographic voice
might speak in conversation with activists: respectfully, with a recognition of importance of social movement work, but with a reluctance to
presume that such work should enjoy transcendent privilege. I think
that this stance has something to offer black movement activists in

Brazil. Howard Winant has recently argued that in the Brazilian context a strategy for the future might be to open up rather than narrow the options of identification available to people who wanted to join in the antiracist struggle. In his view, "mobilization might appear as a series of options for identification, in which blacks could recognize themselves—at least partially—in various organizational and ideological forms."[7] The idea is intriguing and important. It would mean, in the words of Wendy Brown, disentangling a politics of being from the politics of wanting.[8] The point is not to downplay, let alone abandon, black identity; it is, rather, to make room for a variety of identities in which the valorization of blackness plays an emotionally important part. In Brazil, making this kind of room could have an important effect on antiracist politics. It would mean placing on a plane of political equality the activist who identifies herself as *negra* with the activist who identifies herself as *mestiça* but who deeply values her African ancestry.[9] It would mean moving away from a stance that regards such differences as inherently threatening or weakening to one that regards their public articulation as a source of strength and forward movement. Stuart Hall has argued that as we move into the next century the political agenda of antiracism calls for a progressive move away from essentialized ethnicity and toward the articulation of a common political project and vision that respects the internal differentiation within ethnic groups.[10] Paul Gilroy's notion of "double consciousness"—that of simultaneously being heir to Europe's imposed suffering as well as its universal human values—is sometimes offered as the ideological ground upon which a new antiracist, anti-essentialist politics might be built.[11]

Perhaps. But here again is where the ethnographic perspective may be of some use. For all the honorable antiessentializing impulse of writers like Hall and Gilroy, they seem once again to be slipping into the mode of thought that a "correct" politics now requires transcendence of essentialism. What then are we to do about those voices heard at the grass roots about the importance of mystical connection with Africa? Are they to become the new outcasts from the movement?

It is important to head off this question at the pass. Is it possible to conceive of a pluralism in which nonpluralizing views have an important role to play, a key contribution to make? Or is this yet another utopian liberal fantasy? I don't think that it is. The fate of antiracist struggle in the next century will hinge, at least in part, upon paying close attention and learning more about the everyday experiential correlates of both ethnic essentialism and human universalism. Delving more deeply into "double consciousness" can only be the answer if that exploration respects the integrity and specificity of those who declare that their consciousness is not "double" at all. It will have also to deal with the deepest experiential meanings of Christianity and other world religions, which include the creation of subjectivities that transcend difference altogether.

Throughout these explorations, listening carefully will be as important as pronouncing. And that is why the political work of ethnography has only just begun.

Notes

INTRODUCTION

1. Wagley (1952); Harris (1956); Azevedo (1951); Hutchinson (1957).
2. Cardoso and Ianni (1960); Cardoso (1962); Bastide and Fernandes (1971); Fernandes (1972); Azevedo (1975); Nogueira (1985).
3. Hasenbalg (1979); Silva (1978); Silva and Hasenbalg (1992).
4. Much of this work was published during the 1980s and 1990s in the journal of the Centro de Estudos Afro-Asiáticos (Center for Afro-Asian Studies), *Estudos Afro-Asiáticos*. Other important work includes Barbosa (1983); Pacheco (1986); Berriel (1988); Souza (1983); Turra and Venturi (1995); Santos (1993, 1984); Moura (1988, 1994); Berquó (1988); Scalon (1992); Twine (1997).
5. Hasenbalg and Silva (1990).
6. Hasenbalg and Silva (1991): 245.
7. Rosemberg (1987); Figueira (1990); Sant'Anna (1996); Rosemberg (1985).
8. Oliveira et al. (1981); Hasenbalg (1988): 41; Bento (1992).
9. Adorno (1995).
10. Turra and Venturi (1995): 24.
11. Gomes dos Santos (1992); Valente (1986); Hanchard (1994): 133–137.
12. Abreu et al. (1994); Bento (1995); Lima (1995); Ferreira da Silva and Lima (1992); Reichmann (1995); Lovell (1992); Queiroz (1994); Castro (1990).
13. Roland and Caneiro (1990).
14. On the movement of the 1930s, see Andrews (1996, 1991); Fernandes (1969).

15. Hanchard (1994): 104–141; Monteiro (1991); Fontaine, ed. (1985); Santos (1993, 1985); Gonzalez and Hasenbalg (1982).
16. Santos (1988); Hanchard (1994): 111–119; Moura (1994): 219–228.
17. Santos (1988).
18. Berriel (1988).
19. Moutinho (1996): 92–129.
20. Moreira Alves (1984).
21. Guimarães (1996): 84–95; Guimarães (1995).
22. Silva (1995).
23. Alves (1996): 21; Skidmore (1996).
24. Figueiredo (1994).
25. *Black People* (1996).
26. Twine (1996).
27. CONEN (1996).
28. Damasceno (1988).
29. Moura (1994): 211–249; Santos (1993).
30. Borges Pereira (1982): 59; Valente (1986); Hasenbalg (1992).
31. Castro (1991).
32. Winant (1994a): 149.
33. Hasenbalg (1992): 160.
34. Degler (1986 [1971]); Harris (1964); Casa Dandara (1992); Skidmore (1974); Borges Pereira (1983); Hasenbalg (1992): 156.
35. Winant (1994a): 154; Marx (1996).
36. Twine (1996): 40.
37. Hasenbalg (1992); Telles (1992); Oliveira (1996).
38. Valente (1986).
39. Hasenbalg (1992): 160.
40. Hess (1995); Brandão (1980); Birman (1996).
41. For example, Theodoro (1996); Serra (1995); Elbein Santos (1977); Prandi (1995).
42. Turra and Venturi (1995): 92.
43. This view of social movements is partly influenced by the discussion of "cognitive praxis" initiated by Eyerman and Jamison (1991).
44. Morris (1992, 1984); McAdam (1996).
45. Goffman (1974).
46. The literature on "frames" in the sociology of social movements is rich and expanding every day. The seminal article of this literature is Snow et al. (1986). A recent effort (with mixed results) to tie together the literature on framing with that on identity is Hunt, Benford, and Snow (1994). A good overview of how frame analysis fits into the history of social movement research is Gamson (1992).
47. Snow and Benford (1992).
48. On identity movements, see Cohen (1985); Melucci (1996).
49. Melucci (1989): 209; Stein (1995): 144; Werbner (1991): 24.

50. Turner (1993).
51. Pryce (1990).
52. Morgen (1988).
53. Benford (1993).
54. Sociologists define "frame resonance" as "the degree of fit between . . . framings or products of that work and the life situation and ideology of potential constituents." Snow et al., (1986): 477. For more detailed sociological discussion of frame resonance, see Snow and Benford (1988); Benford (1993); Benford and Hunt (1992).
55. Benford (1993).
56. Snow et al. (1986): 477. It is telling that sociologists concerned with frame resonance have focused most of their attention on the success of frames; they have been reluctant to attend to situations in which frames fail to resonate. The tendency is not, however, limited to sociologists. Recent anthropological treatments of ethnic movements (Keesing [1989]; Jackson [1995]; Mato [1996]; Rappaport and Dover [1995]; Rogers [1995]), because of their methodological focus on leaders, fail to represent the ideological positions of people who, although members of the targeted ethnic group, feel alienated and separate from the purveyed essentialisms.
57. Snow and Benford (1988).
58. Tarrow (1994): 123.
59. As Stuart Hall has observed, "[identification] is the process by which groups, movements, institutions, try to locate us for the purpose of regulating us" (Hall [1996]: 130). Paul Gilroy observes as well that "the political rhetoric of leaders is, after all, not a complete guide to the motivations and aspirations of those who play a less prominent role" (Gilroy [1987]: 235–236). Yet Gilroy seems reluctant to acknowledge that black leaders may have often alienated significant portions of their own social bases. Rather, he prefers to represent social movements as engaged primarily in an expressive, rather than marginalizing, process. It may be Gilroy's desire to skirt the problem of ideological leadership that leads him in his discussion of urban social movements to focus on acephalous rioting. In contrast, Everton Pryce has addressed directly the failure of black leaderships in the 1970s to resonate with the everyday existential longings of their main constituency, urban black youth. See Pryce (1990).
60. Lorde (1984).
61. Klandermans (1997): 72.
62. Benford and Hunt (1992).
63. Rogers (1995); Epstein (1995): 3–19.
64. Melucci (1989).
65. Cohen (1991): 177.
66. Muniz Sodré (1988).

67. By "field" I have in mind here an arena of social activities that include, but are not limited to, highly organized or institutionalized action. My notion of "field" is thus a bit broader than that of Klandermans (1992).

68. Scott (1985, 1990). Examples of work that seek to show various forms of everyday and symbolic resistance include Willis (1990); Comaroff (1985); Fiske (1994); Ong (1987); Gold and Raheja (1994).

69. Brown (1985). This point has also been made in the most recent wave of writing issuing from British cultural studies, which has taken very much to heart Partha Chatterjee's critique of postcolonial nationalism as a failure to forge an autonomous cultural project. See the various contributions, especially the one by Lawrence Grossberg, to Hall, ed. (1996). Chatterjee's critique was published as Chatterjee (1993).

70. A successful example of this kind of work is Abu-Lughod (1993, 1995).

71. This tends to be the perspective of cultural studies. See, for example, cultural studies' great willingness to celebrate gangsta rap's search for freedom, but its greater reluctance to engage with it as a space for the freedom of play of sexism. Gilroy (1994); and Rose (1996).

72. Scott (1976).

73. Canclini (1993).

74. O'Hanlon (1990).

75. Stokes (1995).

76. Examples of work of the "*cherchez* the colonial story" variety include Wachtel (1977); Taussig (1993); Stoller (1995); Dayan (1995): 65–74.

77. An excellent example of the insights that can emerge when Christian universalism is taken seriously as expressing the deep longings of at least some popular sub-groups, and not simply dismissed as yet another ruse of power, is Toulis (1997).

78. For a more detailed discussion of these socio-material categories, see Burdick (1993): 17–32.

79. Fernandes et al. (1996): 53.

80. For example, see Goldani (1994); Reichmann (1995).

81. Important exceptions include Giacomini (1992); Almada (1995); Casa Dandara (1992); Alves (1995); Medeiros (1987).

82. Stolcke (1991); Newton and Stacey (1995).

83. Sanjek (1971); Harris (1970).

84. Harris (1964); Sansone (1993); Fry (1995).

85. Silva (1988, 1996); Maggie (1995); Skidmore (1993). In response, Marvin Harris has revised and stepped up his census studies. See Harris et al. (1993, 1995); Telles (1995).

86. Sheriff (1995): 8.

87. Statistical evidence also suggests that there is a sizable contingent of

Brazilians who possess a rather stable black identity. The 1976 census reported that for the region of Rio de Janeiro, 8.3 percent of respondents spontaneously identified themselves to census takers as *pretos*. When these same people were offered the category "*pardo*" as a way to identify themselves, only 2 percent of them "migrated" to this category. See Silva (1996): 8. Of five thousand people surveyed nationwide in 1994 by the *Folha de São Paulo*, 7 percent spontaneously identified themselves to researchers as either *preto* or *negro*. When these same people were asked to place themselves into categories that included *branca* and *parda*, 80 percent insisted on remaining in the *preta* category (Turra and Venturi [1995]: 88).

88. For an exception see Wood (1991).

89. It may be objected that the image of relatively stable terms of self-reference is itself a side effect of the in-depth interview. That is, informants may construct in the course of such interviews narratives that lend more coherence to their color identities than is warranted by the more fluid, context-driven reality. "Identity" here becomes primarily a discursive motif or strategy. I think this is a fair objection. I have no doubt that our informants engaged in the usual glossing over of contradiction, inconsistency, and contingency one has learned to expect in most interview situations. Still, it was in practice not too difficult to pose critical questions that helped informants distinguish more enduring terms of self-reference from more conjunctural usages. In any case, ethnographic images are always at least in part an effect of methodological emphases. Thus, it would perhaps be useful to turn the question around and ask whether the image of referential indeterminacy might be viewed as a methodological side effect of the privileging of indexical usage.

90. Moura (1994).

91. Sansone (1994).

CHAPTER ONE

1. On the *funk* craze, see Vianna (1988).

2. *Manchete* (September 1996), 23–24.

3. *Raça Brasil*, 1/2 (October 1996), 35.

4. *O Dia*, 3/10/96.

5. The size of the nonwhite market is discussed in a feature article in *Raça Brasil*, 1/2 (October 1996).

6. Queiroz Junior (1975): 68.

7. Guimarães (1996 [1875]): 13.

8. *Ibid.*, 36.

9. Giacomini (1992,1994). For an interesting discussion of the *mulata* identity as experienced from a North American black woman's point of

view, see Gilliam and Gilliam (1995). More generally, the centrality of
hair in the definition of feminine beauty is discussed in Eilberg-
Schwartz (1995).

10. Skidmore (1974): 55; Moura (1988): 61–64; Nascimento (1978).
11. Degler (1980 [1971]): 189–190; Santos (1993); Parker (1991):
    136–163. More general discussions of the theme of "hybrid beauty"
    as part of the patriarchal and imperialist imagination may be found in
    Pacteau (1994): 123–144; Segal (1993); Lakoff and Scherr (1984): 251.
12. The play of power of the *mulata* to hold off and slow down the pace
    of sexual accostment is poignantly dramatized in Nelson Pereira dos
    Santos' 1955 film, "Zona Norte." The best discussion of this film is
    Robert Stam (1997): 162–165.
13. Moraes (1995): 62–65.
14. Turra and Venturi (1995): 138.
15. On Fillardis's early career, see the special supplement "O Negro" in
    the *Jornal do Brasil,* July, 1994; also see the many interviews with her
    published in 1996 in *Azzeviche, Raça Brasil, Black People, Destino,*
    and *Cabelos e Cia.* Richard Parker has recently argued that the *mulata*,
    through her personification of the sex at the heart of miscegenation,
    may have come to symbolize the ability of Brazilians, through sexual
    passion, to transcend the racial divide. Certainly in everyday discourse
    the public recognition of *mulata* beauty is mobilized as proof that
    racial democracy exists in Brazil. See Parker (1991): 153ff. For more
    general discussion of the relationship between national identity and the
    idealization of national female types, see Cohen et al., eds.(1996).
16. On the distinction between facial and bodily beauty, and their social
    correlates, see Synnott (1993). Also see Doniger (1995).
17. *O Dia*, 7/22/96.
18. Almada (1995): 210.
19. Sansone (1994).
20. Turra and Venturi (1995): 206.
21. I sampled three such magazines throughout 1996: *Black People,*
    Azzeviche, and *Raça Brasil.* Virtually all the advertising space was
    devoted to women's hair-care products, most of them imported from
    the United States.
22. Onik'a Gilliam suggests that this is also why some black women in the
    United States wear braids. See Gilliam and Gilliam (1995): 542.
23. An important exception to this trend in the United States is the position
    taken by Black Islam against any form of chemical intervention in
    black women's hair. See Pierce and Williams (1996).
24. In 1992, a product called "Rio Hair" was exported to the North
    American black female market, with disastrous results: many women
    lost their hair. On this episode see Rooks (1996): 120–123.
25. This logic, of feeling you are appropriating the power of the powerful,

rather than submitting to the powerful's demands, is also present in the process of mimesis of the accoutrements of colonial power. See Taussig (1993); Strathern (1996): 96–106.

26. In the U.S. context, see the discussions of female appropriations and subversions of patriarchal aesthetic norms in Davis (1995); Young (1990); Smith (1990).

27. This view has been alternately criticized as narcissistic, individualist, and alienated by Bartkey (1990): 33–40 and Bordo (1993). It may be all of these things, at any one moment. The question is whether such sentiments have, or do not have, the capacity and potential to lead to new, broader levels of understanding of self and others.

28. For a similar assessment of black women's ambiguous relationship to the beauty salon in the United States, see hooks (1988): 14–18; Dash (1992); Coleman (1983): 221–222; Rushing (1988); Rooks (1996): 1–22.

29. This stereotype has in Brazil a long checkered history. Gilberto Freyre cites a nineteenth-century medical opinion that Negro women were possessed of "boundless apelike lubricity," in Freyre (1956 [1933]): 396. The stereotype is not, of course, limited to Brazil. Winthrop Jordan has discussed it at length for the United States (Jordan [1968]: 150–151). Fely Simmonds (1995) has offered a thoughtful portrait of how such images enter into contemporary everyday love relations in Great Britain.

30. Almada (1995): 123.

31. Stam (1981); see also the splendid discussion of *Black Orpheus* in Stam (1997): 166–176.

32. Similarly, one of Mary Castro's informants declared that "I don't ever want a white boyfiend, because I don't want him to be able to humiliate me. I don't want to be called 'negrinha' or 'graxeirinha' [floor-washer]." Castro (1991): 28.

33. Birman (1990); Da Costa (1991): 109–117.

34. Mattoso (1986): 153–212; Russell-Wood (1972); the best analysis of these processes historically in the hemisphere may be found in Verena Martinez-Alier (1974).

35. Degler (1986 [1971]): 224. The judgment endures today as a kind of popular and elite common sense. It is, for example, present in Darcy Ribeiro's historical work (1995): 238.

36. Pacheco (1987): 85–97.

37. Sheriff (1995); Sansone (1994): 18. See also Twine (1998).

38. In the United States, Russell et al. found that "Biracial families also have the potential to produce enormous variations in color and features among their children, and one might expect them to experience intense color conflicts as well. Instead, in interview after interview that we conducted with adult biracial children of Black-White marriages, all main-

tained that their parents had been very much attuned to color issues."
Russell et al. *(1992)*: 99. Other recent discussions of the subtle inter-
play in the United States between kin values and color hierarchy may
be found in Funderburg (1994), and Azoulay (1997).

39. Lima (1995): 494ff.
40. *Ibid.*, 493.
41. Bento (1995).
42. Lima (1995): 494.
43. Castro (1991).
44. Brookshaw (1986): 24.
45. Figueira (1990).
46. Amaral and Silva (1993): 115.
47. Ferreira da Silva (1994).
48. Almada (1995): 200.
49. Freyre (1956 [1933]): 89, 287, 383.
50. *Ibid.*, 349.
51. Birman (1990): 5–12.
52. Filho (1980); Williams (1994): 201–236.
53. Pacheco (1986): 121.
54. Ferreira da Silva (1994); Birman (1990): 9.

CHAPTER TWO

1. The best overviews of the pentecostal field in Rio de Janeiro are Freston
   (1993); and Fernandes et al. (1996). Also see the special issue of
   Religião e Sociedade 17/1–2 entitled *Pentecostes e Nova Era: fron-
   teiras, passagens* (1994). Chestnut (1997) is excellent on pentecostalism in the Amazonian region. In general, the best way to track
   pentecostal and neo-pentecostal trends is to keep up with the most
   recent issues of *A Folha Universal* (the publication of the Universal
   Church of the Kingdom of God) and *Vinde: A revista gospel do Brasil.*
2. On the liberationist movement, see Smith (1991).
3. On the new movement of Charismatic Catholics in Rio de Janeiro, see
   Machado (1994). On popular Catholic devotions, there is no better
   analysis than the various studies by Carlos Brandão, including (1994):
   179–258. Also see his classic *Os deuses do povo* (1980).
4. The following section is based on interviews with several of the key
   participants in the events described, as well as on documents internal
   to the black pastoral. Among these documents, the most important
   are José Ariovaldo da Silva, "Elementos históricos de adaptação da
   liturgia ás várias culturas," mimeo; and Quilombo Regional Baurú,
   "Agentes de pastoral negros: histórico," mimeo.
5. The story of the rise and consolidation of the progressive Catholic
   movement in Brazil is best summarized by Mainwaring (1986) and by
   Della Cava (1976).

6. The Brotherhood Campaign is an annual national event, in which the Church commits itself for the forty days of Lent to discussing some common theme in all Church venues.

7. Slavery was abolished in Brazil on May 13, 1888. For the historical antecedents to this event, see Conrad (1972).

8. The series of documents that describe these events include "Ecumenismo e religiões afros," mimeo, 1991; "Uma contribuição ao debate em torno do rito católico Afro-brasileiro," mimeo, 1992; "Desafios do processo de inculturação na igreja," mimeo, 1993; Cansi (1990): 7–17; Gantin (1996): 165–171.

9. On the *ginga* in Brazilian culture, see Barbosa (1994): 136–141.

10. Among the many publications focusing on Zumbi and distributed by the black pastoral for free or for sale at the Quilombo, the black pastoral's headquarters in São João, one can find Agentes de Pastoral Negros (1995); Braz (1995).

11. Afro-Catholic theologians situate this effort at theological dialogue in more general post-Vatican II ecumenism. The Vatican Council of 1962–1965 affirmed that there were good and true elements present in various religious traditions, and that these should be regarded as "seeds of the Word." The disciples of Christ should go forth and discover, in the words of Vatican II's final document, "the riches that God liberally spread to all peoples." This pursuit would be the basis of "fruitful dialogue" and the attitude of "respect." This "respect," it should be pointed out, however, was clearly limited. As John Paul II said to an audience in Benin in 1993, it was a "respect for true values, wherever they are found." Put another way, Catholicism is to be liberal in *where* it looks for truth, but orthodox about *what* it finds along the way.

12. Pontifícia União Missionária, Omnisterra 10/II (May 1996).

13. Santos (1990): 2.

14. My account of the history of Anastácia's devotion is reconstructed from many dozens of interviews with all the key participants in the events, or their direct descendants, as well as all extant documents related to the story, which I cite where relevant.

15. Mulvey (1980): 253–279; Russell-Wood (1982); Hoornaert (1987): 15–36; Valente (1994); Bastide (1978 [1960]): 105–129; Karasch (1987).

16. On the logic of devotional relations with the dead in popular Catholicism, see Brandão (1994).

17. Hoornaert (1987): 29; Botelho (1980): 335.

18. Beozzo (1985): Tome III, 281–283.

19. Santos (1990).

20. Silva (1990): 2–3.

21. Card. D. Eugênio de Araujo Sales to Nilton da Silva and Ubirajá

Rodrigues da Silva, August 3, 1984, reproduced in Silva (1990): 4.
22. Schubert, Guilherme. "Escrava Anastácia," *Jornal do Brasil*, 9/15/87.
23. *O Dia*, 12/9/89.
24. *Jornal do Brasil*, 3/25/88.
25. "Her devotees are deluded by charlatans," wrote Luiz Mott, a movement leader in the aftermath of the prohibition. *Jornal do Brasil*, 5/22/89.
26. There has been surprisingly little written about Anastácia as a religious phenomenon. The little that exists may be found in the following texts: Hale (1997); Lambret Silva (1985); Almeida (1995); Birman (1992); Sheriff (1997).
27. Fernandes et al. (1996): 8ff.
28. Cox (1995): 49.
29. *Ibid.*, 58.
30. *Ibid.*, 58.
31. Freston (1994): 110.
32. Freston (1993): 29.
33. Ireland (1993); Stoll and Garrard-Burnett, eds. (1993); Cleary and Stewart-Gambino, eds. (1997); Toulis (1997); Austin-Broos (1997).
34. Fernandes et al, (1996): 85.

CHAPTER THREE
1. Pierre Sanchis, personal communication, 1997.
2. This research project coincides with the emerging concern in feminist studies to understand how women fit, or do not fit, into ethnic and nationalist struggles. Much of this work has focused at the level of the rhetoric produced by political leaders. "Considerable work remains to be done," writes McClintock, "on the ways in which women consume, refuse, or negotiate the male fetish rituals of national spectacle." See McClintock (1993): 71. Also see Smith (1996); Williams (1996).
3. Rocha (1994): 20.
4. Associacão de Teólogos d. Terceiro Mundo (1988): 35.
5. Theodoro (1996): 135; Sodré (1983).
6. Yuval-Davis and Anthias, eds. (1989): 7.
7. Gilroy (1993): 1–40.
8. ASETT (1988): 30.
9. Giacomini (1994).
10. The black woman's body in the inculturated Mass exemplifies what Yuval-Davis and Anthias suggest is a worldwide aspect of ethnic movements, of representing the woman in her ideal form as "biological reproducer of members of ethnic collectivities" Yuval-Davis and Anthias, eds. (1989): 7.
11. Ethnic movements often work with the logic of spectacle. McClintock has suggested that "nationalism [or politicized ethnicity] takes shape

through the visible, ritual organization of collective fetish spectacle—in team sports, military displays, mass rallies, the myriad forms of popular culture" in McClintock (1993).

12. Rocha (1994): 15.
13. *Ibid.,* 17.
14. Rodrigues da Silva (1990): 171.
15. ASETT (1988): 35.
16. Yuval-Davis points to the symbolic role women play as mothers in the construction of ethnic identity, in their roles as socializers of the young and maintainers of solid families. Yuval-Davis and Anthias (1989): 9.
17. Theodoro (1996): 61.
18. Ibid.: 59.
19. For an extended discussion of the issue of purity in the comparison between *umbanda* and *candomblé,* see Dantas (1988).
20. The inculturated Mass gives plenty of ammunition to the Protestants, who are only too happy to have yet another proof of the Catholic Church's alliance with the devil.
21. In a similar case, recently a *mãe-de-santo* actually took a samba school to court for having used symbols of the *orixás.* Her argument was that one could not mix the "profane" of Carnaval with the "sacred" of *candomblé.*
22. Gomes and Santos (1996): 2.
23. Chagas (1996): 33.
24. *Folha de São Paulo,* 6/25/95.
25. Eyerman and Jamison (1991): 45–65.
26. In the United States, of course, there has been a long, often searing, debate about this question. See especially Michele Wallace, *Black Macho and the Myth of the Superwoman,* and bell hooks's retrospective analysis of the debate in *Black Looks.*
27. Gilroy (1993).

CHAPTER FOUR

1. Movimento Terreiro e Cidadania, "Documento Sumário," xerox, 1996: 3–4.
2. This link is documented in Viotti da Costa (1966): 237–241; Hauck (1985): 263ff.
3. Damasceno (1990); Valente (1994).
4. Passos (1995): 5.
5. Dolhnikoff et al. (1995): 24.
6. Freston (1993); Fernandes, et al. (1996).
7. *Ibid.,* 10.
8. Turra and Venturi (1995).
9. Verger (1992): 19–26
10. Bastide (1989 [1960]): 512.

11. Novaes and Floriano (1985): 58
12. Contins (1992, 1995).
13. Csordas (1992); Sanchis (1994); Johannesen (1988): 558; Mariz and Dores Machado (1994): 24–34.
14. *Black People*, 3/96
15. Dolhnikoff et al. (1995): 23–24.
16. *Folha Universal*, 5/13; 5/27; 6/21
17. Certainly, from a comparative perspective, there is no irreconcilable contradiction between pentecostal beliefs and ethnic identity. Indeed, throughout Latin America and the world, ethnic identities have frequently drawn direct sustenance from pentecostal faith. See for example Burnett (1986); Wedenoja (1978); Rappaport (1984); Muratorio (1980); Scotchmer (1991); Comaroff (1985); Roswith (1994).
18. Cunha (1993): 120–137
19. Fernandes et al. (1996): 56.
20. These numbers are drawn from my calculations upon the raw data generated by the Instituto de Estudos de Religião's 1994 survey.
21. In October 1994, the Institute for the Study of Religion (ISER) carried out the most comprehensive survey of evangelicals undertaken in Brazil. In the project known as "Novo Nascimento" ("Born Again"), a team of seventy researchers posed some fifty questions to nearly twelve hundred evangelicals in the greater Rio area. The questions ranged over the topics of religion, family, sexuality, and politics. Among the questions posed, researchers asked "What is your color?" and recorded three answers: the subject's spontaneous self-identification, her self-classification according to the categories of the national census, and the interviewer's own judgment in relation to national census categories. Researchers also asked if the subject was married, and if so, various items of information about the spouse, including his or her color.
22. Turra and Venturi (1995): 186.
23. *Ibid.*
24. ISER data.
25. Turra and Venturi (1995): 187.
26. The full biblical text is the following: "My brothers, as believers in our glorious Lord Jesus Christ, don't show favoritism. Suppose a man comes into your meeting wearing a gold ring and fine clothes, and a poor man in shabby clothes also comes in. If you show special attention to the man wearing fine clothes and say 'Here's a good seat for you' but say to the poor man, 'You stand there' or 'Sit on the floor by my feet' have you not discriminated among yourselves and become judges with evil thoughts?" There is no ambiguity here: "If you show favoritism, you sin and are convicted by the law" (James 2:1–10).
27. I should point out that black men report similar experiences of disillusionment, but theirs tend to revolve not so much around the court-

ing market as around mobility in the authority hierarchy of the church.

28. Gramsci (1971): 373.
29. Passos (1995): 5.

CHAPTER 5

1. "Negra Tambem Tem História,"Black Women's Collective in São Paulo, 1993, 13.
2. Odo-Yá, "Informativo Odo-Yá: AIDS," July 1994.
3. For a discussion of the vicissitudes of the black movement's relationship with the devotion, see Burdick (forthcoming).
4. Anastácia's increasing presence in *umbanda* does not alter this sentiment, for *umbanda* also is regarded as impure, an unacceptable mix of Catholic and African elements. "Unfortunately," explained an activist, "Anastácia is now connected to syncretic, mixed religions in which the original character of the *negro* has been lost." Furthermore, when one regards *candomblé* as the only proper religiosity of the black, this renders discussion of Anastácia difficult, for in *candomblé* she is regarded as an *egungun*, a spirit of the dead, of whom one is supposed neither to have images nor mention the name.
5. Equipe de Religioso Negro, *Vocação ao Som dos Atabaques* (1993).
6. In the sense I am suggesting here, spiritism can also act as a brake on the articulation of race/color issues. Adepts of spiritism believe that some spirits are assigned by God to be so purifed by their patience in the face of suffering that after death they become entirely free of all earthbound demarcations of class or color.
7. Joan Dayan has described a similar historic-mythical memory in Haiti. In the figure of the vindictive spirit named Ezili is realized the "blunt recollection of what those who were abused first by the master and then by the mistress had come to know." For in Haiti, as Moreau de Saint-Mery wrote: "Nothing equals the anger of a Creole woman who punished the slave that her husband had perhaps forced to dirty the nuptial bed. In her jealous fury she doesn't know what to invent in order to satisfy her vengeance." Dayan (1995): 65.
8. The centrality of this "no" to rape in black women's understanding of Anastácia was revealed also in their belief that matters of romantic love and marriage remained entirely outside the slave saint's purview. Having been tortured at the hands of men for refusing to give in to them, asking Anastácia for a husband would be like rubbing salt into an open wound. Black devotees explicitly stated that one could ask anything of Anastácia "except a husband."
9. A corollary of this is suggested by our very surprising discovery that dark-black women devotees, as a group, tended to reject the idea that Anastácia was of royal blood. This is surprising, because on the whole,

Brazilian blacks have a long-standing cultural tradition supporting royalism, rooted in among other things the importation of kingship and queenship from West Africa and their embedding in the Catholic *congada* and Carnaval, and gratitude to the Brazilian royal family for having abolished slavery. (Blacks were, for example, actively courted, with some success, by monarchists in the 1994 plebiscite on the form of government.) Yet for black women, it seems, attributing noble blood to Anastácia would entail diluting the impact of her moral victory and triumph, her refusal of the master. Aparecida, in a statement typical of the views of other black devotees, insisted that for her the image of Anastácia as princess or queen "is not important at all. Is it that only women of royal blood have the ability to stand up for themselves?" "For me," said Gegê, "she was much more than a princess, much more than a queen."

10. *Morenas* with such views not only are willing to turn to Anastácia for help in matters of love and romance; some even regard her, in contradiction to the beliefs of black devotees, as a patron saint of childbirth and midwives.

11. Interestingly, in several accounts gathered from domestic servants, a key flashpoint in their humiliation on the job was being obliged to eat separately from the family, and usually inferior food. The image of Anastácia as a servant whose mouth had been closed to food by the face-iron resonated for at least one domestic servant by reminding her of her own deprivation on the job.

12. hooks (1995): 269; also West (1993); Dalton (1995).

13. Dalton (1995).

14. Quoted in Murphy and Hampton (1988): 17.

15. In a broader discussion of the association in Western culture between beauty, women, and death, Elizabeth Bronfen points to the importance in literary iconography of dying women forgiving all wrongdoing against them as a means to reestablish the social order a "bad" death might create. See Bronfen (1992): 78.

16. This is in contrast to the United States, where the image of the docile, affectionate slave prevailed so strongly that for many masters their slaves' quick rejection of them after abolition was something of an emotional earthquake. On the image of docility in the United States and the reaction and feelings of betrayal on the part of masters after abolition, see Genovese (1972): 97–112, 595–596.

17. Brookshaw (1986): 29.

18. *Ibid.,* 31

19. Marotti (1987): 256.

20. In a recent survey, a quarter of white men who admitted having color prejudice said that they would be troubled and might try to leave a job in which a black had been assigned as their boss. See Turra and Venturi (1995): 175.

CHAPTER SIX

1. Hymes (1972).
2. Schensul (1974).
3. Stull and Schensul (1987).
4. Harrison (1991); Gordon (1991); Starn (1994).
5. Escobar (1992).
6. Moran (1996).
7. Some, of course, skeptical of all these, call for a restful abandonment of this pretentious activity called anthropology altogether. (Enslin, 1994).
8. Gail Omvedt and Faye Harrison have, similarly, suggested that ethnography can communicate to movement leaders the various levels of receptivity, both actual and potential, to their message. See Omvedt (1979); Harrison (1991).
9. For a review, see Van Willigen (1993).
10. *Ibid.*, 341.
11. Barger and Reza (1989): 272–273.
12. Scheper-Hughes (1992, 1995); and see the opposing view of D'Andrade, (1995).
13. Anglin (1997): 38.
14. Cunha (1996).

CONCLUSION

1. Tarrow (1994); Diani (1992); Melucci (1996): 1–41.
2. The point of view I am suggesting here is different from the "submerged network" idea espoused by Melucci (1989). A submerged network proves itself as such by eventuating in collective action. But one might participate in a network, and sites for the articulation of alternative ways of seeing the world, without ever translating those ways into collective action.
3. The "problem" of freeloading was first articulated by Olson (1965). Although Olson's view has been roundly criticized in recent years, the research problem of trying to understand how "freeloaders" turn into good upstanding social movement participants or activists remains central to the sociological project. See, for example, Klandermans (1997).
4. Much of the literature on social movements produced by sociologists treats the cultural milieu of a social movement organization in precisely these terms, as a sort of "toolkit" from which activists may choose their tools. See Swidler (1986). The view espoused here, in contrast, calls for attention to the ability of *non*-social movement groups to bring about social change *independently* of self-identified social movement organizations.
5. For the argument that Colombian women's involvement in evangelical churches is a more socially effective approach to women's liberation than self-conscious feminist organizing, see Brusco (1995).

6. This is one of the reasons Paul Gilroy's cultural analyses, despite their lack of engagement with the cultural users' own voices, has a certain integrity: they are, without apology, evaluative, as when he counterposes cultural practices that embody a "politics of fulfilment" (good, but not the best) to the politics of transfiguration (the best) (1993: 137).

7. Winant (1994a): 156. For a fuller exposition of Winant's recent views on "racial formation theory" see Winant (1994b).

8. Brown (1996).

9. Appiah (1996). In the United States, of course, the issue of miscegenation carries its own culturally and historically specific freight. Yet as the current debate about reformulating the U.S. census to include the category "biracial" or "multiracial" shows, the U.S. will not be able to put off much longer a public debate about the specificity of "mixed-race" people. On this see Spencer (1997). It is revealing that those who are quick to heap contempt upon such people's claims that they have historically distinct experiences are denying them the very hearing they themselves have been denied by racist society. There has in the last ten years been a virtual explosion of compendia of "mixed-race" voices in the United States, including Sollors (1997); Camper (1994); Root (1992); Zack (1993, 1995); Russell, et al. (1992). It is illustrative of the growing social importance of awareenss of mixed race in the post-1989 world that the World Wide Web now has literally dozens of "mixed-race" homepages. Some of the irritation that "mixed-race" people's claims to a public hearing can provoke is present in Angela Gilliam's review of Maria Root's collection, in the pages of *American Ethnologist*.

10. See for example Hall (1996): 129–135. This is a view echoed on this side of the Atlantic by bell hooks, and to some extent by Cornel West (1993). The politicization of this perspective seems to be more advanced in Great Britain than in the United States, probably because of the history of inter-ethnic solidarities that have emerged with greater force among British youth, especially across the various postcolonial migrant groups to London. On this demographic basis to the new ethnic politics in Great Britain, see Back (1996), and, to a lesser extent Alexander (1996). The case, however, is far from closed about the political potentialities of inter-ethnic mobilization among youth in the United States. Studies of the social and political meanings for ethncity at work in North American urban youth culture pervaded by hip-hop are still in their infancy.

11. Gilroy (1993).

Bibliography

Abreu, Alice Rangel de Paiva et al. 1994. "Desigualdade de gênero e raça: o informal no Brasil em 1990." *Estudos feministas* 2/2: 153–178.

Abu-Lughod, Lila. 1993. "Finding a Place for Islam: Egyptian Television Serials and the National Interest." *Public Culture* 5/3: 493–513.

———. 1995. "The Objects of Soap Opera: Egyptian Television and the Cultural Politics of Modernity." In Daniel Miller, ed., *Worlds Apart: Modernity Through the Prism of the Local*. New York: Routledge, 190–210.

Adorno, Sérgio. 1995. "Discriminação racial e justiça criminal em São Paulo." *Novos estudos CEBRAP* 43 (November): 45–63.

Agentes de Pastoral Negros. 1995. *Zumbi Vive: Tricentenário de Zumbi dos Palmares*. Belo Horizonte: Quilombo Regional Grande Belo Horizonte.

Alexander, Claire. 1996. *The Art of Being Black: The Creation of Black British Youth Identities*. Oxford: Oxford University Press.

Almada, Sandra. 1995. *As damas negras*. Rio de Janeiro: Mauad.

Almeida, Marcus Vinicius. 1995. "Anastácia: mito e lenda." Baccalaureate term paper, Universidade Federal de Rio de Janeiro.

Alves, Miriam. 1995. *Finally Us: Contemporary Black Brazilian Women Writers*. Colorado Springs: Three Continents Press.

Alves, Wendecley. 1996. "Empresário negro." *Black People* 1/3 (March): 21.

Amaral, Rita de Cassia, and Vagner Gonçalves da Silva. 1993. "A côr do axé: brancos e negros no candomblé de São Paulo." *Estudos Afro-Asiaticos* 25 (December): 99–124.

American Friends Services Committee (AFSC). 1997. "Report on Study of Treatment of African Americans by Storeowners in Syracuse." Mimeo.

Andrews, Reid. 1996. "Brazilian Racial Democracy, 1900–1990: An American Counterpoint." *Journal of Contemporary History* 31/3 (July): 483–508.

———. 1991. *Blacks and Whites in São Paulo, Brazil, 1888–1988* Madison: University of Wisconsin Press.

Anglin, Mary K. 1997. "Activist Praxis and Anthropological Knowledge." In M. Tim Wallace, ed., *Practicing Anthropology in the South*. Athens, GA: University of Georgia Press.

Appiah, Anthony. 1996. *Color Conscious: The Political Morality of Race*. Princeton: Princeton University Press.

Associação de Teólogos do Terceiro Mundo. 1988. *A historia e a fé do povo negro no Brasil e na América Andina*. São Paulo: ASETT.

Austin-Broos, Diane. 1997. *Jamaica Genesis*. Chicago: University of Chicago Press.

Azevedo, Thales de. 1951. *As elites de côr: Um estrado de ascençao*. São Paulo: Companhia Editora Nacional.

———. 1975. *Democracia racial: Ideologia e realidade*. Petrópolis: Vozes.

Azoulay, Katya Gibel. 1997. *Black, Jewish and Interracial*. Durham: Duke University Press.

Back, Les. 1996. *New Ethnicities and Urban Culture: Racisms and Multiculture in Young Lives*. New York: Saint Martin's Press.

Barbosa, Irene M. F. 1983. "Socialização e relações raciais: um estudo de familias negras em Campinas." Master's thesis, Universidade de São Paulo.

Barbosa, Wanderley. 1994. "A ginga." *Atrás do muro da noite*. Brasília: Fundação Cultural Palmares.

Barger, W. Ken, and Ernesto Reza. 1989. "Policy and Community-Action Research: The Farm Labor Movement in California." In John van Willigan et al., eds., *Making Our Research Useful*. Boulder: Westview.

Bartkey, Sandra Lee. 1990. *Femininity and Domination: Studies in the Phenomenology of Oppression*. New York: Routledge.

Bastide, Roger. 1978 [1960]. *The African Religions of Brazil*. Trans. Helen Sebba. Baltimore: Johns Hopkins University Press.

———. 1989 [1960]. *As Religiões africanas no Brasil*. Graal: Rio de Janeiro.

Bastide, Roger, and Florestan Fernandes. 1971. *Brancos e negros em São Paulo*. 3rd. ed. São Paulo: Companhia Editora Nacional.

Benford, Robert. 1993. "Frame Disputes Within the Nuclear Disarmament Movement." *Social Forces* 71: 677–701.

———. 1995. "Cultural Power and Social Movements." In Hank Johnston and Bert Klandermans, eds., *Social Movements and Culture*. Minneapolis: University of Minnesota Press, 25–40.

———. 1993. "You Could Be the Hundredth Monkey: Collective Action Frames and Vocabularies of Motive within the Nuclear Disarmament Movement." *Sociological Quarterly* 34: 195–216.

Benford, Robert, and Scott A. Hunt. 1992. "Dramaturgy and Social Movements: The Social Construction and Communication of Power." *Sociological Inquiry* 62: 36–55.

Benmayor, Ruth. 1991. "Testimony, Action Research, and Empowerment: Puerto Rican Women and Popular Education." In Sherna B. Gluck and Daphne Patai, eds., *Women's Words: The Feminist Practice of Oral History.* New York: Routledge, 159–174.

Bento, Maria Aparecida. 1992. "Resgatando a minha bisavo: discriminação racial no trabalho e resistência na voz dos trabalhadores negros." Ph.D. thesis, Pontificia Universidade Católica.

———. 1995. "A mulher negra no mercado de trabalho." *Estudos feministas* 3/2: 479–488.

Beozzo, José. 1985. *História da Igreja no Brasil.* Tome III. Petrópolis: Vozes.

Berquó, Elza. 1988. "Demografia da desigualdade: algumas considerações sobre os negros no Brasil." *Novos estudos do CEBRAP* 21 (July): 74–84.

Berriel, Maria Maia. 1988. "Identidade fragmentada: as muitas maneiras de ser negro." Master's thesis, Universidade de São Paulo.

Birman, Patricia. 1990. "Beleza negra." *Estudos Afro-Asiáticos* 18: 5–12.

———. 1992. "As crenças perifericas." In Pierre Sanchis, ed., *Catolicismo: Unidade Religiosa e Pluralismo Cultural.* São Paulo: Loyola, 167–195.

———. 1996. *Fazer estilo criando gêneros.* Rio de Janeiro: Relume.

Black People. 1995–1996. Rio dde Janeiro.

Black Women's Collective. 1993. "Negra Tambem Ten Historia." Mimeo. São Paulo" Black Women's Collective.

Bordo, Susan. 1993. *Unbearable Weight.* Berkeley: University of California Press.

Borges Pereira, João Batista. 1982. "Parametros ideológicos do projeto politico dos negros em São Paulo." *Revista do Instituto de assuntos brasileiros* 24

———. 1983. "Negro e cultura negra no Brasil atual." *Revista de antropologia* 26: 93–105.

Botelho, Carlos. 1980. *107 Invocações da Virgem Maria no Brasil.* Petrópolis: Vozes.

Brandão, Carlos. 1994. "A alma do outro: identidade, alteridade e sincretismo na ética das relações de reciprocidade entre vivos e mortos em religiões do Brasil." In Carlos Brandão, *Somos as águas puras.* São Paulo: Papirus, 179–258.

Brandão, Carlos. 1980. *Os deuses do povo.* Petrópolis: Vozes.

Braz, Julio Emilio. 1995. *Zumbi: O despertar da liberdade.* Rio de Janeiro: Memorias Futuras.

Bronfen, Elizabeth. 1992. *Over Her Dead Body: Death, Femininity and the Aesthetic.* New York: Routledge.

Brookshaw, David. 1986. *Race and Color in Brazilian Literature.* Metuchen, N.J.: Scarecrow Press.

Brown, Michael. 1985. *Tsewa's Gift: Magic and Meaning in an Amazonian Society*. Washington, D.C.: Smithsonian Institution Press.

Brown, Wendy. 1996. "Injury, Identity, Politics." In Avery F. Gordon and Christopher Newfield, eds., *Mapping Multiculturalism*. Minneapolis: University of Minnesota Press, 149–166.

Brusco, Elizabeth. 1985. *The Reformation of Machismo*. Austin: University of Texas Press.

Burdick, John. 1993. *Looking for God in Brazil: The Progressive Catholic Church in Urban Brazil's Religious Arena*. Berkeley: University of California Press.

———. Forthcoming. "The Eyes of Anastácia." *Journal of Afro-Latin Literature and Studies*.

Burnett, Virginia-Garrard. 1986. "A History of Protestantism in Guatemala." Ph.D. diss., Tulane University.

Camper, Carol. 1994. *Miscegenation Blues: Voices of Mixed Race Women*. Toronto: Sister Vision.

Canclini, Nestor Garcia. 1993. *Transforming Modernity: Popular Culture in Mexico*. Trans. Lidia Lozano. Austin: University of Texas Press.

Caneiro, Sueli. 1990. "Saúde da mulher no Brasil: a perspectiva da mulher negra." *Revista da Cultura Vozes* 84/2 (March): 204–210.

Cansi, Bernardo. 1990. "Inculturação, liturgia e catequese." *Revista de catequese* 49: 7–17.

Cardoso, Fernando Henrique. 1962. *Capitalismo e escravidão no Brasil meridional*. São Paulo: Companhia Editora Nacional.

Cardoso, Fernando Henrique, and Octávio Ianni. 1960. *Côr e mobilidade social em Florianopolis*. São Paulo: Companhia Editora Nacional.

Casa Dandara. 1992. *O triunfo da ideologia de embranquecimento: o homem negro e a rejeição da mulher negra*. Belo Horizonte: Projeto Cidadania do Povo.

Castro, Mary Garcia. 1990. "Female Heads of Household, Racism and Ageism in Brazil." Unpublished mss. Belo Horizonte: Universidade Federal de Minas Gerais.

———. 1991. "A alquimia das categorias sociais: gênero, raça e geração na produção de sujeitos politícos: o caso de líderes do sindicato de trabalhadores domésticos em Salvador." Paper presented at the 15th annual meeting of the Associação Nacional de Pós-Graduação em Ciências Sociais, October.

Chagas, Conceição. 1996. *Negro: uma identidade em construção*. Petrópolis: Vozes.

Chatterjee, Partha. 1993. *The Nation and its Fragments: Colonial and Postcolonial Histories*. Princeton: Princeton University Press.

Chestnut. Andrew. 1997. *Born Again in Brazil: The Pentecostal Boom and the Pathogens of Poverty* . New Brunswick: Rutgers University Press.

Cleary, Edward, and Hannah Stewart-Gambino, eds., 1997. *Power, Politics and Pentecostals in Latin America*. Boulder: Westview.

Cohen, Abner. 1991. "Drama and Politics in the Development of a London Carnival." In Pnina Werbner and Muhammad Anwar, eds. *Black and Ethnic Leaderships in London*. London: Routledge, 170–202.

Cohen, Jean. 1985. "Strategy or Identity: New Theoretical Paradigms and Contemporary Social Movements." *Social Research* 52: 663–716.

Cohen, Colleen B., Richard Wilk, and Beverly Stoeltje, eds. *Beauty Queens on the Global Stage: Gender, Contests, and Power*. New York: Routledge.

Coleman, Patti. 1983. "Among the Things That Used to Be." In *Home Girls: A Black Feminist Anthology*. New York: Kitchen Table-Women of Color Press.

Comaroff, Jean. 1985. *Body of Power, Spirit of Resistance*. Chicago: University of Chicago Press.

CONEN (Coordenação Nacional das Entidades Negras). 1996. "Proposta de trabalho." Brasilia: mimeo.

Conrad, Robert. 1972. *The Destruction of Brazilian Slavery, 1850–1888*. Berkeley: University of California Press.

Contins, Marcia. 1992. *Narrativas pentecostais: estudos antropológicos de grupos de pentecostais negros nos Estados Unidos*. Rio de Janeiro: Centro Interdisciplinar de Estudos Culturais.

———. 1995. "Tornando-se Pentecostal: um estudo comparativo sobre pentecostais negros nos Estados Unidos e Brasil." Ph.D. diss., PPCS/UFRJ.

Cox, Harvey. 1995. *Fire from Heaven*. Reading, Mass.: Addison-Wesley.

Csordas, Thomas. 1992. "Religion and the World System: The Pentecostal Ethic and the Spirit of Monopoly Capital." *Dialectical Anthropology* 17: 3–24.

Cunha, Olivia. 1993. "Fazendo a coisa certa: Reggae, rasta, e pentecostais em Salvador." *Revista Brasileira de Ciências Sociais* 8/23 (Outubro): 120–137

———. 1996. "Depois da festa: movimentos negros, culturas e politicas de identidade." Unpublished mss.

Da Costa, Maria Cecilia Solheid. 1991. "A cor não se ve e a cór que se tem: a criança preferencial na adoção em camadas medias." *Estudos Afro-Asiáticos* 21: 109–117.

Dalton, Harlan. 1995. *Racial Healing: Confronting the Fear Between Blacks and Whites*. New York: Doubleday.

Damasceno, Caetana. 1990. "Cantando para Subir." Master's thesis, Programa de Pos-Graduação de Antropologia Social, Universidade Federal de Rio de Janeiro.

Damasceno, Caetana et al. 1988. *Catálogo de entidades de movimento negro o Brasil*. Rio de Janeiro: ISER.

D'Andrade, Roy. 1995. "Moral Models in Anthropology." *Current Anthropology* 56/3 (June): 399–408.

Dantas, Beatriz. 1988. *Vovo nagô e papai branco: usos e abusos de Africa no Brasil*. Rio de Janeiro: Graal.

Dash, Julie. 1992. *Daughters of the Dust: The Making of an African American Woman's Film*. New York.

Davis, Kathy. 1995. *Reshaping the Female Body: The Dilemma of Cosmetic Surgery*. New York: Routledge.

Dayan, Joan. 1995. *Haiti, History, and the Gods*. Berkeley: University of California Press.

Degler, Carl. 1986 [1971]. *Neither Black nor White: Slavery and Race Relations in Brazil and the United States*. 2nd ed. Madison: University of Wisconsin Press.

Della Cava, Ralph. 1976. "Catholicism and Society in Twentieth Century Brazil." *Latin American Research Review* 11/2: 7–50.

Diani, Mario. 1992. "The Concept of Social Movement." *Sociological Review* 40.

DIEESE (Divisão de Estudos e Estatistícas Socio-Económicas). 1988. *Pesquisa de emprego e desemprego da grande São Paulo*. São Paulo: DIEESE.

Dolhnikoff, Miriam, Fernando Peixoto, Omar Ribeiro Thomaz. 1995. "Raça e Política: Entrevista com Benedita Da Silva." *Novos Estudos CEBRAP* 43 (November).

Doniger, Wendy. 1995. "'Put a Bag Over Her Head': Beheading Mythological Women." In Howard Eilberg-Schwartz and Wendy Doniger, eds., *Off with her Head! The Denial of Women's Identity in Myth, Religion and Culture*. Berkeley: University of California Press, 15–31.

Elbein Santos, Juana. 1977. *Os nagôs e a morte*. Petrópolis: Vozes.

Eilberg-Schwartz, Howard. 1995. "The Spectacle of the Female Head." In Howard Eilberg-Schwartz and Wendy Doniger, eds., *Off with her Head! The Denial of Women's Identity in Myth, Religion and Culture*. Berkeley: University of California Press, 1–14.

Enslin, Elizabeth. 1994. "Beyond Writing: Feminist Practice and the Limitations of Ethnography." *Cultural Anthropology* 9/4 (November): 537–568.

Epstein, Barbara. 1995. "'Political Correctness' and Collective Powerlessness." In Marcy Darnovsky, Barbara Epstein, Richard Flacks, eds., *Cultural Politics and Social Movements*. Philadelphia: Temple University Press, 3–19.

Equipe de Religiosos Negros. 1993. *Vocaçáo ao som dos atabaques*. Petrópolis: Vozes.

Escobar, Arturo, and Sonia Alvarez, eds. 1992. *The Making of Social Movements in Latin America*. Boulder: Westview.

Eyerman, Ron, and Andrew Jamison. 1991. *Social Movements: A Cognitive Approach*. University Park: Pennsylvania State University Press.

Fernandes, Florestan. 1969. *The Negro in Brazilian Society*. New York: Columbia University Press.

———. 1972. *O negro no mundo dos brancos*. São Paulo. Difusão Européia do Livro.

Fernandes, Rubem Cesar et al. 1996. *Novo nascimento: os evangelicos em casa, na igreja e na política*. Rio de Janeiro: ISER.

Ferreira da Silva, Denise, and Marcia Lima. 1992. "Raça, gênero e mercado de trabalho." *Estudos Afro-Asiáticos* 23: 97–111.

Figueira, Vera Moreira. 1990. "O preconceito racial na escola." *Estudos Afro-Asiáticos* 18: 63–71.

Figueiredo, Angela. 1994. "O mercado de boa aparência: as cabelereiras negras." *Bahia: análise e dados* 3/4 (March): 33–36.

Filho, Abreu. 1980. "Raça, sangue e luta." Master's thesis, Universidade Federal de Rio de Janeiro.

Fiske, John. 1994. *Media Matters: Everyday Culture and Political Change.* Minneapolis: University of Minnesota Press.

Folha Universal. 1992–96. Rio de Janeiro.

Fontaine, Pierre-Michel, ed., 1985. *Race, Class and Power in Brazil.* Los Angeles: UCLA Press.

Freston, Paul. 1993. "Protestantes e política no brasil: da constituinte ao impeachment," Ph.D. diss., Department of Social Science, Universidade Estadual de Campinas, Campinas.

———. 1994. "Uma breve história do pentecostalismo brasileiro: a Assembléia de Deus." *Religião e Sociedade* 16/3: 104–129.

Freyre, Gilberto. 1956 [1933]. *The Masters and the Slaves.* New York: Knopf.

Fry, Peter. 1995. "O que a Cinderela negra tem a dizer sobre a 'politica racial' no Brasil." *Revista USP* 28 (December): 122–135.

Funderburg, Lise. 1994. *Black, White, Other.* New York: William Morrow.

Gamson, William. 1992. "The Social Psychology of Collective Action." In Aldon Morris and Carol Meuller, eds., *Frontiers of Social Movement Theory.* New Haven: Yale University Press, 53–76.

Gantin, Bernard. 1996. "Valores universais das religiões tradicionais africanas." *Pontificia União Missionaria: Omnis e Terra* 2/10 (May): 165–171.

Genovese, Eugene. 1972. *Roll, Jordan, Roll: The World the Slaves Made.* New York: Vintage.

Giacomini, Sonia. 1992. "Profissão mulata: natureza e aprendizagem em um curso de formação." Master's thesis, Universidade Federal de Rio de Janeiro.

———. 1994. "Beleza mulata e beleza negra." *Estudos Feministas*: 217–229.

Gilliam, Angela, and Onik'a Gilliam. 1995. "Negociando a subjetividade de mulata no Brasil." *Estudos feministas* 3/2: 525–543.

Gilroy, Paul. 1987. *There Ain't No Black in the Union Jack.* London: Hutchinson.

———. 1993. *The Black Atlantic: Modernity and Double Consciousness.* Cambridge: Harvard University Press.

———. 1994. "'After the Love Has Gone': Bio-politics and Ethno-poetics in the Black Public Sphere." *Public Culture* 7/1 (Fall): 49–76

Goffman, Erving. 1974. *Frame Analysis.* Cambridge: Harvard University Press.

Gold, Ann, and Gloria Raheja. 1994. *Listen to the Heron's Words: Reimagining Gender and Kinship in North India.* Berkeley: University of California Press.

Goldani, Ana Maria. 1994. "Retratos de familia em tempos de crise." *Estudos feministas* 2/2: 303–334.

Gomes, André Luiz, and David Raimundo Santos. 1996. "O negro e a política." Mimeo. São João de Merti: Quilombo.

Gomes dos Santos, Revanilda. 1992. *Partidos políticos e eleitorado negro.* Master's Thesis, São Paulo: Pontifícia Universidade Católica.

Gonzalez, Lélia, and Carlos Hasenbalg. 1982. *Lugar do negro.* Rio de Janeiro: Marco Zero.

Gordon, Edward. 1991. "Anthropology and Liberation." In Faye Harrison, ed., *Decolonizing Anthropology.* Washington, D.C.: American Anthropological Association.

Gramsci, Antonio. *Prison Notebooks.* 1971. Ed. and trans. Quintin Hoare and Geoffrey Smith. New York: International.

Guimarães, Antônio. 1995. "Racismo e antiracismo no Brasil." *Novos Estudos CEBRAP* 43 (November): 26–44.

———. 1996. " O recente anti-racismo brasileiro: o que dizem os jornais diários." *Revista USP* 28 (December-February): 84–95;

Guimarães, Bernardo. 1996 [1875]. *Escrava Isaura.* 30th ed. Rio de Janeiro: Ediouro.

Hale, Lindsay. 1997. "Preto velho: Resistance, Redemption and Engendered Representations of Slavery in a Brazilian Possession Trance Religion." *American Ethnologist* 24/2 (May): 392–415

Hall, Stuart. 1996. "Politics of Identity." In Terence Ranger, ed., *Ethnic Identity in Britain.* Aldershot: Avebury.

Hall, Stuart, ed. 1996. *Questions of Cultural Identity.* London: Sage.

Hanchard, Michael. 1994. *Orpheus and Power: The Movimento Negro of Rio de Janeiro and São Paulo, 1945–1988.* Princeton: Princeton University Press.

Harris, Marvin. 1956. *Town and Country in Brazil.* New York: Columbia University Press.

———. 1964. *Patterns of Race in the Americas.* New York: Walker and Co.

———. 1970. "Referential Ambiguity in the Calculus of Brazilian Racial Identity." *Southwestern Journal of Anthropology* 14/4: 1–14.

Harris, Marvin, Josilbeth Gomez Consonte, and Bryan Byrne. 1993. "Who are the Whites? Imposed Census Categories and the Racial Demography of Brazil." *Social Forces* 72/2: 451–462.

Harris, Marvin, Josilbeth Gomez Consonte, Bryan Byrne, and Joseph Lange. 1995. "What's in a Name? The Consequences of Violating Brazilian Emic Color-Race Categories in Estimating Social Well-Being." *Journal of Anthropological Research* 51/4 (Winter): 389–400.

Harrison, Faye, ed. 1991. *Decolonizing Anthropology.* Washington, D.C.: American Anthropological Association.

Hasenbalg, Carlos. 1979. *Discriminação e desigualdades raciais no Brasil.* Rio de Janeiro: Graal.

———. 1988. *Estrutura social, mobilidade e raça.* São Paulo: Vertiço.

———. 1992. "O negro na indústria: proletarização tardia e desigual." In Carlos Hasenbalg and Nelson do Valle Silva. *Relações raciais no Brasil.* Rio de Janeiro: Rio Fundo Editora, 101–118.

Hasenbalg, Carlos, and Nelson do Valle Silva. 1990. "Raça e oportunidades educacionais no Brasil." *Estudos Afro-Asiáticos* 18: 73–91.

———. 1991. "Raça e oportunidades sociais no Brasil." In Peggy Lovell (org.), *Desigualdade racial no Brasil contemporâneo.* Belo Horizonte: MGSP Editions.

———. 1992. *Relações raciais no Brasil.* Rio de Janeiro: Rio Fundo Editora.

———. 1992. "Negros e mestiços: vida, cotidiano e movimento." In Carlos A. Hasenbalg and Nelson do Valle Silva. *Relações raciais no Brasil.* Rio de Janeiro: Rio Fundo Editora, 149–164.

Hauck, João, Hugo Fragoso, Josí Oscar Beozzo, Klaus Van der Grijp, and Behno Brod. 1985. *História da Igreja no Brasil: segunda epoca.* Petrópolis: Vozes.

Hess, David. 1995. "Hierarchy, Heterodoxy, and the Construction of Brazilian Religious Therapies." In David Hess and Roberto Da Matta, eds., *The Brazilian Puzzle.* New York: Columbia University Press, 180–208.

hooks, bell. 1988. "Straightening Our Hair." *Z Magazine* (Summer): 14–18.

———. 1992. *Black Looks: Race and Representation.* Boston: South End Press.

———. 1995. *Killing Rage: Ending Racism.* New York: Holt.

Hoornaert, Eduardo. 1987. "A devoção dos beatos negros." *Revista de ciências sociais* 18/19: 15–36.

Hunt, Robert D. Benford, and David A. Snow. 1994. "Identity Fields: Framing Processes and the Social Construction of Movement Identities." In Enrique Laraña, Hank Johnson, and Joseph Gusfield, eds., *New Social Movements: From Ideology to Identity.* Philadelphia: Temple University Press, 185–208.

Hutchinson, Harry W. 1957. *Village and Plantation Life in Northeastern Brazil.* Seattle: University of Washington Press.

Hymes, Dell. 1972. *Reinventing Anthropology.* New York: Pantheon.

Ireland, Rowan. 1993. *Kingdoms Come.* Pittsburgh: University of Pittsburgh Press.

Jackson, Jean. 1995. "Culture, Genuine and Spurious: The Politics of Indianness in the Varpés, Colombia." *American Ethnologist* 22(1): 3–27.

Johannesen, Stanley. 1988. "The Holy Ghost in Sunset Park." *Historical Reflections*, 15/3.

Jordan, Winthrop. 1968. *White Over Black: American Attitudes Toward the Negro, 1550–1812.* Chapel Hill: University of North Carolina.

Karasch, Mary. 1987. *Slave Life in Rio de Janeiro, 1800–18.* Princeton: Princeton University Press.

Keesing, Roger. 1989. "Creating the Pat: Custom and Identity in the Contemporary Pacific." *Contemporary Pacific* 1(1–2): 19–42.

Klandermans, Bert. 1992. "The Social Construction of Protest and Multiorganizational Fields." In Aldon Morris and Carol Meuller, eds., *Frontiers of Social Movement Theory*. New Haven: Yale University Press, 77–103.

———. 1997. *The Social Psychology of Protest*. Oxford: Blackwell.

Lakoff, Robin, and Raquel Scherr. 1984. *Face Value: The Politics of Beauty*. Boston: Routledge.

Lambert Silva, Rosângela Martius. 1985. "O mito e o culto da escraua Anastácia: Notas de um processo social." BA Thesis, Universidade do Estado do Rio de Janeiro.

Lima, Marcia. 1995. "Trajetória educacional e realização socio-econômica das mulheres negras." *Estudos feministas* 3/2: 489–505.

Lorde, Audré. 1984. "Age, Race, Class and Sex: Women Redefining Difference." In *Sister Outsider*. Trumansburg, N.Y.: Crossing Press.

Lovell, Peggy. 1992. "Raça, classe, gênero e discriminação salarial no Brasil." *Estudos Afro-Asiáticos* 22: 85–98.

Machado, Maria Das Dores. 1994. "Adesão religiosa e seus efeitos na esfera privada: um estudo comparativo dos carismáticos e pentecostais do Rio de Janeiro." Ph.D. diss., IUPERJ.

Manchete. 1996. September.

Maggie, Yvonne. 1995. "Aqueles a quem foi negada a côr do dia: as categorias côr e raça na cultura brasileira." Unpublished paper.

Mainwaring, Scott. 1986. *The Catholic Church and Politics in Brazil, 1916–1985*. Stanford: Stanford University Press.

Mariz, Cecilia, and Maria das Dores Machado. 1994. "Sincretismo e trânsito religioso: comparando pentecostais e carismáticos." *Comunicações do ISER* 45: 24–34.

Marotti, Georgia. 1987. *Black Characters in the Brazilian Novel*. Los Angeles: Center for Afro-American Studies.

Martinez-Alier, Verena. 1974. *Class and Color in Nineteenth-Century Cuba*. Cambridge: Cambridge University Press.

Marx, Anthony. 1996. "A construção da raça e o Estado Nôvo." *Estudos Afro-Asiáticos* 29: 9–36.

Mato, Daniel. 1996. "On the Theory, Epistemology, and Politics of the Social Construction of Cultural Identities in the Age of Globlization." *Identities* 3(1–2): 61–72.

Mattoso, Katia. 1986. *To Be a Slave in Brazil*. New Brunswick: Rutgers University Press.

McAdam, Douglas. 1996. "The Framing Function of Movement Tactics: Strategic Dramaturgy in the American Civil Rights Movement." In Doug McAdam, John D. McCarthy, and Mayer N. Zald, eds., *Comparative Perspectives on Social Movements: Political Opportunities, Mobilizing Structures, and Cultural Framings*. Cambridge: Cambridge University Press.

McClintock, Ann. 1993. "Family Feuds: Gender, Nationalism and the Family." *Feminist Review* 22 (Summer).

Medeiros, Maria Alice de Aguiar. 1987. "Mulheres negras: histórias de vida." *Revista de ciências sociais* 30/2: 207–222.

Melucci, Alberto. 1989. *Nomads of the Present*. Philadelphia: Temple University Press.

———. 1996. *Challenging Codes*. Cambridge: Cambridge University Press.

Monteiro, Helena. 1991. "O ressurgimento do movimento negro no Rio de Janeiro na decada de 70." Master's thesis, Universidade Federal de Rio de Janeiro.

Moraes, Aparecida. 1995. *Mulheres da vila: prostituição, identidade social e movimento associativo*. Petrópolis: Vozes.

Moran, Emilio, F. 1996. *Transforming Societies, Transforming Anthropology*. Ann Arbor. University of Michigan Press.

Moreira Alves, Helena. 1984. *Estado e oposição no Brasil*. Petrópolis: Vozes.

Morgen, Sandra. 1988. "'It's the Whole Power of the City Against Us!': The Development of Political Consciousness in a Women's Health Care Coalition." In Sandra Morgen and Ann Bookman, eds., *Women and the Politics of Empowerment*. Philadelphia: Temple University Press, 97–115.

Morris, Aldon. 1984. *Origins of the Civil Rights Movement*. New York: Free Press.

———. 1992. "Political Consciousness and Collective Action." In Aldon Morris and Carol Mueller, eds., *Frontiers in Social Movement Theory*. New Haven: Yale University Press, 351–373.

Moura, Clovis. 1988. *Sociologia do negro brasilerio*. São Paulo: Atica.

———. 1994. *Dialetica radical do Brasil negro*. São Paulo: Atica.

Moutinho, Laura. 1996. "Negociando discursos: análise das relações entre a Fundação Ford, os movimentos negros e a acadêmia na decada de 80." Master's thesis, Universidade Federal de Rio de Janeiro.

Mulvey, Patricia. 1980. "Black Brothers and Sisters: Membership in the Black Lay Brotherhoods of Colonial Brazil." *Luso-Brazilian Review* 17/2 (Winter): 253–279.

Muratorio, Blanca. 1980. "Protestantism and Capitalism Revisited in the Rural Highlands of Ecuador." *Journal of Peasant Studies* 8/1: 37–60.

Murphy, Jeffrie, and Jean Hampton. 1988. *Forgiveness and Mercy*. Cambridge: Cambridge University Press.

Nascimento, Abdias do. 1978. *O genocídio do negro brasileiro*. Rio de Janeiro.

Newton, Judith, and Judith Stacey. 1995. "Ms. Representations: Reflections on Studying Academic Men." In Deborah Gordon and Ruth Behar, eds., *Women Writing Culture*. Berkeley: University of California Press, 287–305.

Nogueira, Oracy. 1985. *Tanto preto quanto branco: estudos das relações raciais*. São Paulo: TA.Queiroz.

Novaes, Regina and Maria da Graca Floriano. 1985. *O negro evangélico*. Rio de Janeiro: Institudo de Estudos de religião.

O Dia. 1996. Rio de Janeiro.

Odô-Yá. 1994. *Odô-Yá: Informativo*. Rio de Janeiro: ACRA/ISER.

O'Hanlon, Rosalind. 1991. "Issues of Widowhood: Gender and Resistance in Colonial West India." In Douglas Haynes and Gyan Prakesh, eds., *Contesting Power*. Berkeley: University of California Press, 62–108.

Oliveira, L . E. G. 1981. *O lugar do negro na força de trabalho*. Rio de Janeiro: Instituto Brasileiro de Geografia e Estatísticas.

Oliveira, Santos. 1996. "Favelas and Ghettos: Race and Class in Rio de Janeiro and New York City," *Latin American Perspectives* 23/4 (Fall): 71–90.

Olson, Mancur. 1965. *The Logic of Collective Action*. New York: Schocken.

"O Negro," *Journal do Brasil* (July 1994).

Ong, Aihwa. 1987. *Spirits of Resistance and Capitalist Discipline: Factory Women in Malaysia*. Albany: State University of New York.

Pacheco, Moema. 1986. "Familia e identidade racial: os limites da côr nas relações e representações de um grupo de baixa renda." Master's thesis, Universidade Federal de Rio de Janeiro.

———. 1987. "A questão da côr nas relações de um grupo de baixa renda." *Estudos Afro-Asiáticos* 14: 85–97.

Pacteau, Francette. 1994. *The Symptom of Beauty*. Cambridge: Harvard University Press.

Parker, Richard. 1991. *Bodies, Pleasures and Passions: Sexual Culture in Contemporary Brazil*. Boston: Beacon Press.

Passos, Walter de Oliveira. 1995. *Teologia negra*. Salvador: Edição Independente.

Pierce, Paulette, and Brackette Williams. 1996. "And Your Prayers Shall Be Answered Through the Womb of a Woman: Insurgent Masculine Redemption and the Nation of Islam." In Brackette Williams, ed., *Women Out of Place: The Gender of Agency and the Race of Nationality*. New York: Routledge, 186–215.

Prandi, Reginaldo. 1995. "As religiões negras do Brasil: para uma sociologia dos cultos afro-brasileiros." *Revista USP* 28 (December/February): 64–83.

Pryce, Everton. 1990. "Culture From Below: Politics, Resistance and Leadership in the Notting Hill Gate Carnival: 1976–1978." In Harry Goulbourne, ed., *Black Politics in Britain*. Aldershot: Avebury, 130–148.

Queiroz Junior, Teófolo. 1975. *Preconceito de côr e a mulata na literatura brasileira*. São Paulo: Atica.

Queiroz, Ana Maria. 1994. "Mulheres negras, educação e mercado de trabalho." *Bahia: análise e dados: o negro* 3/4 (March): 78–81.

Raça Brasil. 1996. 1/1–5.

Rappaport, Joanne, and Robert Doner. 1996. "The Construction of Difference by Native Legislators." *Journal of Latin American Anthropology.* 1/2 (Spring): 22–45.

Rappaport, Joanne. 1984. "Las misiones protestantes y la resistencia indígena en el sur de Colombia." *América Indigena* 44/1 (January–March): 111–126.

Reichmann, Rebecca. 1995. "Mulher negra brasileira: um retrato." *Estudos feministas* 3/2: 496–514.

Ribeiro, Darcy. 1995. *O povo brasileiro.* São Paulo: Companhia das Letras.

Ribeiro de Oliveira, Pedro. 1985. *Religião e dominação de classe.* Petrópolis: Vozes.

Rocha, Geraldo. 1994. *Cadernos de teologia negra: Deus na roda com a gente.* Rio de Janeiro: Pilar.

———. 1994. *Teologia negra: retalhos de nossa história.* Rio de Janeiro: Pilar.

Rogers, Joel. 1995. "How Divided Progressives Might Unite." *New Left Review* 210 (March–April): 3–33.

Roland, Edna and Sueli Carneiro. 1990. "Saúde da mulher no Brasil: a perspectiva da mulher negra." *Revista de Cultura Vozes* 84(2): 204–210.

Rooks, Noliwe. 1996. *Hair Raising: Beauty, Culture, and African American Women.* New Brunswick: Rutgers University Press.

Root, Maria, ed. 1992. *Racially Mixed People in America.* Newbury Park, Cal.: Sage.

Rose, Trisha. 1996. "A Style Nobody Can Deal With: Politics, Style, and the Postindustrial City in Hip Hop." In Avery F. Gordon and Christopher Newfield, eds., *Mapping Multiculturalism.* Minneapolis: University of Minnesota Press, 424–444.

Rosemberg, Fúlvia. 1985. *Literatura infantil e ideologia.* São Paulo: Global.

———. 1987. "Relações raciais e rendimento escolar." *Cadernos de pesquisa* 63 (November): 19–23.

Roswith, Gerloff. 1975. "Black Power and Pentecostalism." In *Pentecost and Politics.* Bristol: SCM Publications.

Rubinstein, Robert. 1986. "Reflections on Action Anthropology: Some Developmental Dynamics of an Anthropological Tradition." *Human Organization* 45: 270–79.

Rushing, Andrea Benton. 1988. "Hair-Raising." *Feminist Studies* 14 (Summer): 325–335.

Russell, Kathy, Midge Wilson, and Ronald Hall. 1992. *The Color Complex: The Politics of Skin Color Among African-Americans.* New York: Harcourt Brace Jovanovich.

Russell-Wood, A. J. R. 1972. "Brazil in the Eighteenth Century." In Jack P. Greene and David W. Cohen, eds., *Neither Slave nor Free.* Baltimore: Johns Hopkins Press.

———. 1982. *The Black Man in Slavery and Freedom in Colonial Brazil.* New York: St. Martin's Press.

Sanchis, Pierre. 1994. "O rapto pentecostal a cultura católico-brasileiro." *Revista de Antropologia* 37: 145–182

Sanjek, Roger. 1971. "Brazilian Racial Terms: Some Aspects of Meaning and Learning." *American Anthropologist* 73: 1126–1143.

Sansone, Livio. 1993. "Pai preto, filho negro: trabalho, côr e diferenciais geracionais." *Estudos Afro-Asiáticos* 22: 143–74.

———. 1994. "The Local and the Global in Today's Afro-Bahia." Paper presented at the 18th meeting of the Associação de Pôs-Graduação em Ciências Sociais.

Sant'Anna, Rosângela. 1996. "A fileira da catástrofe: o que a côr pode representar no sistema educacional?" Working Paper, Núcleo da Côr, Universidade Federal do Rio de Janeiro.

Santos, David Raimundo dos. 1990. "Raça e cultura." Mimeo. São João de Meriti: Quilombo.

Santos, Joel Rufino dos. 1984. *O que é racismo*. São Paulo: Brasiliense.

———. 1985. "O movimento negro e a crise brasileira." *Política e Administração* 2/2 (July-September): 287–307.

———. 1988. "IPCN e Cacique de Ramos: dois exemplos de movimento negro na cidade do Rio de Janeiro." *Comunicações de ISER* 7/28: 5–20.

———. 1993. "A luta organizada contra o racismo." In *Atrás do muro da noite*. Brasilia: Fundação Cultural Palmares, 89–146.

———. 1993. "Clara dos Anjos."In *Atrás do muro da noite*. Brasilia: Fundaçao Cultura Palmares.

Santos, Micênio. 1990. "O treize de maio e o 20 de novembro." Master's thesis, Universidade Federal de Rio de Janeiro.

Scalon, Maria. 1992. "Côr e seletividade conjugal no Brasil." *Estudos Afro-Asiáticos* 23: 17–36;

Schensul, Stephen L. 1974. "Skills Needed in Action Anthropology: Lessons for El Centro de la Causa." *Human Organization* 33: 203–209.

Scheper-Hughes, Nancy. 1992. *Death Without Weeping*. Berkeley: University of California Press.

———. 1995. "The Primacy of the Ethical: Propositions for a Militant Anthropology." *Current Anthropology* 36/3 (June): 409–420.

Schubert, Guillermo. 1987. "Escrava Anastácia." *Journal Brasil* 9/15.

Scotchmer, David. 1991. "Symbols of Salvation: Interpreting Highland Maya Protestantism in Context." Ph.D. diss., State University of New York, Albany.

Scott, James. 1976. *The Moral Economy of the Peasant: Rebellion and Subsistence in Southeast Asia*. New Haven: Yale University Press.

———. 1985. *The Weapons of the Weak*. New Haven: Yale University Press.

———. 1990. *Domination and the Arts of Resistance*. New Haven: Yale University Press.

Segal, Daniel. 1993. "'Race' and 'Colour' in Pre-Independence Trinidad and Tobago." In Kevin Yelvington, ed., *Trinidad Ethnicity*. Knoxville: University of Tennessee Press, 81–115.

Serra, Ordep. 1995. *Aguas do rei*. Vozes: Petrópolis.

Serrano, Carlos. 1995. "Ginga, a rainha quilombola de Matamba e Angola." *Revista USP* 28 (February): 136–141.

Sheriff, Robin. 1995. "'Negro é um apelido que os brancos deram aos pretos': discursos sobre cor, raça e racismo num morro carioca." Unpublished paper, Programa de Raça e Etnicidade, Instituto de Filosofia e Ciências Sociais, UFRJ.

———. 1997. "Negro is a Nickname that Whites Call Blacks." Ph.D. diss., Dept. of Anthropology, City University of New York.

Tarrow, Sidney. 1994. *Power in Movement*. Cambridge: Cambridge University Press.

Silva, Nelson. 1978. "Black-White Income Differentials: Brazil, 1960," Ph.D. diss., University of Michigan.

Silva, José Ariovaldo da. 1994. "Elementas históricos da adaptação da liturgia ás várias culturas." Mimeo. São João de Meriti: Central Pastoral Quilombo.

———. 1988. "Côr e processo de realização socio-econômica." In Carlos Hasenbalg and Nelson Silva, eds., *Estrutura social, mobilidade e raça*. Rio de Janeiro: Vertice, 144–63.

Silva, Benedita da. 1995. *Dia internacional para a eliminação da discriminação racial*. Brasilia: Congresso Nacional,.

Silva, Nelson. 1996. "Mocenidade: modo de usar." Paper presented at the 7th Congress of Brazilian Sociology. Rio de Janeiro.

Silva, Marcos. 1990. "Pistas para uma teologia negra de libertação." Master's thesis, Faculdade de Teologia Nossa Senhora da Assunção.

Silva, Nilton. 1990. *Milagres e graças*. Rio de Janeiro: Ordem Universal Escrava Anastácia.

Simmonds, Fely. 1995. "Love in Black and White." In Lynne Pierce and Jackie Stacey, eds., *Romance Revisited*. New York: New York University Press, 210–222.

Singer, Merrill. 1994. "Community-Centered Praxis: Toward an Alternative Non-dominative Applied Anthropology." *Human Organization* 53/4 (1994).

Skidmore, Thomas. 1974. *Black into White: Race and Nationality in Brazilian Thought*. New York: Oxford University Press.

———. 1996. "Affirmative Action in the United States and Brazil." Paper presented at the Brazilian Commission on Human Rights, Brasilia.

———. 1993. "Bi-racial U.S. vs. Multi-racial Brazil: Is the Contrast Still Valid?" *Journal of Latin American Studies* 25: 373–386

Smith, Carol. 1996. "Race/Class/Gender Ideology in Guatemala: Modern and Anti-Modern Forms." In Brackette Williams, ed., *Women Out of Place: The Gender of Agency and the Race of Nationality*. New York: Routledge, 50–78.

Smith, Christian. 1991. *The Emergence of Liberation Theology: Radical Religion and Social Movement Theory*. Chicago: University of Chicago Press.

Smith, Dorothy. 1990. *Texts, Facts and Femininity*. New York: Routledge.

Snow, David, and Robert Benford. 1988. "Ideology, Frame Resonance, and Participant Mobilization." In Bert Klandermans, ed., *From Structure to Action: Social Movement Participation Across Cultures*. Greenwich, Conn.: JAI.

———. 1992. "Master Frames and Cycles of Protest." In Aldon Morris and Carol Meuller, eds., *Frontiers in Social Movement Theory*. New Haven: Yale University Press. 133–155.

Snow, David, E. Burke Rocheford, Jr., Steven K. Worden, and Robert Berford. 1986. "Frame Alignment Processes, Micromobilization, and Movement Participation." *American Sociological Review* 51: 464–81

Sodré, Muniz. 1983. *A verdade seduzida: por um conceito de cultura no Brasil*. Rio de Janeiro: Codreci.

———. 1988. *O terreiro e a cidade*. Petrópolis: Vozes.

Sollors, Werner. 1997. *Neither Black nor White Yet Both: Thematic Explorations of Interracial Literature*. New York: Oxford University Press.

Souza, Neusa Santos. 1983. *Tornar-se negro: as vicissitudes da identidade do negro brasileiro em ascensão social*. Rio de Janeiro: Graal.

Spencer, Jon. 1997. *The New Colored People: The Mixed Race Movement in America*. New York: New York University Press.

Stam, Robert. 1981. *Brazilian Cinema*. Rutherford, NJ: Farleigh Dickinson University Press.

———. 1997. *Tropical Multiculturalism: A Comparative History of Race in Brazilian Cinema and Culture*. Durham: Duke University Press.

Starn, Orin. 1994. "Rethinking the Politics of Anthropology. The Case of the Andes." *Current Anthropology* 35(1): 45–75.

Stein, Arlene. 1995. "Sisters and Queers: The Decentering of Lesbian Feminism." In Marcy Darnovsky, Barbara Epstein, and Richard Flacks, eds., *Cultural Politics and Social Movements*. Philadelphia: Temple University Press.

Stokes, Susan. 1995. *Cultures in Conflict: Social Movements and the State in Peru*. Berkeley: University of California Press.

Stolcke, Verena. 1991. "Sexo está para gênero assim como raça para etnicidade?" *Estudos Afro-Asiáticos* 20 (June): 101–119.

Stoll, David, and Virginia Garrard-Burnett, eds., 1993. *Rethinking Protestantism in Latin America*. Philadelphia: Temple University Press.

Stoller, Paul. 1995. *Embodying Colonial Memories: Spirit Possession, Power and the Hauka in West Africa*. New York: Routledge.

Strathern, Andrew. 1996. *Body Thoughts*. Ann Arbor: University of Michigan Press.

Stull, David D. and Jean J. Schensul, eds. 1987. *Collaborative Research and Social Change*. Boulder: Westview.

Swidler, Ann. 1986. "Culture in Action: Symbols and Strategies." *American Sociological Review* 51: 273–286

Synnott, Anthony. 1993. *The Body Social*. New York: Routledge.

Tarrow, Sidney. 1994. *Power in Movement: Social Movements, Collective Action and Mass Politics in the Modern State*. Cambridge: Cambridge University Press.

Taussig, Michael. 1993. *Mimesis and Alterity*. New York: Routledge.

Telles, Edward. 1992. "Residential Segregation by Skin Color in Brazil." *American Sociological Review* 57: 186–197.

———. 1995. "Who are the Morenas?" *Social Forces* 73/14 (June): 1611–1615.

Theodoro, Helena. 1996. *Mito e espiritualidade: mulheres negras*. Rio de Janeiro: Pallas.

Toulis, Nicole. 1997. *Believing Identity*. Oxford: Berg.

Turner, Terence. 1993. "From Cosmology to Ideology.: Resistance, Adaptation and Social Consciousness among the Kayapó." In *Cosmology, Values, and Inter-Ethnic Context in South America*. Bennington, VT: Bennington College Press, 1–3.

Turra, Cleuza, and Gustavo Venturi. 1995. *Racismo cordial*. São Paulo: Editora Atica.

Twine, France. 1996. "O hiato de gênero nas percepções de racismo: o caso dos afro-brasileiros socialmente ascendentes." *Estudos Afro-Asiáticos* 29: 37–54.

———. 1997. "Mapping the Terrain of Racism in Brazil." *Race and Class* 38/3 (January/March): 49–62.

———. 1998. *Racism in a Racial Democracy*. New Brunswick: Rutgers University Press.

Valente, Ana Lúcia. 1986. "Política e relações raciais: o negro e as eleições paulistas de 1982." Master's thesis, Universidade de São Paulo.

———. 1994. *O negro e a igreja católica: o espaço concedido, um espaço reivindicado*. Campo Grande, MS: CECITEC.

Van Willigen, John. 1993. *Applied Anthropology: An Introduction*. 2nd. ed. South Hadley, MA: Bergin and Garvey.

Verger, Pierre. 1992. *Os libertos: sete caminhos na liberdade de escravos da Bahia no seculo XIX*. São Paulo: Corrúpio.

Vianna, Hermano. 1988. *O mundo funk carioca*. Rio de Janeiro: Jorge Zahar.

Viotti da Costa, Emilia. 1966. *Da senzala á colônia*. 2nd ed. São Paulo: Difusão Européia do Livro.

Wachtel, Nathan. 1977. *The Vision of the Vanquished*. New York: Barnes and Noble.

Wallace, Michelle. 1979. *Black Macho and the Myth of the Superwoman*. New York: Dial Press.

Wagley, Charles, ed. 1952. *Race and Class in Rural Brazil*. Paris: UNESCO.

Wedenoja, William. 1978. "Religion and Adaptation in Rural Jamaica." Ph.D. diss., University of California, San Diego.

Werbner, Pnina. 1991. "Black and Ethnic Leaderships in Britain: A Theoretical Overview." In Pnina Werbner and Muhammad Anwar, eds., *Black and Ethnic Leaderships*. London: Routledge.

West, Cornel. 1993. *Keeping Faith*. New York: Routledge.

Williams, Brackette. 1994. "Classification Systems Revisited: Kinship, Caste, Race, and Nationality as the Flow of Blood and the Spread of Rights." In Sylvia Yanagisako and Carol Delaney, eds., *Naturalizing Power: Essays in Feminist Cultural Analysis*. New York: Routledge, 201–36.

———. 1996. "A Race of Men, A Class of Women: Nation, Ethnicity, Gender, and Domesticity Among Afro-Guyanese." in *Ibid.*, 129–158.

Willis, Paul. 1990. *Common Culture: Symbolic Work at Play in the Everyday Cultures of the Young*. Boulder: Westview.

Winant, Howard. 1994a. *Racial Conditions*. Minneapolis: University of Minnesota Press.

———. 1994b. "Racial Formation and Hegemony: Global and Local Developments." In Sallie Westwood and Ali Rattansi, eds. *Racism, Modernity and Identity: On the Western Front*. Cambridge: Polity Press, pp. 250–280.

Wood, Charles. 1991. "Categorias censitárias e classificações subjetivas de raça no Brasil." In *Desigualdade racial no Brasil contemporâneo*. Belo Horizonte: CEDEPLAR.

Young, Iris M. 1990. *Throwing Like a Girl and Other Essays in Feminist Philosophy and Social Theory*. Bloomington: University of Indiana Press.

Yuval-Davis, Nina, and Floya Anthias, eds. 1989. *Woman-Nation-State*. New York: St. Martin's Press.

Zack, Naomi. 1993. *Race and Mixed Race*. Philadelphia: Temple University Press.

———. 1995. *American Mixed Race: The Culture of Microdiversity*. Lanham: Littlefield.

Index